PRAISE FOR *The Struggle to Be Gay—in Mexico, for Example*

"A dazzling experimental ethnography of Mexican men who love men. Deftly situates an array of human experiences within the warps of the global economy and the local iterations of class and race that sculpt the intimate, liberatory dreams and desires of these men but severely constrain their lived experiences."

—Ramón Gutiérrez, University of Chicago

"Roger Lancaster gently urges us to take stock of why the idea of being gay can sound so outmoded in one place and so utopian in another. With its humane attention to the limits of our theories and the power of our dreams, *The Struggle to be Gay* opens up new paths in the study of 21st-century sexuality."

—Chris Nealon, Johns Hopkins University

"Lancaster captivates us with a deeply personal and satisfying account of Mexican gay men's lives and identities. The picture that emerges in this fascinating book is of a Mexico where gay-identified people grapple with pervasive material inequalities while simultaneously contributing to a growing collective emphasis on diversity and the pursuit of social change."

—Héctor Carrillo, Northwestern University

"This book provides groundbreaking theoretical interventions into the 'material foundations of sexual identity' as well as heart-wrenching descriptions and analyses of how these material realities shape sexual identities and possibilities for gay men in Mexico."

—Tanya Golash-Boza, author of *Before Gentrification: The Creation of DC's Racial Wealth Gap*

"Combining perceptive ethnographic observations, powerful memoir, and deep historical dives, this marvelous book offers an insightful meditation on gay life in Mexico and beyond. This book is a true gem and should be used, discussed, and emulated in the years to come."

—Javier Auyero, University of Texas at Austin

"Casting a gimlet eye over class as 'the dirty secret of gay life,' Lancaster shows that in good measure we are who we are in relation to the resources we bring to bear."

—Matthew Gutmann, author of *Are Men Animals? How Modern Masculinity Sells Men Short*

"From a dazzling scholar-writer, heart-wrenching stories and a refreshing class analysis. In gorgeous prose, Lancaster plumbs details of gay life over the decades of his observations in Mexico and beyond to reveal our universal predicament."

—Alisse Waterston, author of *Light in Dark Times: The Human Search for Meaning*

*The Struggle to Be Gay—
in Mexico, for Example*

The Struggle to Be Gay—in Mexico, for Example

Roger N. Lancaster

UNIVERSITY OF CALIFORNIA PRESS

University of California Press
Oakland, California

© 2023 by Roger N. Lancaster

Names: Lancaster, Roger N., author.
Title: The struggle to be gay—in Mexico, for example / Roger N.
    Lancaster.
Description: Oakland, California : University of California Press, [2023] |
    Includes bibliographical references and index.
Identifiers: LCCN 2023012186 (print) | LCCN 2023012187 (ebook) |
    ISBN 9780520397569 (hardback) | ISBN 9780520397576
    (paperback) | ISBN 9780520397583 (ebook)
Subjects: LCSH: Gays—Mexico. | Gender identity—Mexico. | Social
    classes—Mexico. | Sexual minorities—Mexico.
Classification: LCC HQ76.3.M6 L36 2023 (print) | LCC HQ76.3.M6 (ebook) |
    DDC 306.76/60972—dc23/eng/20230411
LC record available at https://lccn.loc.gov/2023012186
LC ebook record available at https://lccn.loc.gov/2023012187

32 31 30 29 28 27 26 25 24 23
10 9 8 7 6 5 4 3 2 1

Para Quique, por supuesto

Primarily, everybody lives in the future, because they strive, past things only come later, and as yet genuine present is almost never there at all.

—Ernst Bloch, *The Principle of Hope*

One day, in retrospect, the years of struggle will strike you as the most beautiful.

—Sigmund Freud, 1907

No hay peor lucha que la que no se hace.

—Mexican proverb

La lutte elle-même vers les sommets suffit à remplir un cœur d'homme. Il faut imaginer Sisyphe heureux.

—Albert Camus, *Le Mythe de Sisyphe*

We take no delight in existence except when we are struggling for something.

—Arthur Schopenhauer, "The Vanity of Existence"

Contents

Acknowledgments

A long-term project like this, involving false starts, long pauses, and the slow accretion of stories, requires patience and support. I express my gratitude to Fulbright-Comexus for a fellowship in 2006–7 and to George Mason University for yearlong faculty study leaves in 2010–11 and 2017–18. I owe special thanks to the Instituto de Ciencias Sociales y Humanidades at the Benemérita Universidad Autónoma de Puebla (BUAP) for my research affiliation there, for collegial fellowship, and for stimulating conversations with scholars and students on the left. Sociologist Carlos Figueroa Ibarra and anthropologist Mauricio List Reyes were constant friends and helpful interlocutors at BUAP, as were Octavio Moreno and then students Guillermo López Varela and Toño Mendoza Bueno. Ongoing conversations with colleagues and students in the cultural studies program at George Mason have helped shape some of the elements of this book.

Some debts date to the distant past. Although memory fails me on the details, I'm fairly certain that when I was a grad student, either the Anthropology Department or the Center for Latin American Studies at the University of California, Berkeley, helped fund at least one of my summer trips to Mexico to study Spanish in Cuernavaca in 1983 and 1984. Memory is clearer on other matters. A decade later, anthropologists Michael Higgins and Tanya Coen hosted us, my former partner and me, at their home in Oaxaca. Michael continued to be a friend and insightful conversationalist during subsequent visits to Mexico until his untimely death in 2011.

I am deeply indebted to friends and colleagues who have read this manuscript in part or in whole, giving me helpful feedback at different stages in the development of this book. Readers and commenters include Jonathan Aspeitia, Andy Bickford, Vivek Chibber, Todd Cronan, Marcial Godoy-Anativia, Connor Kilpatrick, Jeff Maskovsky, Walter Benn Michaels, Adolph Reed Jr., Nancy Scheper-Hughes, Rafael Silva, Aniruddhan Vasudevan, Krzysztof Wargan, Joanna Wuest, and Daniel Zamora. Héctor Carrillo was exceptionally generous, giving me several pages of detailed feedback and instructive pointers on the penultimate draft of the manuscript. Víctor Macías-González has been an especially helpful interlocutor, filling my ear with a historian's understanding of how gay scenes developed in Mexico City over the long course of the twentieth century. Two graduate students in cultural studies assisted with manuscript preparation over different periods; Chelsea Triggs and Zachary Gehring helped keep me to deadlines.

Experience suggests that one's editor has more to do with the conceptualization and final shape of a book than is usually acknowledged. It has been my distinct pleasure to work with Naomi Schneider, my editor on this and other projects. Cindy Fulton was an attentive production editor, and Steven Baker was insightful and careful in his role as copyeditor.

I am most grateful to my friends, contacts, subjects, and interlocutors in Mexico, who have put up with me and my questions and sometimes my boorishness over many years, and who have shared meals, drinks, conversations, and life with me. They appear here under pseudonyms, to protect their privacy, but not, I hope, as faceless examples of theoretical concepts. Special thanks go to the staff and regulars at Luciérnaga (also a pseudonym), my haunt over many years. My deepest gratitude goes to Enrique Galindo, for open-ended conversation about the content of this work, of course, but also for love and companionship.

Any errors or oversights are of course my own; readers and interlocutors are to be held blameless. The translations of Spanish-language texts are also my own, unless otherwise noted. Excepting public figures, identities and identifying characteristics of all persons have been thoroughly disguised; some places and events have been additionally camouflaged.

Introduction

WHEN THE MUSIC STOPS

It is true: we have another way of not knowing ourselves,
and we speak more freely of our emotional complexes than
of our material condition or of our socio-professional
milieu; we prefer to ask ourselves about the homosexual
component of our characters than about the history which
has made us and which we have made. We too are victims
and accomplices of alienation, reification, mystification. We
too stagger beneath "the weight of things said and done," of
lies accepted and transmitted without belief. But we have no
wish to know it. We are like sleepwalkers treading in a gut-
ter, dreaming of our genitals rather than looking at our feet.

—Jean-Paul Sartre, *Between Existentialism and Marxism*

Zona Rosa, Mexico City, sometime around 2006: It is the wee hours of the
morning, and my ears are ringing after a night of revelry in crowded bars
and dance clubs. Ambling down narrow sidewalks, I have a flash of giddy
optimism which I take for insight: *The gay scene has arrived.* This problematic notion of a sudden "arrival" is a recurring idea in cities of the global south, where gay scenes often developed under dictatorships or repressive conditions—as did Mexico's—and are invariably compared, often
unfavorably, to those of the global north.[1]

The gay scene in the Zona Rosa has "arrived" in the sense that it now
outshines its rivals; it is more jubilant, more carefree, *gayer*, than any of
the comparably staid and claustrophobic scenes in the United States
or Northern Europe. It is certainly younger, in a country where the median
age is twenty-five (compared to thirty-six in the United States and

1

forty-three in Germany at the time).[2] Buoyed by urban density and youthful exuberance, the Zona Rosa (the "Pink Zone") far surpasses the scale and intensity—the buzz—of Castro Street or Greenwich Village in their 1970s heydays. And unlike earlier versions of the gay scene on the same site—I had been visiting the Zona frequently since the mid-1990s—there is nothing discreet or subdued about it. "Gay Disneyland," I call it, an expansive participatory spectacle spread out over a dozen or so compact city blocks in three dense clusters, as though the city itself, its layout and architecture, had been designed for our amusement and happiness. And even if you have no money for admission to clubs or beer in the bars, the sidewalks themselves are dappled rivers of humanity, vibrant happenings in their own right: places to chat with friends, dance, cruise, and have a lively night out.

I gush not altogether coherently to my Chilango (a slang demonym for residents of Mexico City) companion, who tries to douse my unchecked enthusiasm with some insiderly cynicism. "But what happens when the music stops?" he asks me. "You realize that virtually all these kids will go back now to sleep in their parents' houses, right? That by day they work for low wages in call centers or offices or department stores? That this, what you see tonight, is their *reprieve*? Within five years, half of them will succumb to family pressures to be married."

I express skepticism at his final surmise, which dates the speaker (just as my invocation of the Castro and Village scenes date me). There was a time when substantial numbers of Mexican men allowed themselves the indulgence of a gay youth, to be followed by a staid, publicly heterosexual adulthood. This life cycle still exists, of course, perhaps especially in conservative small towns, but it has long been viewed as "backward," especially in big cities across Mexico where one encounters in abundance all the varieties of lifelong "modern" homosexuality (and I place both terms in eyebrow-raising quotation marks for the time being): stable middle-aged same-sex couples; durable circles of gay and lesbian friends who host parties and organize outings; clubbers, barflies, and men who dedicate their free time to cruising in bathhouses or public places or on social media; and so on. More convincing is my interlocutor's sense that spectacular scenes of nocturnal entertainment serve as temporary reprieves—*aplazamientos*, postponements. This strikes me as both sober and true.

His invocation of humdrum workaday routines at anemic wages is indisputable, and his observation about young gays' submission to parental authority rings at least partly true.

So much for my unbridled enthusiasm for "gay [or queer] worldmaking," a recurrent trope of the period's LGBT studies.[3] This bullish phrase was often applied, implausibly, to fleeting scenes, staged performances, or evanescent happenings in nightlife industries. So much, too, for my Disneyland metaphor, which works against me and my upbeat intentions—and not only because it refers to a distinctly North American consumer spectacle but also because what, after all, is Disneyland, if not an elaborate postponement, a suspension, a deferral?

Every nightlife has its opposite, a day life, for which it serves as reprieve. It is not the one thing or the other but rather the relation between them that might count as a "world."

Here, then, are some stories, observations, and notes about how some of us live, love, work, and try to imagine our lives under prevailing conditions. I am drawing on four decades of visits and returns to a number of Mexican cities, stretched out over a period of recurrent economic crises and the country's slow, halting, and uneven transition from dictatorship to democracy, culminating in a fifteen-year period of intermittent participant-observation fieldwork in Puebla.

I relate not just any old accounts of any old "us." I am trying to understand how men who have sex with men live in a globally connected world that is not as brutally hostile as it was in the past but that can scarcely be deemed accepting or supportive. I am especially interested in how such men come to inhabit a gay identity—or not—and how they build networks and communities of various sorts—or not—and how they might join their lives together—or not—but I am also interested in more than that. I want to understand better what this sense of identity, community, and connection might mean for us, and how it corresponds to or clashes with other parts of our lives. With a few notable exceptions,[4] LGBT studies has for too long edited these other parts of our lives—work, debt, economic inequality and precarity—out of the picture, producing idealized, reified, and ultimately false versions of identity and empty narratives about sexual citizenship.

Now, I cannot help but feel that I am going against three strong currents here.

First, my use of words like *us, we,* and *our* will signal something of my approach from the outset. It is a gesture of coidentification that departs from standard ethnographic conventions (including theoretical frameworks I have used in the past[5]), and also from the usual rules of contemporary identity politics, which has progressively narrowed the scope of the "we," fragmenting "us" into ever smaller intersectional blocs. The prevailing protocols respond to important truths about the lived experience of race, gender, sexuality, postcolonial condition, and so on, categories that variously "intersect" in a person's life, no doubt, and have helped produce important insights. But they have become rigidified in academic studies, hardening into complacent assertions about one's *own* tribe and its supposedly unique perspective, fast-freezing into rituals of deference about *other* people's cultural property.[6] More often than not, these rituals of recognition reduce *speech* (an individual act) to *discourse* (a fragment of ideology) to *identity* (membership in a socially defined group): "I" can only ever speak *my* identity; identity expresses itself through my words and actions. Cleaving the world into "distinct, stable territories"[7] of *us* and *them*, these proprietary conventions tend to make us turn away from our commonalities—in this case, shared sexual, emotional, and political interests. They draw our attention to exceptional, spectacularized suffering (the holy grail of both identitarian specificity and liberal charitability) while ignoring all the ways we might share experiences, make points of contact, forge relationships, or build tacit alliances *across* ethnic, cultural, or class divides. We shrink the circle of the "we," the scope of fellow feeling, down to the smallest possible triply or quadruply intersectional communities—when the times cry out for an expansive, all-peoples solidarity based on shared concerns. Or else, as gawking spectators, we reify the exquisite unfathomable alterity of the Other, imbuing it with a sacral aura, when, if anything, we ought to attend to the everydayness of others and the dialogical conversations through which we all negotiate our conjoined and overlapping meanings.

In this book, I take my cue from the way my Mexican friends and subjects typically include *me* within the circle of the "we" when we talk about gay life ("we gays," "us homosexuals")—although I also note, dialectically, that they do sometimes draw a hard line against my perspectives (as an outsider, a North American, a middle-class person with comparably more resources). I try to track both of these propositions in the pages that follow. As against prevailing trends in ethnographic rubbernecking, I try to relate my friends' and subjects' mostly unspectacular, unexceptional suffering. To be sure, it sometimes seems that catastrophe is waiting around every corner: Some die young from the combination of grinding poverty and toxic intolerance. Others despair of ever having a decent life, stop taking their antiretrovirals, and wait for AIDS to take them. A few have been uprooted, displaced, or "disappeared" in the narcoviolence that has engulfed large portions of the country since 2006 and even now shows no sign of abating. But mostly, the people about whom I write—like most people in most places at most times—trudge on in the face of indifference and violence, managing and making do and sometimes even doing well.

In conveying my subjects' stories, I acknowledge their creative strategies, their deep comprehension of their experiential worlds (which includes an acute awareness of tragic outcomes). At the same time, I try to reveal what still too often goes missing in ethnographic work, even after the dialogical turn in cultural theory (which construed knowledge as a give-and-take, a dynamic conversation):[8] the conditions under which our meandering conversations took place. These were usually conditions of camaraderie, amity, affinity. The settings were typically places of "contact" (to borrow a term from Samuel R. Delany) which throw together people from different social and economic walks of life:[9] the Zona Rosa's sidewalks, public squares in city centers, bars, cafés, bathhouses, discotheques. Sometimes, I listen as my friends vent their frustrations over beer. Sometimes, one of us is trying to convince the other of something. I try to show these dynamics as much as possible. I try to plant my own arguments in friendship, solidarity, and accompaniment.[10] I try to take up my dwelling in this text as I tried to make my home in Mexico over many years—mindful of differences but within the abode of commonalities.

Second, for the past thirty years, scholarly works often have eschewed use of the word "gay," making it recede behind once-edgier labels—"queer"— or demoting it to a single grapheme in the ever-expanding acronym that it once broadly connoted: LGBTQIA+. No doubt these successive rebrandings seemed warranted at the time, as activists and intellectuals strove for inclusiveness and sought to outrun the conformism and consumerism that threatened to overwhelm gay life, especially in its urban, middle-class sectors. The unintended result, however, has been new forms of conformism and consumerism, which apparently are not impeded by terminological innovation.

Today, queers on college campuses and in tolerant cities strike social and political poses based on resistance, nonassimilation, and an anti-normative aesthetic, never quite seeing how far these outsiderly gestures are from our own middle-class experiences—or how they serve as badges of status distinction in new hierarchies based on sensibility. We gentrify long-standing commonplace sexual practices, rechristening vernacular terms with ever-more-specific hipster sexological typologies (which are often visibly marked by neoliberal sensibilities, perhaps especially references to flexibility and fluidity: "heteroflexible," "gender-fluid").[11] Meanwhile, however, "gay" still remains the default aspirational signifier for large numbers of gay men, lesbians, and trans people, especially those who live outside the educated, upper-middle-class cosmopolis. Their needs and desires are not easily mapped onto the standard assimilationist–anti-assimilationist spectrum. (Working-class gays are, as often as not, puzzled by or indifferent to the distinctions parsed and arguments hatched by educated, affluent, up-to-date queers. And they do encounter the new classificatory schema; how could they not? It's an online world everywhere, after all. But to encounter is not necessarily to assimilate.)

I will mostly use the term "gay" in preference to "queer," in deference to my subjects' everyday usages. I will also use *de ambiente*, a complex and ubiquitous term that predates local use of "gay" and, up to a certain point, has a parallel history with that term. Educated Mexican speakers, especially academics and activists, sometimes use the word "queer" in English (occasionally transcribed as *cuir*), though the Spanish *raro* might serve as a workable translation. When it comes up, I cannot help but hear the term enclosed in quotation marks, designating what the Bakhtin school calls an alien word (an elite alien word at that) not yet assimilated into everyday speech.[12] This is no longer the case with the word "gay," which also was imported from English but which, like "nice," "sandwich," "coach," "open-minded," and other terms, long ago settled into vernacular Spanish.

(Perhaps someday "queer" will follow suit, the quotation marks around it fading into forgetfulness. This has not yet happened.)

Third, and over a somewhat longer stretch of time, a wider spectrum of scholarship and political writing has repeatedly (and with increasing urgency) denounced the specter of something called class reductionism and implored readers not to focus exclusively (or even at all) on social class. These critiques once packed a wallop, as New Left social movements sought to shake themselves loose from Old Left orthodoxies—which were often, let us be clear, harrowingly homophobic and sometimes, yes, reductionist. This scholarly trend was most obviously associated with British cultural studies from the 1970s onward and with various American schools of writing on race, gender, and sexuality, although it also swept the academic shores of many non-Anglophone countries.

The anti–class reductionists, who were originally grounded in socialist aspirations, began by unveiling an important truth: not every form of inequality under capitalism is reducible to class. (Marx himself said as much![13]) Over time, this intellectual turn, and those of us who participated in it, strove to give specificity to those *other* forms of inequality, to distinguish them from class inequality—and even (sometimes) to locate their origins in epochal historical shifts. This was good and right, for who would deny that the changing institutions of race, gender, kinship, and so on demarcate "material conditions"? And what, after all, could be more "material" than sexuality? The problem is that as this decades-long intellectual movement turned into an academic cottage industry, it lost track of the difference between relations of production (which are principally class relations) and institutions of social reproduction (which cut across class lines in various ways and serve to reproduce the social order). We counterposed the least Marxist conception of Worker (understood as a moral figure rather than as a participant in relations of production) with similarly ahistorical and reified notions of Identity. We began every academic soliloquy with the ritual invocation of the standard formula: "race, gender, and sexuality are social constructs"—and then proceeded to write about these identities as though they were more real than reality itself, existing independently of the ebb and flow of social and political-economic developments. The anti-reductionists have long since ended by contriving all manner of inventive and devious ways to close ranks around an essentially liberal conception of identity and to evade recognition of the central facts of social life under capitalism (which inevitably come down to class distinctions). These are oh-so-convenient elusions if, as now seems apparent, the aim is to build up comfortable enclaves in the neoliberal academic and foundation apparatus, pursuing an accredited and endowed version of social justice whose motto might well be: "Talk about anything except class."

Today's social and theoretical problems are of a different order from those of the recent past, a time when robust welfare states still blunted the impact of capitalist business cycles and tempered the ramifications of class in many people's personal experiences. The newer conditions, which include both widening economic inequalities and waxing toleration of sexual diversity, are dramatically, though not uniquely, on display in Mexico. We live in a social world that has been remade by fifty years of New Left social movements. We understand well enough that LGBT and other identities cannot be reduced to class. Yet we often fail to fully understand that those identities, and the striving for well-being and happiness they encapsulate, are not equally available to everyone who might wish to claim them. The signs and accoutrements of gay life—a certain manner of dress, a fun night out at the clubs, followed by Sunday brunch and banter informed by the sort of cultural capital described in David Halperin's witty and mischievous *How to Be Gay*—exceed the reach of many (perhaps most) aspirants, and not only in Mexico. (The phrase "and not only in Mexico" will be a recurring refrain of this book, which concerns global processes and tendencies.)

And this is precisely where class comes back into the picture: we can scarcely understand what brings us joy or pain, what aspirations we take on or shun in the pursuit of happiness, without also taking into account the material conditions of our existence. These material conditions are the ground or purchase for our strivings, which begin with the struggle for our daily bread; they assert a gravitational pull on our lofty aspirations no less than on our basic wants and needs. They principally involve what Marxists call "the class character of society."[14]

This book is an inquiry into the material foundations of sexual identity.

What we talk about when we talk about class is not always clear. Informally, we use the term "class" loosely, generically, to refer to income, educational level, the possession or not of *personal* property (such as a house or a small plot of land), and so on. A more disciplined approach emerges if we follow Marx's understanding of class as one's relation to *productive*, profit-making property (such as a factory, business, or corporation).[15] In the Marxist accounting, class is not a status or a state, much less an identity, but a *relation*; it is nonetheless an objective situation, ineluctably structured by productive and social forces.

More formally, we also talk about overlapping ("intersectional") identities, or we refer to experiences with conjugated forms of oppression and personal domination. On this point, much of the political and scholarly literature is less disciplined than its authors imagine—as though simply indicating that subaltern women are "doubly in shadow" or pointing to the overlapping forms of oppression that queers of color undeniably face (especially if they also happen to be queers without money) could in itself give us much traction on anything other than the barest of facts.[16] Too often, one imagines an accountant conducting an audit, tallying up identities on an old-style adding machine, with each entry registering a distinct tintinnabulation. It understates matters to say that much of this literature effaces the class character of the experiences it relates. Class appears, if at all, as the least compelling of an intersected subject's experiences of inequality. And when it does appear, confusions abound over even the most basic points. For instance, when Martin Manalansan IV claims that "class issues . . . are subordinated to the immigrant experience" for his subjects, he seems to treat class as though it were a durable personal trait. But what his own evidence actually shows is that his educated and credentialed middle-class informants have been proletarianized, pushed into menial jobs in the immigrant experience.[17] It is not that migration weighs more than class in the balance of discrete objects of analysis, but that immigration clarifies the salience of class.

This book affirms a different understanding of class, beginning with its connection to political economy. Exploitation is the central fact of capitalism, which cannot exist and reproduce itself unless it extracts a profit—that is to say, pays laborers less than the value of the commodities they produce. This dynamic—which *tears* something out of the worker, namely, effort, attention, activity, time—defines class not as an abstract category or identity but as an *antagonism*. This means that classes come into existence only in and through their struggles over wages, working conditions, the length of the workday, and so on, as Marx showed. It also means that class is *the* necessary and ineluctable form of social inequality under capitalism, which progressively resolves the class structure into a small class of owners (or stockholders) who seek profits and a very large class of non-owners who effectively have nothing except their own labor to sell in the marketplace. In countries like Mexico or the United States, the vast majority are workers.

It matters not what kind of industry or private enterprise is involved; waiters, salesclerks, and call center employees are workers no less than factory workers—and sometimes they labor under worse conditions, as the reader will see. Early on, Siegfried Kracauer spotted these truths about the so-called new middle classes in his 1929 ethnography, *The Salaried Masses*.[18] It matters, but only a little, whether the worker is directly employed or labors on a small farm to give over the sweat of his brow to the real owners of capital: lenders, banks, grain companies. This, too, was clear enough to late-nineteenth-century populist and socialist movements. For their part, the actual middle classes—who derive their incomes from small properties, or from licenses or credentials, or from managing other people's property—are always under pressure from above and below. From above, they are under constant threat of liquidation and proletarianization. From below, they are hard-pressed by the needs and demands of employees.

The sad fact is that class remains the dirty secret of gay life, and it is seldom expressly treated in LGBT studies. This is perhaps especially true of the field's queer theory variants, and this has been by design, not oversight. Opening with the line, "What do queers want?" Michael Warner expressly read class perspectives out of the field in his introduction to the influential collection *Fear of a Queer Planet*. "Class," he writes, "is conspicuously useless . . . unintelligible" for queer theorizations of the social.[19] Warner only gave explicit expression to an injunction that others were already implicitly following. And over thirty years, queer theory mostly heeded Warner's counsel, though a few have sometimes claimed the mantle of "materialism" to launch abstract notions that scrupulously avoid the nitty-gritty of economic inequalities.[20]

"Class is barely indexed in most Queer Studies scholarship," writes Matt Brim in a timely new book.[21] There have been notable exceptions to this trend, of course. Brim rightly pays homage to the nonacademic community historian Allan Bérubé.[22] Kath Weston always seems to have her eye on social class in the experiences of black, brown, and white LGBT people, and George Chauncey's *Gay New York* comes prominently to mind, with its close attention to class dynamics in the formation of gay communities.[23] In *Sexual Hegemony*, Christopher Chitty attempted to correlate the regulation of same-sex relations over the long development of the world system with crises of capital accumulation and how these have resonated in class relations.[24] But perhaps a more significant thematic exception to the rule is Didier Eribon's *Returning to Reims*, an autoethnographic reflection on the author's early life in a French working-class slum and how his sense of gay pride aligned with a sense of class shame. "It doesn't seem exaggerated to assert," Eribon writes, "that my coming out of the sexual closet, my desire to assume and assert my homosexuality, coincided within my personal trajectory with my shutting myself up inside what I might call a class closet."[25] Édouard Louis covers similar ground in his novel, *The End of Eddy*, an unflinching depiction of class violence that, like Eribon's *Returning*, also serves as an indictment of the French Socialist Party's progressive abandonment of the working poor. There are problems with these accounts, which treat class suspiciously like an identity or subculture and pay less attention to political-economic factors than one might hope. But France's gay intellectuals still care about class, even if their neoliberal governments do not; they understand that being poor, being lower-working-class, exposes you to the most brutal and unrelenting forms of homophobia. Their accounts also remind us that "being working class isn't just defined in terms of wages and economic indicators: it means that beauty has been stolen from your life," as Italian novelist Alberto Prunetti eloquently put it.[26]

Mexicans know this as well and are quite explicit about it. Mexican and binational scholars make frequent recourse to depictions of class conditions and class dynamics in their analyses of gayness—typically in combination with other factors, to be sure, but without making class disappear behind the other factors. Thus, for example, Víctor Macías-González keeps a close eye on class dynamics in the development and repression of mid-twentieth-century gay nightlife in Mexico City.[27] In *Pathways of Desire*, Héctor Carrillo shows how his migrant subjects' understandings of sexuality were shaped in no small part by their "geographic location" and "social class position."[28] Guillermo Núñez Noriega examines economic inequality in his study of identity and intimacy in rural northern Mexico, suggesting at the outset that the idea of a "gay world" "does not always offer a comfortable fit with class and ethnic experiences."[29] And in a work that attends to how class placement affects the understandings, experiences, and possibilities of gay existence in Mexico City, Mauricio List Reyes glances at the cruelties of subcultural life in a biting remark: "But we must be realistic: even among gay sectors there is intolerance and rejection, mainly due to social class and age."[30] The effects of social class on sexual cultures are not always foregrounded in the Mexican literature; class is not always given its full due. But it is not a dirty secret, either.

Americans have largely forgotten all of this, if they ever really knew any of it. Of course, some American scholars on the cultural studies Left do write the word "class" from time to time, typically embedded as an afterthought in a string of references to other forms of social inequality—"race, gender, sexuality, class"—but it's clear that they don't really mean it when they say the word and often don't even understand what it means: they see class basically as an effect of discrimination ("classism," a term introduced by Audre Lorde early on in the development of identity politics[31]) and not as the form that social relations inevitably take under the inexorable dynamics of capitalist production and circulation. Or else, in typical American style, they conflate class with one of its manifestations, poverty, conceptually aligning the bulk of ordinary working-class people with elites in the moral drama of rich versus poor.[32]

So far I have laid out a straightforward narrative, but I am not naïve about the complexities involved in social class. People experience greater or—more often—lesser forms of social mobility under modern class systems. Any given person's location in the class system thus might be unstable, transitory, in flux. Inequalities also exist within the working class. Some sectors of the labor force are better remunerated, enjoy more perquisites, or have more job security than others. This, their success at claiming a bigger chunk of the value they produce and asserting some control over their working conditions, nuances the question of nonownership but does not thereby transform workers into owners.

Then there are what Max Weber called "status" distinctions, which flow from one's relation to consumption as opposed to production. Through dress, dwelling, and myriad acts, I affect a "style of life": I display my education, my respectability or lack thereof; I adhere to an ethnic group; I claim higher or lower standing.[33] Gay subcultures have always planted themselves here, more or less, where the circuits of consumption define identity.

But not all inequalities under capitalism are of a strictly economic nature (production, consumption). Gender inequality, as Friedrich Engels realized, predates the capitalist mode of production and is rooted in the institutions of family and kinship, that is, in the mode of social reproduction.[34] This material site is also where homophobia comes into the picture: in modern industrial societies, the prohibition or devaluation of same-sex relationships has played an important role in regulating gender norms, structuring personal life, and consolidating the institutions of social reproduction.

Some inequalities are closely related to but not quite reducible to class; some are "holdovers" from precapitalist relations of production, subsequently assimilated into the capitalist system. Thus, when Marx wrote about the enclosure acts, conquest, colonialism, and slavery, he glossed these varied "takings" under the term "primitive accumulation," which he contrasted with the usual regime of capitalist accumulation: the former acts of theft and plunder predate or lie outside the economic system of capitalism proper, which extracts wealth as profits in the production and circulation of commodities. But it turns out that what is "primitive" about primitive accumulation is never finished once and for all and consigned to the past; instead, capitalist planners make recourse to looting, plunder, and other forms of brute expropriation whenever the circuits of capital are obstructed, whenever the system is in crisis.[35]

Capitalism as a social system also makes recourse to forms of coercion that augment and secure class exploitation, some of which derive from conditions of primitive accumulation. Thus, in writing about the Irish question, Marx observed that it benefits capitalists to maintain that one sector of the working class is inferior to the other, to pay members of that sector less, and to stoke ethnic, racial, and national divisions among the proletariat. He likened the status of the Irish worker in England to that of African Americans in the former slave states of the United States.[36] It goes without saying, then, that the history of conquest, colonialism, and slavery and, with it, the invention of racism and race form an important part of the history of global capitalism and the development of modern institutions. The implications of these histories unfold in different, conflicting, and changing ways at different moments.

All of these and other sorts of complication come into play in Mexico, where everyday insults and ascriptions refer to uncultured taste (a status distinction closely linked to gauges of class privilege), to homosexuality (specifically promiscuous, passive-role, lower-class homosexuality)—and perhaps especially to skin color and rural origins, typically in a condensed manner: having a rural or small-town background is tantamount to indigeneity; having dark skin and indigenous features implies rural roots in manual labor. But if there are good reasons to take into account how the history of colonial conquest and systems of race, caste, or ethnic domination have shaped the making of the Mexican working class, or to take stock of the way society still distinguishes intellectual from manual labor, masculine from feminine actions, light-colored from dark-colored skin, and so on, there are better reasons for distinguishing central from contingent facts of the present-day system—and for taking into account some of the contradictory ways peoples' lives play out among these intractable facts. The total situation of working-class people today depends on the meshing and crosshatching of all these factors, but the elements are not equally weighted.

This book, then, is a sustained argument about the strong draw of class on gay life in Mexico—and by extension in other places as well. It queries the ongoing antinomies of globalization, especially as these are involved with both a rising tide of economic inequality *and* the spread of LGBT sexual identity formations. It also asks: How do different modalities of inequality and identity hang together, "articulate," under changing regimes of modern capitalism?

The work unfolds in two parts. The first part seeks to understand how commonplace crises and predicaments play out in the lives of gay men, specifically around the question of coming out: to be, or not to be, gay? The first chapter provides a quick first immersion in the section's themes and problems as seen through the experiences of "Erik," a young working-class man from one of the pueblos (villages, towns) clustered on the outskirts of the city of Puebla. (Names and identifying traits have been changed throughout.) Erik arrives at his "moment of truth" when same-sex desires come into direct conflict with religious beliefs and intense family pressures to marry—at a propitious moment when he and his family are caught up in economic catastrophe. His approach is illustrative of how working-class people often deal with similar climacterics. He neither embraces the public mantle of gay pride nor retreats from gay life, he neither comes out nor remains in the closet. The second chapter is an interlude, not much longer than a title card in a silent film. It sketches an approach to the themes emergent in Erik's life and anticipates ideas to be tracked in subsequent chapters: Identity is essentially a type of story. Specifically, it is a "modern" story, by which we learn to live our lives.

Chapter 3 expands and deepens the themes broached in the first two chapters, giving up-close looks and fleeting glances at some of the ways some (more than a dozen) of my (mostly) working-class gay subjects' lives have played out over decades up until now. How have they resolved, or not, the inevitable crises of identity? What are some of the ways they have plotted their life stories between the rock of scarcity and the hard place of intolerance? How do storylines about modernity and self-possession work out for people of different upbringings, dispositions, and temperaments from different sections of the working class? If I have done my work in this, the book's longest chapter, the reader will get a sense of the tension between freedom and constraint, self-possession and privation, in the different paths working-class people take on life's journey. The fourth chapter briskly sketches some of my own coming-out experiences to suggest that my informants' life crises are commonplace occurrences in a globalizing world. Chapter 5 then concludes this self-enclosed first part. Contrasting my subjects' life histories with long-standing sociological models, it shows not that "class explains everything" nor that the working class is simply more culturally conservative than the middle or upper classes, but rather that at critical junctures, a great many urgent questions about sexuality, identity, and intimacy really do come down to what economic and cultural resources one possesses, that is to say, to one's class position, and to how one acts (and is acted upon) from that basis.

The second part returns to the problematic theme of advent, which opens this introduction: the arrival of a highly visible, public, "modern" gay scene. But such a scene did not pop up all at once; it developed over a long period, stretched out across different neighborhoods and classes. A homosexual underground was already present in 1901, when Mexico City's police infamously raided an upper-class homosexual dance ball, splashing scandal across tabloids and everyday conversations.[37] Homosexual milieux, including working-class scenes, remained planted in the rapidly growing, transnationally connected city over the decades of the early- to mid-twentieth century, as studies by historian Víctor Macías-González and others have shown.[38] Countercultural youth movements of the 1960s and 1970s gave new impetus to the development of this preexisting subculture, which grew and became more visible under liberalization in the 1990s, then exploded in the 2000s, arriving finally in second-tier cities like Puebla, the main site of my study. Inevitably, given the stretches of time involved, the series of meditations in part II are more historical and expressly *historicist* in their approach. From shifting vantages, they examine how what it means to be *de ambiente*—"on the scene" or "in the life," for want of a better immediate translation—has metamorphosed under changing political-economic conditions.

Chapter 6 begins to sketch these changes by relating how it happened that I came to make Puebla my home over so many years. Chapter 7 then takes a step back from scenes of everyday life to adumbrate a thumbnail history of Mexico's transition from center-left dictatorship to neoliberal democracy, tracing some of the ways that identity has been a constant and vexed theme in Mexican history. It also begins to suggest how the narrative threads for the construction of different sorts of identities (gay, indigenous, mestizo) borrow from one another's storylines and interweave with national dramas about modernity. It ends by showing how political and economic liberalization (neoliberal deregulation) along with the spread of global new media cultivated the terrain in which "modern," visible gay identities and institutions could take root. The connections between economic and cultural liberalization challenge complacent notions about identity and its placement in social formations; these challenges have not always been clearly marked, not even by local activists.

The eighth chapter examines these questions through the experiences of a young migrant from an indigenous village. It relates elements of his life story over some fifteen years, probing points of tension between universalization and particularism, freedom and constraint, and how ubiquitous ideas about "modernization" and "backwardness" shape gay life. (I continue to bracket such terms in eyebrow-raising quotation marks.) The chapter's protagonist, Diego, left one identity (indigenousness) behind to embrace another (gayness). He longs for what he understands to be up-to-date modern freedoms. But ambiguity and contradiction, it turns out, haunt the supposedly open field of gay possibilities. In reflecting on the course of his life, I begin an explicit discussion of a theme that resonates across the text: How are we to understand *frustrated* longings? I try to shape an understanding that departs from the prevailing academic approaches to want and affect, which, it seems to me, assume what the earnest scribblers already want to show.

The most daring because it is the most obvious premise of this book can be put succinctly: economic inequality—which is to say, social class—affects sexual subjects and subjectivities in ways both crude and subtle; it shapes gay life not only from the *outside* (through limited resources, which push against people's aspirations and propel their life stories along certain tracks) but also from the *inside* (that is, through the economically valenced definitions that structure those very aspirations). Chapter 9, a series of reflections on the uses of the term *puto* (fag, queer) and its relationship to "gay," spells out how this works. It shows first how class—the inescapable fact of people's existence under capitalism—constrains people's options; second, how it defines ranked social spaces and sexual identities; third, how it consequently structures gay men's symbolic worlds; and, finally, how submerged class struggles and manifest class anxieties resonate directly and indirectly in gay aspirations. The book's conceptual epicenter, this chapter shows how longing, economic limitation, and frustration come together in the struggle to be gay.

Chapter 10 continues to probe the preceding chapter's themes by examining them across changing sexual geographies. Through vignettes

and scenes—a series of postcards, if you will—it constructs a novel argument about how the terms "gay" and *de ambiente* functioned during years
of repression under the dictatorship; how they differently divide up the
conceptual terrain today; what sorts of subcultures they predicate; and,
not least, how they inevitably mark class differences. Delving into how
"gay life" was lived before broad dissemination of the term "gay," this chapter also suggests some of the ways gay life still goes on outside the gay
subculture. Two figures cast long shadows across this chapter: Juan
Gabriel, the Mexican singer-songwriter pop icon, who neither concealed
nor revealed his sexuality; and Carlos Monsiváis, Mexico's gay leftist public intellectual, whose writings often reflect on his compatriots' unrequited
longing for modernity. My framings across part II, including the "postcards" conceit in this chapter, owe a great debt to Monsiváis.[39]

A penultimate microchapter glances at the urban surround and recaps
the history of subcultures. Then the twelfth and final chapter tracks how
the gay scene has changed in two cities, eighty miles apart (Mexico City
and Puebla), since the florescence of gay nightlife in the 2000s. If the
onset of neoliberalism was associated with openness, toleration, and liberalization, a second phase soon set in and in some ways replicated forms
of repression associated with the dictatorship—albeit under new stated
rationales. What neoliberalism gives with one hand it takes away with the
other.

The conclusion adumbrates something of the (historical, sociological,
and above all political-economic) limits of gay identity, but also revisits
some of gaiety's open-ended promise.

My intent is to write about such matters as passion, love, and the desire for
freedom—which, for us, assert themselves in the guise of identity and
involve the struggle to be clear about it—as these play out under prevailing conditions, which set the terms that all too often undermine our
heartfelt strivings. My main method consists in trying to scratch just
below the surfaces of events, to get at what messier stuff might be lurking
underneath the sign of gay identity: to try to understand how people with
such-and-such pasts really do make their own meanings, their own histories, not just any way they please but under conditions constrained by the
past and structured by present-day inequalities. I hope it is clear that I am

trying to avoid the prevailing conventions of identity politics, which stage people's life stories as events in the Oppression Olympics, a conceit whose reactionary class politics becomes clearer every day. The point is not to find out which section of the working class suffers the most onerous compounded oppressions but to show that the coordinates of identity formations can be made fully intelligible only when plotted against the class condition of society. And I have tried to write about this business accessibly, often in the vernacular.

It may not always be clear to what extent I am rubbing my accounts against existing scholarship, much of which remains on the surface of events in the realm of abstract identities, canned performances, mechanistic intersectionalities, whimsical psychologisms, ahistorical temporalities, idle performances of recreational pessimism, free-floating culturescapes, windy denunciations of ordinary people's mundane goals—or even, it must be said, flyover Marxisms (which give us a picture of the terrain as seen from a very far distance but lose track of its meandering footpaths and kinked trails, to say nothing of the people who wend their ways along them). If I say that I have become wary of many of the received wisdoms and trending colloquies of the professional chattering classes (to which I belong, in which I inevitably participate), I will seem ungenerous or presumptuous or un-self-aware. So let me say instead that I try to be attentive to both the empirical demands of ethnography, with its attention to real people's agencies and aspirations over the course of everyday life, and to the exigencies of the wider capitalist system, which frames people's experiences and understandings. We are thrown into a world not of our making and we try to make a home there, with what resources we can muster, sometimes fixing our eyes on distant possibilities. We struggle, we love, we hope, we get by. The prospects of gay life look very different if we start there, with the struggles of real people immersed in ordinary, mundane problems, rather than in the prepackaged bundles of idealist concepts that define the rise and fall of the strictly academic movements that purport to speak in our names.

If I have made my mark, the reader will see that gayness, as the concept actually circulates in everyday life among ordinary people, is in no small part an unfulfilled desire, a frustrated wish, a receding referent: a capacious utopian longing for a better life that takes shape under definite material conditions and aims at a discernible horizon of happiness. This might sound something like José Muñoz's inventive claims in *Cruising Utopia*, but perhaps it might be better to invert Muñoz's assertions about an abstracted "queerness," which he sees as the future utopian idea.[40] Actually, the concept of queerness, which carries with it stigma and social exclusion as the price of pleasure or love, is very much part of the lived "here-and-now" for most LGBT people, who long to escape this estranged reality or at least to seek reprieve from it.[41] What people who work, worry, and wish[42] generally aspire to is a *gay* future, that is to say, a happy, unfettered one. The reader will come to make out something of the class content of these very strivings in the following pages. Reflection on this, the class character of gay struggles, is largely absent in Muñoz's book and other works that purport to delve into the utopian dimension of LGBT life. (Occasional references to class notwithstanding, the nucleus of Muñoz's utopia seems to be found in a curiously segregated social imagination: in ethnically homogenous bars and clubs where participants, free at last of the white gaze, pose and model conjugated race-ethnic-sexual identities.)

It seems to me that this—acknowledgment of what we do when we aspire to gayness, recognition of the primacy of the class condition of our evanescent scenes and flickering identities—neither closes off nor "reduces" or narrows the meanings of gay life; much less does it augur their retreat into ethnic enclaves; rather, it opens us up to wider solidarities and connects us with other struggles for dignity and a decent life.

Or such, at any rate, is a sentimental gay socialist's utopian wish for us: that life might be more pleasant and more fulfilling—gayer—even after the music stops. This is a book about Mexican gay men, of course, but this is also a book about all of us. The reader will judge whether I have been reductive or synthetic.

PART I

Predicament and Crisis

THE STRUGGLE FOR SELF-DETERMINATION

I can only answer the question, "What am I to do?" if I can answer the prior question, "Of what story or stories do I find myself a part?"

—Alasdair MacIntyre, *After Virtue*

No mode of production and therefore no dominant order and therefore no dominant culture ever in reality includes or exhausts all human practice, human energy, and human intention.

—Raymond Williams, *Marxism and Literature*

Sweet are the uses of adversity.

—William Shakespeare, *As You Like It*

1 Moment of Truth

My young friend Erik was in the grips of despair. A twenty-one-year-old farm boy from a tough, grimy pueblo just outside the city's expanding core, he confided to me that although he was gay and was falling deeply in love with another man, he did not plan to remain in *el ambiente* ("the gay life") much longer. He wanted a "normal" life. And he feared for the fate of his soul, which he believed would be lost to eternal darkness. The setting is Puebla, Mexico, in 2011, but the young man's moment of crisis will scarcely seem alien to gay readers from any number of backgrounds in any number of settings or countries.

The youngest of thirteen siblings, Erik had quit school when he was sixteen to take care of his aging parents and to tend the family's small farm. His brothers and sisters had all left home and scattered to far-flung cities, putting some distance between themselves and a violent, domineering father. School had been a frustrating experience in any event. He had had a difficult childhood—if you go to school barefoot and unwashed, many teachers will view you as a lost cause—and had fallen three grades behind his peers.

When he first began venturing onto the gay scene at about this time, Erik had thought of his activity there as an experiment, a passing stage, a youthful adventure to be enthusiastically embraced before eventually returning to the fold of church and family. In this case, the church was Jehovah's Witnesses, a proselytizing millenarian religion that has made substantial inroads among indigenous and recently mestizoized members of Mexico's lower classes. (By "recently mestizoized," I refer to people who have recently shed the primary markers of indigenous identity: language, dress, residency.) Erik's long-suffering mother was an iconic convert: she and her husband had both spoken Nahuatl in their youth. She had joined the church when Erik was a small boy, after enduring years of domestic violence, and had pulled much of the family along with her into a soberer and less violent life. Erik had grown up in the church and had attended weekly meetings. Now, after five years of wandering, it was the fact that he was falling in love with an older man, a gentle, doting doctor—precisely at a time when he should have been beginning his retreat from the lures of the flesh—that brought the young man to his moment of truth.

"I AM ERIK AND I AM GAY"

I, too, had inadvertently contributed to Erik's existential crisis by asking him to write a short life history. He took up the call with vigor and produced scores of introspective pages relating a life of poverty and struggles with his sexual feelings. In a telling passage, he narrates that he had *resigned* himself to being gay—and yet, as though by contrast, he put a positive spin on the title of his *testimonio*: "Soy Erik y Soy Gay."

I mark at the outset Erik's title: it is written in the indicative mood, a simple straightforward assertion of fact. In actuality, there was nothing simple or straightforward about Erik's declaration, which resembles a great many kinds of utterances on the gay scene. Perhaps his title is better understood as the expression of a hope or wish, that is, a statement in the optative mood. Or, to shift analytical gears (while keeping in view our premise, that ideas about gayness embody a certain *striving* for happiness), perhaps it reflects what J. L. Austin dubs an "infelicity," that is, an honest performative utterance that fails because it lacks the material and institutional conditions to support it.[1] In either case, emphatic declarations are the stuff of writing but proved more difficult to sustain in real life.

In our conversations, I urged him to reconsider his plans for retreat and told him, quite simply, that he was naïve if he thought that "normal" people were any happier than *we* were. My use of the words "normal" and "we" were deliberate and considered: the former because Erik had introduced the idea of a "normal life" while reflecting on the married lives of his siblings; the latter because, following the communal precedent of friends in the bars, I was claiming comembership in the identity he dreaded. "You wouldn't understand," he said. "It's not easy being gay in Mexico."

This was not the first time I had heard this exact phrase, which, perhaps more than anything, serves to locate speakers within the coordinates of a world imagined along the axes of wealth and tolerance. I don't know whether it's easy being gay anywhere, or whether the worst difficulties are of our own making or of someone else's, but my thoughts at the time were steeped in the rose-colored literature on globalization and its associated transformations of conservative sexual cultures. I pressed what I thought were obvious points, a veritable catalog of changes associated with liberalization and globalization: "But things are changing quickly, and life is getting better for gays here in Mexico. There are bars, cafés, meeting places everywhere. You can't stroll in the *centro* without running into gay or lesbian couples holding hands. More people are living outside the closet, and there are gay role models on TV and in the movies. In Mexico City, you can even get married now. So, in the emerging reality, you do have a place." Thus I, too, mapped the coordinates of an imagined world.

Erik was unimpressed by my sunny account. "Maybe," he replied. "But when I was seven, my cousin came out. His family ran him out of the house and disowned him. He lived in the streets for several months and now no one even mentions his name." To tide over his sixteen-year-old cousin, Erik had stolen small amounts of money, undetected, from his parents' "secret" safe-keeping spot, the family Bible; the two remained in furtive contact during this season of family drama until the cousin, who never could find a place in Mexico, made his way surreptitiously across the border into the United States.

Erik went on to relate to me some of his own experiences, which narrated the dark underside of gay modernity in Mexico: he had been lured into robberies and subjected to extortion attempts by other gay men; he had experienced varied forms of police harassment. He talked about his mistreatment in gay establishments because of his dark skin and, more important, his work-hardened, sun-burnt hands, which betrayed his class position and the fact that he was a manual laborer. (There were plenty of people with skin as dark as Erik's in the bars and clubs; there were not so many whose bodies were marked by hard physical work.) He talked about the claustrophobia of a gossipy neighborhood and intense family pressures to marry. In fact, a year before, his ailing mother had stepped up her campaign to see him married before she died; he yielded to family pressures and proposed to a childhood friend. The girl proved to be wise beyond her years. With wedding plans set and invitations sent out, she proposed that the two of them have sex. "My spirit abandoned me," he explained elegiacally, and his fiancé told him, "So, it's true what they say. You are gay. Don't worry, I'm not going to tell anyone. But we are *not* going to get married." The two of them, still maintaining an old friendship, sent out notices retracting the wedding invitations.

Looming over the present scene like an inescapable dark cloud was unfinished mourning and the nightmare of bad debt. When Erik had taken out a loan to buy an expensive new tractor, it seemed a good idea: his crops had good placement in local markets and fetched what he thought of as good prices. He was also working full-time at the Volkswagen plant, so reliable money was coming in and there were few expenses. Then his mother's health went into rapid decline, and the family mobilized all of its resources to cover her medical and private hospital expenses. She died after a pacemaker proved ineffective. Erik continued making payments on the loan, but the debt was growing, not shrinking, and he found himself on the brink of losing the farm to the bank that had engaged him in a predatory lending scheme. When he missed a payment, the bank had him tossed into jail until his father could sell a patch of land and scrape together enough money, not to pay off the ballooning debt, but only to bring the account up-to-date.

Ultimately, it was neighborhood gossip that brought things to a head. A week after our weighty conversation, neighbors told Erik's father that he had been seen holding hands with his boyfriend in an area frequented by gays. The old man broke into the boy's locked desk to find incriminating photos, memorabilia—and his life story notes. The father then summoned two of Erik's brothers, and the three of them kidnapped and sequestered the boy, taking his cell phone and subjecting him to beatings, reproaches, and emotional blackmail for the better part of a week: Do you think this is what God wants for you? Don't you know you're going to get AIDS and die? Is this how you honor the memory of your mother? Get yourself back into alignment with your family!

In the midst of this tribulation, Erik sneaked up to the rooftop and used a secret cell phone that he kept stashed away, for emergencies, to call his boyfriend. He told the forbearing doctor that he now wanted to leave home, leave the ambiente, and rejoin the church somewhere in a city where no one knew his name. And he explained, dejectedly, that if he rejoined the church, he would have to shun homosexuals, including his lover. I do not know how all of the conversation went. The doctor was visibly shaken when I saw him the next day. He tells me that on his end of the conversation, he was loving and supportive but also firm and perhaps resigned. "You do whatever you think you have to do, and I'll even try to help you if you choose to escape. But you won't be very happy, and neither will I. Think about what you're doing. Think about how crazy it is that you've let yourself be kidnapped by someone you support. Think about how your church's taboos are out of step with the rest of the modern world. And if you can't think about me, think about yourself: Is this really the kind of life you want?"

Much to my surprise, Erik toughed out his week of family abuse: adversity seems to have stiffened his resolve; perhaps his partner's words had struck some chord. And, although he never uttered the phrase, "I am gay and I am proud of it," he steadfastly refused to renounce his lover, even with threats of disinheritance hanging in the balance. Emotional blackmail (*chantaje*), I suppose, is a two-way street: it requires, on the one side, a party who imposes extortion and, on the other side, a party willing to receive it. Knowing how to play the game requires savvy: cultural and emotional competence. At the end of it all, his father grudgingly announced a new set of conditions, a sort of uneasy truce. His words bear scrutiny; they reveal much about the conditions of gay existence for many working-class youth: "First, I do not want to talk about it anymore. Second, I don't want to hear about it again, either. And third, you will *not* bring men to this house."

After this moment of crisis, Erik's behavior did not much change— except that whenever he was out with his partner or a group of gay friends, he could be seen casting furtive glances to make sure that none of his siblings or members of their families were on the street and that no one from his pueblo was around.

SUFFERING IT

No doubt Erik's ordeal was extreme, though not as extreme as for some. It will serve as an illustration of the predicaments and strategies of many, a rebuttal to (or at least a forceful qualification of) my initial upbeat assessment of globalization's tonic effects on local culture: "but everything is changing . . ." Some things were changing, yes, and some of those things indeed had to do with liberalization and openness, with the spread of global new media, with the arrival of rainbow-flag-festooned bars declaring gay identity, and so on. But at the same time, visibility implies exposure—and institutional opposition to assorted cultural changes was also stiffening. Narratives of "family unity" (the Mexican version of "family values") were spreading in conservative religious and political circles, perhaps the most obvious response to young people's changing sexual mores. The varied pluses and minuses, liberations and repressions, were unequally distributed across uneven geographies.

What Jon Binnie observed early on in *The Globalization of Sexuality* remains relevant today: "Globalization has reinforced the importance of space and place precisely because places are differently impacted upon by globalization." This observation is especially germane if we keep in view how sexual geographies are bisected and fragmented by class differences (a problem to which Binnie was finely attuned).[2] What little research exists on the question—to say nothing of garish newspaper headlines buried in the back pages of local newspapers—suggests that violence, discrimination, and family rejection often take brutal forms (beatings, kidnappings, even lynchings) in low-income barrios and poor pueblos.

And so for Erik, as for others in his class situation, there was no resplendent "coming out," no heroic moment of gay triumph in an enlightened world, no tidy final resolution to all of the conflicts over what it might mean to desire or love someone of the same sex. His agency, his uneasy struggle for a gay life, is better described by an all-purpose verb that Mexicans use to describe their strivings in the face of hardship: *aguantar*—to hold on, hold out, put up with, suffer, withstand, resist, endure; to suck it up.

We need to balance opposed propositions to understand this suffering.

On the one hand, some might celebrate Erik's strategy of passive endurance as an authentic Mexican alternative to the supposedly Anglophone notion of gayness, with its storyline of self-discovery and self-expression, its rites of coming out, its insistence on publicity and transparency. Suspicion of the idea of coming out has waxed in the academic literature over many years, and subaltern stealth is sometimes offered as an alternative to the pageantry of self-disclosure. (I take Martin Manalansan IV to be making a case like this in his discussion of the legacies of Stonewall: his Filipino immigrant informants are said to see coming out as "the primary preoccupation of gay men from other ethnic and racial groups."[3]) I am not impressed: the celebrants themselves (economically comfortable academics who are "out" for all the world to see) are invariably far removed from the scene of suffering and the very real toll that it takes on those who endure a life in the shadows. No one wants to live a life of shame and concealment—that much ought to be axiomatic. Erik's life is experienced as painful precisely because he cannot quite partake in the coming-out storyline, which he understands all too well.

On the other hand, some might (and some of his Poblano friends do) rebuke Erik for his lack of independence, his inability to stand up to his family, his attempt at straightening up his life with a poor unwitting barrio girl, his failure to embrace a proud, public gay identity. But then, the scolds do not have to live in his skin, which is the color of the earth; they do not have to endure his class situation, or the weight of family histories and local institutions that make it unique. The better course would be to empathize and try to understand how identity flickers into awareness, or not, and how it is announced to the world, or not, under specific conditions.

And what, after all, is an identity?

"US" AND "THEM" AND THE WRITER'S PREDICAMENTS

Fussy writers invariably struggle with pitch, tone, wording, and the placement of details in wider narrative arcs. Perhaps the most vexing problem for contemporary ethnographic writing is the placement of the narrator within his or her narrative, a problem that inevitably implies discomfiture and embarrassment. For, from the moment one takes the view that culture or experience is a possession or property, a sense of shame attaches particularly to anthropological writing—telling stories about other people's stories. Perhaps the better, more productive course would be to work with this sense of shame rather than disowning it.[4]

More than a few times in the process of assembling this work, I have heard the phrase "Gringo, you couldn't possibly understand" and others like it. It's true. There are things I couldn't possibly understand. I will never understand from the inside what it is like to have grown up in a dictatorship or to have the Virgin of Guadalupe watch over me. I will always hear Nahuatl words, which are abundant in Mexico, as magical sweeping and swishing sounds punctuated by staccato consonants. Although I can decompose a few place-names into coherent meanings (Popoca+téptl, "smoking mountain"; Chapul+tepec, "grasshopper hill"), I will never hear them as echoes and fragments of a musical language that in my childhood I heard parents or grandparents speaking. But I do know a thing or two about repressive institutions and family blackmail, having grown up in the Bible Belt. Rural poverty is not foreign to me. I understand the terror of putting a loved one in the hands of doctors who might not be up to the task; I also know what it's like to spend my paycheck before the next payday and to wonder how I'm going to make ends meet. I know very well what it means to give something up for the love of men. I know how it feels to anxiously await the results of an HIV test. And whether our experiences converge or diverge, I like to think that I'm reasonably capable of that mysterious faculty, empathy: the ability to share feeling, to put oneself in the shoes of another, to walk a common ground. The power of empathy in fostering what Max Weber called *Verstehen*, sympathetic understanding, is no doubt underrated in the identity politics vulgate today. It is also probably true that people tell me things precisely because I'm an outsider that they would never tell someone who was an insider, a "member of Mexican society" as one interlocutor put it, blushing, in a confessional moment.

When I say such things, my writing sometimes seems to me like a rearguard action, a contretemps with my own allies in ongoing academic culture wars. "Difference," "otherness," and "identity" have been the watchwords of the scholarly left for most of my adult life. But if the unfurling of these battle flags and the pursuit of their implications in the academe have had positive effects—putting an end to the reign of an official public white monoculture; making way for other voices to be heard—they have also had negative ones. In training our gaze on differences, we progressively lose sight of long histories of interconnection. We fix our gazes on the local, the particular, and our experience of it, when what ought to command our attention is universality, the system, and especially how what Marxists used to call "the totality" shapes our experiences. In stilted academic works, we construct a monadic and monological cosmos in which each of us is enjoined to act as representational proprietor of his or her own identity: a flat, loveless, and ultimately uninhabitable universe. We could at least have companionship on this imperiled planet if we greeted one another, in Schopenhauer's elegiac terms, as "fellow sufferers" in a world of fallen subjects.

I insist, in any event, that mindfulness of the other person's unique point of view is only the starting point, not the end point, of productive conversation, which must, like the work of labor or the work of art, produce something independent of and distinct from the activity that produced it. For this the Greeks used the word *poiesis*, linked to poetry but also to other forms of creativity, including material production. I should like to think that the labor that produces such a work is collaborative, that here in these pages you encounter the intellectual work of Erik and the doctor and countless others, even if the ethnographic product typically appears under an individual author's name. I also suggest that the idea that our cultures and experiences are impossibly far apart—the conceit that once buttressed anthropological expertise and now props up identitarian claims—is belied by everyday shared experience. For the most part, we live out of one another's pockets, co-involved in exchanges, conversations, intimacies, and conflicts that all go into the making of the modern world. This much was well known thirty years ago, at the peak of the dialogical turn in cultural studies, when James Clifford recast our understanding of culture not as a property or possession but as a "predicament."[5]

My own predicament is of a specific sort: I long ago lost any sense that the people I write about here are a *them*, cultural others subject to troubles, struggles, and desires that are readily distinguishable from those of a cultural *us* (educated readerships, who invariably turn out to live in cities or suburbs or on college campuses but not in working-class slums or trailer parks—where, after all, the rules of everyday struggles really *are* different). Over the past fifteen years, I have made a home as much in Mexico as in the United States; my friendships, social life, and love life are all centered here.

I can say this only haltingly, as might be appropriate for a "predicament." Yes, I understand that such travel on such terms is a privilege. (The word "privilege" is often misused today but is appropriate here.) I obtained a Mexican permanent resident visa by maintaining a temporary resident visa in good standing for five continuous years; the authorities required little more of me than a copy of my bank account records, some paperwork, and a modest application fee. They did not count up how many days I had actually been in Mexico over this five-year period but verified only that I had periodically renewed my temporary visa in a timely manner. When my friends travel in the opposite direction, as they sometimes do, their journey invariably takes one of two forms. For middle-class people, it involves elaborate paperwork, a long wait, an interview, and perhaps a background check and physical examination. For working-class people, it is likely to involve a fraught and dangerous three-day crossing through the desert.[6] No, I have not forgotten how inequalities pervade social relationships, not only between ethnographer and subject but also among friends and lovers. I do not delude myself into thinking that I can "speak for" my subjects or that I can present the "native's point of view" (the vanishing point of twentieth-century anthropological ethnography), much less that I have "crossed over" or "gone native" (one of the many false lures of participant-observation research). I am staking a different claim here.

Ethnography, like history, is (to steal a line from Frederic Jameson) in part an account of "what hurts."[7] As Erik's experience suggests, many of our hurts are shared: oppressive norms and exploitative conditions cut across national, cultural, and ethnic borders. Ethnographic accounts ought to convey empathic understandings of suffering, underlining our commonalities where appropriate, the better to underscore our shared human condition; drawing out differences where necessary, the better to understand the uneven workings of the world system. Might ethnography also be an account of everyday aspirations, reckless wagers, and fleeting triumphs against the odds? A resident alien, I describe scenes and place my bets. I claim only that I try to understand my friends' stories and experiences empathically, no doubt imperfectly, from within the horizon of shared interests and experiences. These "others" are my fellow sufferers; they are also fellow gamblers, fellow revelers, fellow travelers. What they tell me, sometimes implicitly and often explicitly, is that it isn't easy being gay in Mexico—and that the odds are doubly, triply stacked against you if you're working-class or poor.

In relating Erik's story, and other stories like it, I have tried to engage in sufficient depth with frustration and ambiguity. I have tried to capture what suffering endures and where hope might glimmer.

ERIK TODAY

The main elements of Erik's predicament ought to be familiar enough to empathic readers from any modern culture or class; a world-weary queen might even regard them as a pile of clichés. They include all the elements, in succession, of a timeworn story: repression, self-discovery, climax, denouement. It is their constellation under specific social conditions (including the place of suffering in Mexican culture) that makes them unique.

A decade later, Erik's crisis of self-acceptance and family turmoil seems long past. His struggles have equilibrated. By some miracle of dumb luck and the intervention of a rich distant relative—a story worthy of its own Mexican telenovela—he escaped the bank's clutches and kept the family farm (though, in the process, the farm and the family home were stripped bare, shorn of anything that could be sold). He now works full time, studies full time, and tends the farm on such free time as he can snatch from his weekly routine. He still lives at home and still takes care of his aging father, who is afflicted with diabetes, has had cancer, and is now in the early stages of Alzheimer's. Whether he gives this care out of a sense of love or a sense of duty—is there ever a simple choice between the one and the other?—I cannot say, but such is often the fate of the youngest son, especially in rural cultures (as Nancy Scheper-Hughes told us a long time ago): they are the ones left behind.[8] He has mentioned once that he stands to receive property—a patch of land, the family home—when his father dies, but that this is not his foremost motivation.

It cannot quite be said that he has renounced his faith. Although he left the church, he still believes in many of its precepts. For a time, he wore a bracelet prohibiting hospital medics from giving him a blood transfusion in the event of an emergency. He still corrects me when I refer to Jehovah's Witnesses as a "sect"; it is a church, I am told. Rather, he has developed a less intolerant, more generous framework for thinking about matters of salvation and damnation; he brackets off the church's denunciation of homosexuality, which he views as a doctrinal error, from the idea of a loving God. This is not a new story. Gays and lesbians who grew up in conservative churches seldom abandon their childhood beliefs entirely. (In a generous and affirming book, Ellen Lewin has illuminated some of the creative ways that black LGBT Pentecostals in the United States keep the faith while practicing radical inclusivity.[9])

Part of what defines emotional maturity is knowing whom to cling to in a clutch: knowing who is good for one's stability and emotional well-being. Erik remains connected to the ambiente through gay friends and in a relationship with his partner, the doctor, who paid tuition for him to finish high school (on a one-year accelerated plan) and now pays tuition and fees as he completes an undergraduate degree in biology at one of the local private universities affiliated with the public state university. Hypergamy, as sociologist Judith Stacey once observed without any hint of sarcasm or mockery, is one of the potential benefits for (young, attractive) men in gay relationships.[10] Stacey draws out one of the ways class and desire might intersect in gay life. But perhaps this is to put matters too clinically, to say nothing of how it takes emotional attachments out of the picture. Mexican culture, like American culture, has elaborate vocabularies for describing all the ways that any two people might share material circumstances, economic predicaments, class situations: some are approved, some are disapproved, and it is not always clear what earmarks distinguish good transfers from bad.

The strapping young man, whose body was formed by years of hard work, has heard that some of the doctor's friends—upper-middle-class professionals—disapprove of their relationship, which he contrasts with that of age-and-class-disparate heterosexual relationships: "Society will never view our relationship in positive terms," he says matter-of-factly. "They will always say that someone is exploiting someone else." The doctor, who has a well-preserved gym body of indeterminate age, waxes enigmatic on the subject: "The fish can't see the bowl they swim in." I take him to mean that emotional relationships inevitably have a material dimension, which respectable heterosexual society of the modern liberal era goes to great lengths to deny or conceal. "But I love him, and he loves me." He then adds impishly: "And perhaps it's good that Erik is spending so much time taking care of his sick father. By the time we finally get to live together, I'll be old and will need someone to take care of me."

Mexican jests often mock misfortune or fate. It is difficult to imagine that the doctor, who runs, lifts weights, and maintains himself in good trim, will ever need such care. But time and chance happeneth to us all, and here he, too, expresses his relationship to the ubiquitous Mexican concept *aguante* (noun form of *aguantar*), the guardian spirit of those who suffer, put up with, or endure: the ancient hope that suffering or waiting is an activity that might prove productive.

2 A Provisional Answer to the Question

Identities are not a priori, universal, or timeless; they never simply "express" themselves; they do not come ready-made, as much as this might seem to be the case. They are always cultivated, coaxed, contested, and coerced under specific conditions.

What, after all, is an identity?

To give a preliminary answer to the question: It is an artefact, fabricated on the lathe of history. A poetic residue, elaborated by the anonymous chorus. A name, bestowed as either malediction or blessing—and, thus, a contestable claim. A type of story whereby we learn to live our lives. Of course, the idea that one's life might be a story, a movie, a show, is itself a distinctly modern one, as Anthony Giddens reminds us.[1] It relies on techniques and technologies: the diary, the novel, the autobiography, cinema, TV. Ideas about the self as a self-contained and self-consistent story, along with attendant practices of self-knowledge and self-care, inaugurate the quest for truth that we call "modernity." This unevenly developed and distributed modernity cannot be understood without reference to its motor: changing regimes of capital accumulation that, from the beginning, have operated on global scales.

But I get ahead of myself. This remains to be shown.

3 Life's Rich Pageant

Ethnographic writing, like narratives of self-identity, is based in storytell-ing. Stories get richer as they get older, until we forget the enthusiasms that gave rise to them, whereupon they begin to decompose, subject to the law of entropy.

One of the advantages of long-term fieldwork in a specific location—in this case, Puebla—is the experience of accompanying people on life's jour-ney over a sustained period of time; of trying to understand their stories, both as they might appear from the outside and as their protagonists might understand them; of watching, sometimes up close and sometimes from a distance, some of the ways an identity is claimed or denied, some of the ways concupiscence might mesh with class, status, and power.[1] One of the disadvantages is that the resident alien starts to lose that sense of detachment that marks contemplative, academic writing. Or is that an advantage? Whether the result is a scholarly study or a set of personal reflections, I cannot say.

On this palette, I sketch the contours of a number of people's biogra-phies. What I hope I can give is a sense of how life's rich pageant unfolds under different circumstances, of the specificity or "thisness" of gay, mostly working-class men's experiences. In drawing these stories, I hope to show some of the ways my friends and subjects work through their inevitable crises and predicaments, and thus to paint a picture of how gay life is lived in a particular place and time. I dwell on the beautiful, sad, messy details in order to show two things: first, that individual storylines are swayed by their material conditions—specifically, by their placement in a class system; and, second, that this sway is not absolute, that the course of an individual's life over time might follow not just one or two but many possible trajectories, subject to temperament, whim, or luck.

LOCATION

The stories are set in Puebla de Zaragoza, a city with a grand colonial past and a reputation for cultural conservatism. Conservatives invariably still call the place Puebla de los Ángeles, its religiously inflected colonial-era name, which antedates its secular, patriotic, Liberal-era title. The colonial downtown, supposedly drafted by angels, is well preserved and is recognized by UNESCO as a World Heritage Site.[2] Developers and officials have tried with varying degrees of success to position the city's scenic historic center as a destination for international tourism. So much is "tradition" and the savvy marketing of it, but more importantly, Puebla is the home of what was, until 2011, North America's only Volkswagen (VW) plant. It is still the company's largest factory outside Germany and is the city's largest employer. The VW plant has been joined by an Audi plant on the other side of town, to say nothing of a host of suppliers and services to support car manufacturing, plus a handful of assorted *maquilas* that make clothing, machine parts, or plastics. In addition, the city has evolved over time into a hub for higher education; it is said to have more institutions of higher learning per capita than any other Mexican city.

For all that, the city cannot be said to have a diversified, developed economy. Despite its eponymous capital city's standing as an education hub, the state of Puebla ranks low on the Human Development Index, an aggregation of education, income, and life expectancy statistics: just above three states stigmatized in the public view by poverty and underdevelopment—Oaxaca, Guerrero, and Chiapas.[3] Workers in the informal sector—who work "off the books" for cash in unregistered positions, or who are precariously self-employed, or who work in black or gray markets (and in all cases receive no protections or benefits)—far outnumber those in the formal sector.[4]

Puebla thus hosts a large student population, a cosmopolitan middle class, and a much larger class of workers who toil at anemic wages, even by Mexican standards. But with its polite airs and small-town, middleclass sensibility, the city seems livable, even attractive. Personal security has been an important draw in recent years. Owing, it is rumored, to a durable understanding between the governing class and the drug lords, the city has been a safe haven in a country overwhelmed by narcoviolence. Many thus come to Puebla to get away from one thing or another. Here, one encounters exiles from the hustle-bustle of Mexico City, refugees from personal insecurity in Veracruz, and escapees from rural poverty in the mountainous countryside of the state of Puebla and surrounding states, perhaps especially Oaxaca. The wider metropolitan area has grown rapidly in recent years and now has a population of some 3.25 million people, the fourth largest in Mexico.

Like most places, then, but in its own sort of way, the city is a site where the old and the new meet, where the tensions between the stubbornly local and the insistently global are worked out, where people from a wide variety of different backgrounds are thrown together to sort out their relations as best they can. It can also be a zone of itinerate wanderings, a place that people pass through on their way to someplace else: New York City is one of the main destinations for Poblanos emigrating to the United States. (A local play, "Puebla, New York," tried to make sense of these connections for theatergoers in the city's surviving eighteenth-century playhouse.)

Tales of the city, at least for the young, are invariably tales of how people orient and discover themselves in this vibrant mix and clash. These are stories of self-discovery and self-avoidance: personal pilgrimages plotted against the backdrop of class relations, road trips along the imagined timeline of modernity. For the great bulk of humanity, stories about personal striving are tied up with stories about economic striving: trying to make ends meet, toiling to get ahead, struggling against the currents of downward mobility. I shall try to keep my eye on both sides of this struggle.

TWO BOYS

Alex, the bashful teenager who was working at a local coffeehouse while attending high school, could not speak to me without blushing. So intense was his reaction to me that others commented on it: either he felt "burned" to be talking to a gay man, or he was intensely attracted to me, or both. Nonetheless, his doting grandmother implored me to practice English with him so that he could score well on his college entrance exam. Our only practice was basic coffee, sandwich, and pastry orders, with Alex blushing the whole time, but the boy passed his exam and went on to study at a fine university, one of Mexico's best. It was there that he experienced his crisis of identity and came out of the closet. "I had to come to terms with myself," he told me later, in English. After graduation, he went to work for an international digital consulting firm. Today, Alex seems the epitome of what American newspapers are always touting as the "new Mexican middle class," though his middle-class status is actually not so new: his Poblano family was comfortably upper-middle-class, and his grandparents were successful entrepreneurs. He was working at a café in high school not because he needed the money but because his old-fashioned parents thought it important that he understand something about labor.

Now in his mid-thirties, Alex seems emblematic of modern global gay identity, if in a somewhat toned-down manner. Rainbow flags adorn his Facebook page during Pride Week, and he is discreetly coupled up with a coprofessional from Argentina with a similar biography. In their spare time, they advocate for the interests of children with disabilities. (One of his older sister's children has a disability, and he grew up helping take care of her.) Because he works in a creative high-tech industry, his love life is not an issue. Of course, part of what allows him the freedom of a gay life is geographic mobility. After going off to study in a distant city, he never returned to live in stodgy, gossipy Puebla, where his family and its connections are lodged. He thus could make an independent life for himself without immersing his kinfolk in scandal.

Readers may well consider his story, with its detachment of the free agent from local convention and control, to be a "modern" one—though I would be remiss not to note that there is a counternarrative: some Mexicans also find it sad that to follow the path to self-determination, he had to leave his kin behind. Not only in Mexico, family sentiment coexists with family strictures.

For the same fifteen or so years, I've known Daniel, the affable young boxer and baby-faced athlete whom I met when he worked in a downtown internet café. His life has traced the opposite course, an arc of downward mobility and social isolation. Daniel never went to college, never left home, never separated from family controls, never could accept himself, and never got traction on anything other than a string of odd jobs. Still single in his mid-thirties, he lives with his parents in a working-class neighborhood. Because I am an outsider, not likely to come into contact with his kith or kin, I have sometimes been his confessor, a friendly listener and nonjudgmental ear.

"Why do people always think I'm gay?" he asked me many years ago, when he was a broad-shouldered lad in his mid-twenties. Parents, friends, girlfriends, the psychologist he had briefly seen—everyone seemed to think that Daniel was gay. I gave him the standard-issue response. I told him that he shouldn't be concerned with what other people thought and that only he could decide whether he was gay.

Then, much later, in a candid moment, he recounted his first and only gay experience, which he suggested was traumatizing. He was twenty-nine and was spending the evening drinking and chatting in the home of a close male friend. "We were sitting close together on his sofa," he told me.

> I was leaning into him and he rested his hand on my crotch. We sat there like that for a while, warm and comfortable, and a little buzzed, and I asked him how he knew that he was gay. He responded not with words but by, well, unzipping my pants and showing me what he had discovered that he liked to do with other guys. . . . He had never made a move on me before, and there was always this tension. We both wanted it. We kissed, touched, and embraced. I was so excited! It was like I'd waited all my life for this moment, and I let myself go. He sucked my cock and I sucked his. It felt . . . good! I came quickly—but then immediately afterwards I felt waves of shame and anxiety. What have I done? I thought of my father and how he would disapprove. My friend kept trying to talk to me but I couldn't speak. I ran home and cried to my mother, who understands me.

After hearing this sad story, I told the gentle boxer that he had done nothing wrong. I urged him to seek appropriate counseling, perhaps free services available through some of the progressive nongovernmental organizations (NGOs). He refused, invoking a familiar framework. "You don't understand what families are like here," he told me. "I can't be gay." I recalled stories he had told me before: how his father had beaten him, severely, when he was an adolescent, because he thought the boy was gay. Ultimately, Daniel decided that his fleeting moment of pleasure had defiled him. His strategy, then, would be resignation, retreat into the embrace of family, and ultimately, retrogression. And as though by some secret principle of autoanthropophagy, his own body turned against him. He became emaciated and sickly, and his hair began to fall out. When I see him in the streets now, he appears a thin, wan ghost of his former athletic self. I try to talk to him, but he has become distant and evasive.

His story, which might yet have twists and turns, may be considered tragic, at least by readers who imagine themselves to be modern and who think that identity is, or ought to be, a heroic venture, a quest for authenticity and happiness.

Two boys, roughly the same age, both bright and sensitive, the one upper-middle-class, the other lower-working-class, go down different paths to adulthood. Who knows how many times they actually crossed paths in Puebla's crowded centro? They worked two blocks away from each other. They might as well have lived on different continents.

TWO COUPLES

By contrast, the perky baby-butch lesbian whose cheerful smiles and warm hugs greeted clients at one of Puebla's gay clubs has stayed the course, becoming a hospitality fixture on the gay scene while parenting two beautiful children with her partner, an older woman who works as a clerk with the social security administration. Rejected by their natal families, they have made their own family and embedded it within a dense network of gay and lesbian friends. Their humble lives are joined in informal gay matrimony; the four of them live crammed into a tiny, two-bedroom apartment in a neighborhood on the city's farthest outskirts. Their children play with the neighbors' children, and—from what I could see on visits for birthday parties and holiday events—they all seem to have found an accepting community in their low-income gated apartment complex. (A high percentage of housing in Mexico—high, middle, and low income— is in gated communities.)

They are close friends and socialize frequently with a pair of gay men. One of them waits tables at a restaurant in a mid-price chain, now some twenty years after immigrating to the big city from a small pueblo far from the city and fifteen years after graduating from college with a degree in tourism and hospitality. His partner works as a lower-level clerk in a government office. Over the years, the two have quarreled over money and affairs, broken up, and reconciled a few times. Such is modern love, a contract underwritten not by kinsfolk or church or state but by mutual agreement. They are currently separated but still living together in a distant, gritty suburb, not quite willing to hold on yet not quite willing to let go.

Two couples, whose members go down parallel paths: their joined gay lives give unremarkable testimony to some of the new personal freedoms and standard-issue frustrations that come with urbanization and education, even for working-class people.

THE EDUCATED POOR

In Mexico, as in the United States and Europe, the new working poor are as likely as not to be educated. As a group, recent university graduates have not fared well, especially if they come from working-class or rural backgrounds and lack business or political connections: they make their lives piecemeal, with short-term gigs and part-time jobs. A few of my friends and acquaintances with four-year degrees in psychology or sociology do unpaid work with LGBT NGOs, committing to a vision of progressive gay modernity while driving for Uber to get their daily bread. Above all, they confront a tight labor market with few entry positions in their professions.

A graduate fresh from law school describes his recent job offer at a call center that outsources services for a major corporation: he was offered MXN$4,500 a month (roughly US$220 at the time) to work six 8-hour shifts per week. I marvel at the mingy offer, which was scarcely enough to cover daily transportation and workday lunches. The recruiters also told him that he'd have to be available for overtime and work on Sunday, if needed—with no additional pay. "A clear violation of labor law," the lawyer dryly added, "but this is Mexico." The lawyer told the incensed interviewers that he wasn't available to work for free, but many do accept such jobs—out of either a sense of desperation or a sense of honor. (Working-class Mexicans, like working-class Americans, take a dim view of not working, of being idle: if others in your family work, then so should you.)

Another, who struggles in his mid-thirties to maintain a definition of himself as anything *but* gay, labored in restaurants and warehouses for a long time before taking an unpaid internship with a local news organization to try to get traction in his profession, communications. This was fully seven years out of college, and two years later he still has an unpaid internship, supplemented by odd jobs and short-term gigs.

In the details are the stories of young working-class people striving for love and connection, of course, but also for a better material life, an elusive comfortable middle-class existence. The one struggle is tied to and resonates in the other.

Maybe I'm Just Weird, or a Coward

It is no secret that modern gay life eludes many strivers. This elusion is often tied to economic limitations.

Santiago was finishing college at the age of thirty when he bitterly related over beer how he thinks hardship and precarity have shaped his sexual life and constrained his choices. He left home when he was sixteen, shaken loose from a small farm in the far north of the state during the "Tequila Crisis" of the mid-1990s, when there was no money for seed and thus no crops to plant; his family, like millions of others, had been reduced to barest necessities. "I came to the city and I didn't know anybody here. At first, I slept on sidewalks until a kindly storekeeper took me in, gave me work, and helped me get set up. I worked while eventually finishing high school, then I went on to college." Over this time, he also brought two sisters and three brothers down from the Sierra to Puebla, to work and study as well.

Thanks to his selflessness, all but one of Santiago's younger siblings graduated from the university ahead of him and, at the time of our conversation (2010), he had only just now had his first homosexual experience. "I always fantasized about men, but . . . it just never happened for me before." I note, perhaps boorishly, that plenty of guys in his circumstances were having plenty of sex. I could see that the remark stung. "Maybe I'm just weird, or ugly, or skittish. Maybe I'm a coward. I don't know." Santiago sees how others are living different lives and giving themselves over to flings and romances. He envies them for their openness, their enjoyments, their freedoms. "I hear how my classmates talk about their gay lives, their nights out at the clubs. They gossip about their adventures with rough trade and exotic foreigners." Yet, despite his claim to being liberal and "open-minded," he is unable to coax himself to join in. As he relates his story, with its distinct lack of adventures, tears come to his eyes: "I've never done these things because I've worked all my life. I've always been the responsible one, the older brother. I've never had any free time. So here I am today, and I don't even know if I'm gay or bisexual or what."

Habits die hard. Many years later, after first owning, then rejecting a gay identity, then resigning himself to it, or some semblance thereof, Santiago remains an outsider to the gay life he both desires and fears. From time to time, he tells me, he gets drunk with friends, they sometimes end up in bed together, and whatever happens, happens. Sometimes his overtures are accepted, and sometimes they are brusquely rebuffed when a bedfellow awakens to a blowjob. I worry about where this may someday take him.

This sort of lonely, frustrated life still exists in the era of gay pride, which portends a modern dispensation of personal freedom and enlightened understanding. Santiago attributes his unhappiness to his economic conditions and constraints. But I was surprised to learn that one of his brothers had come out of the closet and was living with his partner.

Two brothers, the same circumstances, born a year apart, went down different paths. Santiago's predicaments cannot be understood as necessary and inevitable consequences of his class position, but they cannot be understood apart from his economic conditions, either, or from the way, as the oldest boy, he took on and internalized the deferrals and constraints that he narrates as economic necessities.

What Can I Tell You about Working in a Maquiladora?

The quest for a modern identity sometimes produces mixed or ambiguous results, even for those who embrace it with courage and open hearts.

Héctor hails from a solidly working-class family that lived in an extension of metropolitan Puebla near the state border with Tlaxcala. His father was a skilled, unionized worker in a machine-parts factory and made what family members describe as a good living until he became ill with HIV. Soon thereafter, he went to live with another woman, and when she died, he disappeared without a trace from the family's lives. Héctor dropped out of high school and went to work for several years, helping his older brother support their mother and two younger siblings.

I met him when he had returned to school to finish his high school degree on an accelerated, one-year course of study, as is common in Mexico. He was then in the process of coming out of the closet. He, Erik, the doctor, and other friends would sometimes gather at my apartment for drinks, music, and chitchat. By the time Héctor finished high school, his brawny older brother, a single father, was supporting the family, having set up a small workshop in the downstairs garage, in Mexican can-do style; he and two employees were turning out small-batch orders of mechanical equipment for farms and small factories. And so, with family encouragement, Héctor went on to study, without further interruption, at the public university and graduated in communications. (Communications is one of the most common liberal arts degrees in Mexico.)

He soon landed a white-collar job with one of the city's larger car dealerships, managing the company's website advertisements and Facebook campaigns. This was hardly the job (or salary) of his dreams, but even so, the young man felt some contentment: he was in a relationship with a well-built, butch, straight-identifying number whom some might describe as handsome. Unfortunately, neither the job nor the relationship lasted much longer than a year, and Héctor was thrown willy-nilly into a series of short-term jobs doing similar work for car dealerships, English-language schools, and the like, each gig more frustrating than the last.

(Young Americans and Europeans will instantly recognize the mismatch between university training and employment market for graduates with degrees in the humanities. Angela McRobbie surveys this brave new world of part-time, short-term contract work without benefits or protections in *Be Creative.*[5])

One day, Héctor vented, mixing an account of job frustrations with insecurities about his looks and despair over his personal life: "I chose the wrong major. There's not much work in my field. Successful communicologists are young, attractive, dynamic, and I'm no longer any of those." I protest—he was barely thirty—but he retorts, "Don't humor me. I've had braces three times and my damned teeth still aren't straight. And I've had no success in personal relationships, either. *Activos* ("tops") are looking for young, thin guys, and just look at me." (Héctor's peers do not view his preference for straight-identifying activos as maladaptive—his orientation is not exceptional in Mexico—though some do view such channeling of desires as old-fashioned.) I remind him that he is, in fact, successful in bars and bathhouses, and he retorts: "That's sex. I want a relationship." Héctor jokes about having hormonal treatments to acquire more feminine characteristics; thus he might make himself more attractive to straight men. "But darling," I jest, "you have big feet and a broad back. I don't think this would really work for you, if what you're trying to obtain is a thin wisp of a body." Trying to reestablish the topic, I ask him what kind of job he would like. "I want a job like yours!" He blurts. "I want to read, write, teach, travel."

Héctor went on to recount the fate of his best friend, who had died a month before. Unbeknownst to friends and family, he had stopped taking his HIV medication and succumbed to a drawn-out and excruciating death. (This was not the first time I had heard this story or variations on it.) Héctor wondered whether the death was his fault, whether he might have made more insistent inquiries so as to monitor the young man's health. I tell him that his friend had basically committed suicide and that, although we are all our brothers' keepers, he could not have known what was happening after his friend had moved to Mexico City.

As we circle around jest, despair, and encouragement, I recall how Héctor had bought a book at my recommendation in an open-air market we passed through one afternoon. I had had in mind the grander themes of French existentialism, but his oral book report a few weeks later was revelatory. "I didn't like *The Little Prince*. The way I read it, it says basically that if you don't do what you want, you're wasting your life. OK. But who does what he wants? Only people born into wealth can do as they please." This was not an ill-informed critique of the work.

It was about this time that we, Héctor's friends and I, set in on a nagging campaign. When he had a cold for two continuous months, we told him that he should get tested for HIV. Then, when he began losing weight, we offered to all go in for testing together, and to receive our results together, so that he wouldn't be alone. He told us that he had taken the rapid test and that it had come back negative.

Still wasting when the 2020 COVID-19 crisis set in, he was laid off from two jobs in brisk succession and decided to head north to the border to work in a maquiladora for several months and, he hoped, claw back some savings. From there, he sent me a long text message on WhatsApp describing his experiences in the American factory, which exports scientific instruments and medical equipment to the United States. His report gives an accurate snapshot of everyday working conditions and uneven development across regions in Mexico.

What can I tell you about working in a maquiladora?

It's a strange experience, since I have normally worked in an office. Have you heard the expression "work like an ant"? Well, that applies here. When we enter to work, we all go in a line, well-marked and with routines, from registration to the entry check in our area. We work for 12 hours in two shifts: from 6:00 am to 6:00 pm, or from 6:00 pm to 6:00 am. To be clear, I work the night shift, since it earns a little more, MXN$2250.00 [roughly US$101 at the time] net per week, working 4 days a week. . . .

Frankly, it's incredible to me what's earned here. Ok, it's not much for my first week: MXN$2250. But despite that, this would be the average salary earned by a university-educated person with a bachelor's degree in Puebla. [Maquiladora workers in Puebla tell me that they earn half as much, putting in six 8–10 hour shifts a week instead of four. Also note that the border maquiladora paid twice as much in a month as what the call center in Puebla was offering the young lawyer at about the same time.] But that's not all. As I mentioned before, it's only 4 days a week. You can work extra shifts and earn MXN$800.00 [US$36] per day. Now if you work for 6 days, which is the standard workweek in Puebla, you can earn almost MXN$4000.00

[US$180] per week, and most workers in this factory have only a middle school education. Does that sound good? It won't sound good to you, but in Mexico, it's quite good.

The activities to be carried out are not complex, anyone with common sense can do them. But they're repetitive. And sometimes you have to stand up all night. Anyone gets stressed. Errors are examined in the product; details are checked, and defective products won't pass review. Inevitably, the machines beat you, and that becomes tedious.

The majority of employees in my area are women. I would estimate that 80% of them are—and it should be added that there are many lesbians among them. (This may not be important, but it was interesting to highlight.) [In fact, Héctor highlights an important sociological finding: self-sufficient women workers in the maquiladoras are liberated from family controls and reliance on a male breadwinner.[6]]

Anyway, maybe for me it was a bad experience since I had never done this kind of work. I will be here for 3 more months. However, there are many people who have put in up to 20 years. The organizational climate is good. Apparently, they try to retain you with hiring bonuses, birthday bonuses, referral bonuses, and bonuses for Kaizen ideas. [Kaizen is a Japanese concept referring to continuous improvement; the American-owned factory had adopted the practice of rewarding employees for coming up with ideas to improve production.]

Héctor never made the kind of money he had planned on earning at the factory. He sent friends a few "selfies" from the beach, but his health was deteriorating rapidly. By the end of his stay, his feet were so painfully swollen that he could barely walk across the room, much less take on overtime shifts. When he finally got tested, he was anemic, and his T-cell count was low—almost low enough for his maladies to be classified as full-blown AIDS.

He returned home abject, with empty pockets. We lent him money for his return flight and met him at the airport a few days before Christmas 2020. He was, at last, a thin wisp of his former self, but his face was marred by dark chancre sores. We all embraced, wept, and reminded him of how good the current treatments are. I told him that I had seen people rise from the dead in the mid-1990s when efficacious HIV/AIDS treatments finally became available. Although the doctor tried to interrupt, Erik burst into tears and could not refrain from admonishing him: "Why?

Why? *Why* did you wait so long to get tested?" We had all pondered just that question. The answer, I suppose, should be obvious: "I was afraid."

I call stop here to the interpretive chain that, in scholarly works, is often quite speculative on matters like these. Nor will I badger the witness to attend to his own suffering. I have described the intimate lives of subjects, friends, and loved ones, baring their scars and sometimes giving their own interpretations of some of their actions. I will not feign to perform the mind-reading tricks and interpretive legerdemain of depth psychoanalysis, or try to square generic sociological maxims with the zigs and zags of a unique individual's personal life. He waited until late; his friends fretted. That is all.

By New Year's Day, Héctor was already visibly improving: his chancre sores had vanished, and his swollen feet were returning to normal size. He had told his siblings one by one and finally his mother that he was in treat-ment for HIV. Now, there are storylines in which the young man tells his family members that he has HIV; this is how they find out that he's gay, and they ostracize him. This is not a story in that genre, or at least it did not appear to be so in the beginning. Héctor's family members already knew that he was gay—in fact, they sometimes hosted us, his friends, on special occasions like Christmas Eve in their modest home above the workshop. His mother calmly said that she already knew that he had HIV: she had seen the symptoms of wasting before. His sister contacted his friends, including me, and told us that she, too, had been nagging him to get tested. She insisted on taking him to his medical appointments at Capacits (the Outpatient Center for the Prevention and Care of AIDS and Sexually Transmitted Infections), perhaps so as to monitor his compliance with treatment. She already knew the score because she had accompanied her father there many years ago, before he disappeared.

And when he told his older brother, the grease-stained, rough-hewn provider walked out of the house, to Héctor's initial alarm. He came back half an hour later with boxes of protein drinks. "Here. You need these. And you have my support."

I wish that the story stopped here, an instructive reversal of stereotype, with Héctor basking in the uninterrupted love and support of family. But within a couple of weeks, his brother had a change of heart. He told Héctor that he was confusing his six-year-old daughter—that now she didn't know whether she liked boys or girls (a strange question to pose to a six-year-old), that she didn't trust him anymore—and that he was to stay away from her and to stop bringing gay friends to the house, seeing how they (we) set a bad example. Héctor's mother, his sister (who sometimes accompanied us to gay bars), and his younger brother dissented from such strictures but in the interests of "family unity" (a recurring trope in Mexican family culture) did not actively oppose the older brother. He was technically "the man of the house," a concept propped up in Mexican family law until very recently, and thought of himself as such, though by this time the sister and the younger brother were bringing in a substantial portion of the household income.

Family acceptance thus devolved to the lowest common denominator, at least for a time. If Héctor had had better options, he would have moved out. But his storyline did not take that route. In these and other matters, he did what so many do: he suffered it, endured it, put up with it. But this seems too cold a way of describing his accommodations, which might be "impediments to his flourishing," as the phrase goes; but more than that, they are also real human situations. So let me elaborate a bit on how class conditions come together with living arrangements and emotional factors. In the first place, Héctor lacked the income to rent an apartment on his own. He could have moved in with friends or shared a rental, but these arrangements are only as stable as the incomes of the roommates. Typically, working-class children move out of the house when they get married—if then, an expectation that complicates the lives of gay people. In any case, he loves his mother, his siblings, and compound multigenerational households are not uncommon. And so Héctor accepted his uneasy predicament in the hope that time would temper bad relations.

THE ARRANGEMENT

I have known Oscar since he was a sophomore at the state university. His experiences show that there are viable alternatives to working-class strategies of suffering and enduring, but that the path to practices of identity and dignity is narrow and depends on the outcomes of many twists and turns.

Oscar had felt dejected for several weeks when I first met him, sometime around 2010. When he came out of the closet, his instructor had expelled him in disgrace from karate school for violating the first and second principles of the students' creed:

(1) I will develop myself in a positive manner, avoiding anything that reduces my mental growth or my physical health.

(2) I will develop self-discipline to bring out the best in myself and the best in others.

(3) I will use common sense before self-defense and never be abusive or offensive.

Being stripped of his black belt in front of classmates was traumatizing. Oscar had thrown himself into karate with dedication and zeal, and he still describes the training as having been an important part of his personal development. But expulsion did not break him—if anything it made him stronger—for he had in fact internalized the creed's principles of self-development and self-reliance. And within a few months, the young man was finding other avenues for development and self-discipline at the university, calling attention to himself as an exceptional student in art history. We had long conversations about gender, sexuality, and social theory at Luciérnaga (Firefly), a gay café-bar, or at a restaurant over pizza and beer.

Things came to a head when he told his family that he was gay. At first, his parents reacted with shock, though it was muted. But family members were also hearing from disapproving neighbors about Oscar's increasingly visible activism in local LGBT groups. Then one evening his father started drinking and drove from the distant working-class slum where the family lived to the city's centro, where he encountered Oscar and a gaggle of his university chums, a group of mostly straight men and women who were involved in a variety of progressive activist projects. The father began beating and berating the boy on a street corner in front of his horrified middle-class peers. Within minutes, the police arrived. When the father told them that his son had gotten "out of line," the police left the scene, deeming the disturbance a family matter and deferring to the disciplinary authority of the father. The berating and abuse continued for several more minutes. Oscar put up mild protestations, and the martial arts expert made only modest efforts to deflect the worst blows. "Father, I'm a human being." "You're not a human being! You're an animal!" And with that, the father forced his son to get into the car and to go home with him.

A lot went on behind the scenes over the next several hours. Oscar was in cell phone contact with university friends and arrangements were made. I told him bluntly that his father was an idiot and that his first responsibility was to protect himself, not to educate his family. The next morning, his father was surprised to encounter Oscar, suitcase in hand, heading for the door. "What are you doing?" "I'm leaving. I'm not going to live like this." "But where will you go?" "My friends will put me up." "Do they support you in this abnormal lifestyle?" "Not only my friends, but my professors at the university—and a gringo anthropologist, too. There's a world of acceptance for me out there, papá." (The young man's invocation of me gestured at international support and solidarity: There I was in his narrative, symbolizing the whole of the educated modern world, I suppose.)

The father then sat with the boy at the kitchen table and asked, "How long did it take you to accept that you were gay?" "Years," Oscar responded. "Well, then, maybe don't you think you could give us a little time to come to terms with it, too?" Perhaps Oscar's father wasn't the idiot I had taken him to be. Oscar agreed and remained in contact with his parents and siblings but still left home that day and went to live, rent-free, with four other university students in a large apartment that they collectively rented. In exchange for room and board, he did some housekeeping and cooking and eventually, as his skills developed, worked on funding applications for the NGOs with which some of his housemates were involved. The arrangement allowed Oscar to finish his degree without interruption and to work with LGBT consciousness-raising and educational projects. It also allowed for a rapprochement with his parents and siblings. One afternoon, I encountered mother, father, Oscar, and a couple of siblings out for a stroll in the centro and greeted them all in that certain Poblano style involving handshakes and curt half-hugs for the men and cheek kisses for the women. The love of family is not necessarily inconsistent with personal and sexual freedom, though their coexistence is not a given.

Narrow was the path for this working-class boy, who is now regarded by everyone as a paragon of progressive modernity, at least on some matters. That path depended on a self-confident subject willing to stand up to patriarchal authority, as well as the emotional support and material aid of better-off friends. But the arrangement did not allow for much of a change in Oscar's material circumstances. Even though he had made traction on a master's degree, job openings in any line of work remotely related to his training were elusive—doubly elusive for graduates from working-class backgrounds who lack social capital: connections, *palanca* ("leverage," "pull"), as they say in Mexico. Unable to afford his own apartment, he eventually moved back in with his parents. He now divides his time between activism, driving for Uber, periodic stints with call centers, and catching construction and renovation odd jobs—most of them with his father—to keep body and soul together.

THE EMIGRANT, THE RETURNEE

Some have given up on economic advancement in Mexico and emigrated to the United States on a perilous clandestine passage. They now cook in restaurants or bus tables, often in New York City. I visited one of them, a young man I knew from the gym in Puebla, some three years after his journey to the North. As we wandered around Macy's and Times Square in the winter cold, he related the remarkable story of his three-day journey through the desert: of a storm with lightning strikes all around and nowhere to take cover; of waking up beside a rattlesnake on the second day; of evading border patrols, visible on the highway in the distance; of finally arriving, dehydrated and exhausted, at a spot where someone had left bottles of water bearing labels reading "suerte" (luck) and "éxito" (success). Then came a crowded, three-day ride down backroads from Arizona to New York, mostly at night—with the minivan's lights off to evade detection.

When he got around to tallying the numbers, he told me that his daily income doing restaurant work in Gotham exceeded his weekly income doing the same in Puebla. But he also related his sense of loneliness and isolation in the Big Apple. He said that his social world was far smaller than it had been back home; that he was far more dependent on networks of family and kin than he had been in Puebla; and that in consequence, he felt more observed, more surveilled—and thus had less freedom. (This same dynamic has been described by Carlos Decena in his book about Dominican immigrants in New York.[7]) He wanted to go back home. There he would be poor, but he would at least have more freedom.

I remembered that in Puebla, he had been very conservative and had taken a dim view of gay clubs, though he could be seen on Sundays strolling downtown with his then boyfriend and his boyfriend's mother. I told him that he needed to go out more—that there were plenty of Latino gay bars where he could meet people who spoke Spanish and make friends. Maybe he took my advice. Three years after our conversation, he legalized his stay when he married his boyfriend, a Colombian American. Their marriage was at the end of the Obama administration, before Trump's ICE (Immigration and Customs Enforcement) began arresting and deporting undocumented immigrants when they showed up for the marital interview.

In such varied storylines are all the elements of social realism, hints and traces of the ways our lives are swayed and steered by forces beyond our control, with plucky protagonists seeking out gaps and openings in the ineluctable force field that stands between them and their freedom.

I'm told that Erik's outcast cousin eventually came back to Mexico after working for fifteen years as a cook in the United States. To everyone's surprise, he returned with a wife and two small boys. But Erik knows about his cousin's doings only through rumors and limited Facebook views. He told Erik, who had remained in contact with him over the years by email, that he wanted to have nothing more to do with anyone in the family: "Leave me alone and do not remain in touch." His story is thus a dead end for me, though not for him: it is inaccessible, it continues in a different register.

THE LOST BOY

The poorest of the poor, queers among them, strive for happiness as much as anyone. But whereas working-class youth risk being thrown away or rejected by the families if they disclose themselves, young people from the poorest sectors belong to a sub-class that has already been thrown away and rejected. Their lives are already unstable. In many cases, what signals their agency is personal resilience in the face of adversity and family dysfunction.

Dancer

Andrés was the tall, dark, doe-eyed leader of an informal street dance school, one of the city's many groups of mostly poor kids who perfect their breaks, pops, whacks, and other dance moves in the *zócalo* (the central plaza) or nearby parks on weekend afternoons and evenings. "Liquid dance is my life," the twenty-year-old explained of his preferred genre. (Others would specialize in break dancing, electro, funk, electric booga-loo, and a bewildering array of hip-hop and electronic styles.) Andrés was talented: his body really did appear to be made of water when he undu-lated, and he would sometimes mix in moves from other genres, then laugh when I'd exclaim, "That's vogue!" or "You're whacking!" He would sometimes try, with mixed results, to induce my two left feet to learn a few moves.

In our conversations, little pieces of his backstory came out. "My mama wasn't able to take care of me anymore," he said without rancor, describing how he had ended up on the streets at the age of twelve. Soon, he was in a group home for adolescent boys, the charitable work of a famous rich cou-ple. He sometimes showed me pictures of himself at the time, among them candid shots with other residents having group meals or engaged in learning activities. His favorite photos showed him standing beside the matron philanthropist, taken when he was fourteen or fifteen, and he later mourned his protector's untimely death from cancer like the death of his own mother.

Andrés describes his "first time" as a crossroads between terror and desire, coercion and consent. He had been loitering on side streets early one evening when he was sixteen, drawn to a cluster of gay establishments but too timid to enter one. Overcome by necessity, he discreetly urinated in an empty dark corner—only to have a policeman walk by as he was zipping up. The cop saw the wet stream and simply said, "Come with me." Once in the patrol car, the boy began to protest, "But I wasn't doing anything!" The burly officer said, "You know that public urination is against the law." After what seemed an interminable drive, the two arrived at the policeman's home. "We were sitting on his sofa, and my heart was pounding—I didn't know what he was going to do to me. Neither of us was saying anything. Then the policeman said, 'You're not such a bad boy' and leaned in and kissed me. And even though I was afraid, I immediately got excited and kissed him back. The next thing I knew, he was kneeling between my legs." I tell Andrés that the policeman's behavior was inexcusable. The young man assents, then adds philosophically, "But I didn't get hurt. And I didn't have to take responsibility for my first time; it was just something that happened to me. In a way, that was good. Anyway, the policeman gave me 200 pesos [roughly US$13 at the time] and drove me back to the group home. We sat outside for a few minutes. He gave me his number and said that if I liked what we had done and wanted to do it again, I could call."

A keen observer of gay life, Eve Kosofsky Sedgewick once wondered whether in a homophobic world it was really possible for most gay youths' first sexual experience to conform to evolving standards of consent and to evade changing definitions of abuse.[8] Not only in Mexico, a great deal of sex takes place in that gray zone where there is neither agreement nor refusal—and this is especially true, I think, for gay boys who are poor or who live on the streets or in various kinds of shelters. Let me be clear again: Andrés's account begins in unconscionable coercion; he was abducted. Not all versions of this sort of tale come out so well, and I know Poblanos who were traumatized by "copnappings" (for want of a better word) whose motives were robbery or extortion, not sex. But I have heard variations on Andrés's story of extorted sex set in Los Angeles, Washington, DC, and other US cities; they were related with the same attention to interpersonal inequalities—and were sometimes balanced by the same impassive calculation of positive effects. These are not heroic narratives of self-possession and self-discovery, of sex distilled down to purest, self-directed, and frictionless desire, of sober and deliberate negotiations between autonomous, informed adult subjects; rather, they address the murkier place of sex in contending relations involving duress and surrender, experience and inexperience, making out and making do.

Andrés was eventually restored to family; he joined the household of his older sister once she had gotten settled. He began studying at the public university by day and organizing dancers in the Parque del Carmen (a small downtown plaza) in the evening. This was how I met him; he was leading a Sunday afternoon dance session.

"Why don't you write about us dance kids?" he suggested. And so I will, if only briefly and tangentially. Street dance schools and similar skill-developing youth subcultures that involve, for instance, capoeira or acrobatics or sports focus the mind, discipline the body, afford a sense of camaraderie, and provide some relief from the crushing boredom of poverty. They structure time for young people for whom unstructured time, according to common sense in many working-class settings, might come to mischief. They provide venues for displays of competency, physical prowess, and derring-do, an important outlet for sleek athletes of ambiguous sexuality and rough boys from tough neighborhoods. They are abundant in Mexico, perhaps because the ensemble of needs for them is so abundant.

I marvel at the physical and mental adroitness developed by ordinary people in these everyday settings. So, too, the capacity of these groups for spontaneity, dynamism, and inclusivity.

A brief digression: In 2020, when COVID lockdowns were in full force and the gyms were closed, my Poblano husband and I started shooting hoops on a basketball court in a working-class neighborhood not far from our apartment in Puebla's historic center. We were soon joined by a pair of brothers, then another pair of brothers, then many more sets of singles, friends, and so on: students, senior citizens, young working-class men, an occasional group of Venezuelan immigrants, a half-dozen Mazatec construction workers, a gay couple in middle school who addressed each other with feminine names, a young trans man, a growing number of girls and women, some accompanied by sisters or grey-streaked mothers, and so on. From time to time, an aging sports enthusiast and ambulatory street vendor would show up with a whistle to act as referee.

One evening I overheard a teenager confide to his companion, "There are some well-kept courts in La Noria [an affluent neighborhood not far away], and I went there a few times—but they never let me play there like I do here, because they're so stuck up." Our group of players, by contrast, was welcoming, downscale, and friendly. Familiarity bred nicknames:

"Blue" (because he was wearing a blue T-shirt the first time he played, and since no one knew his name, players would shout out "Blue!" in English), "Marcos" (the green-eyed young man from Chiapas, and thus a reference to the Zapatistas' Comandante Marcos), "Gelatinas" (the ambulatory street vendor who sold gelatin deserts), "Frijol" and "Pulguita" (the two smallest boys, brothers, though the former nickname fell into disuse when the boy went into an impressive growth spurt, his height surging three inches in as many weeks—I'm not sure how his body withstood it). Before too long, many of us were on a WhatsApp messaging group.

Within three months, we were forty or fifty mostly young, mostly working-class people, who passed time arranging five- and ten-point pickup games every evening. (We had three-point matches when very large numbers showed up so as to rotate play more quickly and give everyone some court time.) No one was ever turned away, no one was ever sent home for lack of skill; rather, the players usually adjusted their play to include slower, clumsier people like me, shouting encouragements like "Throw it!" or "Well done!" There was competition, of course, and our varying abilities were there for all the world to see, but there was also a (mostly) male ethos of competition, care, and solidarity, with players taking an interest in one another's development and well-being. On those few occasions when fights seemed imminent, a half-dozen or so bodies would immediately interpose themselves, separating the antagonists—or even escorting them away from the courts—until tensions waned. (Fractious players who genuinely wanted to brawl were told not to come back.)

Alas, the group dynamics changed somewhat when young men and women who played for neighborhood and college sports teams began showing up. They treated evening time on the public courts as practice sessions and alienated some of the players with their constant scolding and bad humor. No doubt what we needed was a gentle leader, someone like Andrés, who could participate in competitions while maintaining a welcoming environment and training the less skilled.

Conversion

Andrés was soon to be uprooted from school, dance, and tentative explorations of the gay scene when his sister went to work in a maquiladora in

Ciudad Juárez. Accompanying her there, he set his hands to work washing dishes and busing tables in one of the city's large restaurants. This was unglamorous and unpromising work, but it was work. At about the same time, he came under the stewardship of his sister's church, an evangelical sect that had special youth programs involving Christian pop music—but not, of course, dance, which was directly tied to the body's lower regions. In short order, Andrés posted a notice on his Facebook page that he was taking down all of his liquid dance videos (there were scores if not hundreds of them) and began posting instead pictures of his baptism-by-immersion and videos of the youth ministry's singing-and-shouting sessions. These were interspersed with inspirational quotes, spiritual messages, and occasional impassioned sermonettes, many of them given by strikingly handsome youth evangelists.

Organized religious groups have developed myriad ways to induce congregants to sublimate and disown homosexual desires; this is an old story, and today it plays out as much on social media as in congregational spaces. The Facebook banter between Andrés and his church's youth ministers, for instance, included the frequent exchange of compliments such as "*guapo*" (handsome) and other terms of endearment. The price of such belonging included gestures and rituals of self-renunciation. When Andrés published an anti-gay religious message during Pride Week, his old friends, especially those from Puebla, posted sharply critical responses; new friends from the church argued that there was nothing homophobic about telling God's truth.

His dance school back in Puebla was long gone. Leaderless, it had disintegrated quickly after he left town. I suppose some of its constituents integrated with other dance schools, whose members practiced similar genres. Still, from time to time, Andrés posts links to surviving YouTube videos of himself at past events and scattered competitions across Mexico: a lithe, agile youth dancing with the boys, defying the laws of physics. The spirit is willing, but the flesh is weak.

Andrés never really had much of a chance to be clear about his desires, to determine himself. How many of us, thrown into such an unstable life at such an early age, could have even kept our feet underneath us? The arc of the young man's story goes from one kind of institutional care to another, both offering evening programs for lost boys, activities to structure and occupy their time. Where all of this may yet lead is still unclear.

LOS OLVIDADOS (THE FORGOTTEN ONES)

The subclass at the bottom of the class hierarchy constitutes a special case. Its members' options are circumscribed, their circumstances crystalized into distinct caste occupations: beggars, ambulatory vendors, petty thieves, idle dependents, sex workers providing different kinds of services, and so on. Among the entailments of this sorting are certain ambiguities.

On the one hand, members of the lowest orders are effectively excluded from social respectability. This means that sometimes they redouble their adhesion to exaggerated male codes (whose maxim might be "A man takes what he needs"), but it also implies that sometimes the dispossessed feel less compulsion than members of the stable working class to conform to gender and sexual norms. An old market woman thus introduced her son to me playfully and with scarcely a hint of judgment: "He's had three wives—and the third one was a man!" (Had her son been the wife, of course, her response might have been less lighthearted.)

On the other hand, marginalized people's relationship with the ambiente tends to be forged within its most precarious sector, a gay "underclass" that abuts a criminal underworld where sex often presupposes the exchange of money and where rip-offs or interpersonal violence are not uncommon. One young man thus playfully hedged his description of his boyfriend to me in the following deadpan manner: "He's not such a bad guy; it's just that he likes to steal. But he's not very good at it." The speaker implicitly drew a contrast between petty lawbreakers like his beau and violent criminals—an important distinction in the daily lives of the marginalized poor.

Some members of this subclass are more or less openly gay—indeed, some are "obvious," as they say, in manner or dress—but, observant of Puebla's rigid class and status distinctions, they do not often commune with people from other sectors of the gay scene. Still, no system of social stratification is segmented into airtight compartments. With all the weight of a system of social and economic inequality on their backs, some outcasts do venture into gay bars or cafés or seek connection with working- or middle-class others who have caught their attention or reciprocated eye contact. Being gay, after all, is adjacent to other forms of social exclusion. The ambiente, literally "environment," is a diverse ecosystem. And without some degree of porosity, mutuality, or interconnectedness among the scene's ecological niches, I'd scarcely be able to credibly narrate even this cursory examination of these points.

I used to chat from time to time with a broodingly handsome man in his early twenties who dressed impeccably, presented himself as "straight," and discreetly found male sexual clients in the zócalo. I don't know much about his backstory except that he came from the state of Veracruz, had had a difficult home life there, fought with his parents, and left home in his mid-teens. He was usually accompanied by a burly, blocky man, a friend and protector who sometimes worked as a bouncer in gay bars and sometimes found clients for him. The garrulous and overbearing protector eventually disappeared, after which the hustler's appearance, self-presentation, and hygiene began to decline—perhaps from drugs or inhalants, perhaps from a chronic mental illness, or perhaps from the grinding weight of poverty.

The last time I saw him, he was in terrible shape, laughing and talking to himself in the public square. His eyes met mine for a glaring instant. And then he disappeared from view forever, to what fate I dare not imagine.

By contrast, the cheerful young man who resells sushi to go from a cooler strapped to the back of his bicycle, crisscrossing the centro block by block, has innovated for himself a reliable routine in the informal economy. He makes it a point to stop, chat, and discreetly flirt with me whenever we come across each other. He had first hailed me as I passed by with *"Auf Wiedersehen,"* perhaps mistaking me for German, perhaps to show off a bit of arcane knowledge, and no doubt to demonstrate that he knew foreigners.

And then there's the spritely old man who hustles for tips on the street where I live, whistling and thumping the sides of cars to assist people who are parking. He took notice early on of my goings and comings with my partner. Mischievously, he asks: "If I weren't so old and so poor, do you think I might have a chance with you?"

And so on, and so on. These are some of the ways gay life is lived. These are some of the ways working-class people respond to the blows of fate, some rolling with the punches, some persevering, some never quite able to get their feet under them.

4 Commonplaces

I stress the theme of commonalities with a mundane insistence. The crises and predicaments I have laid out here are set in Mexico, but they resonate in far-flung sites, including the settings for my own life story. Aligning these and other such stories just so and tracing their shared components begins to suggest how commonplace the situations of gay life are in a "modernizing," globalizing world. This alignment also prods broader questions about how social class shapes our experiences.

SHARED STORYLINES

I grew up in the 1960s and 1970s, a time when agrarian poverty was giving way to a more consistently proletarianized existence across the rural South. The children of sharecroppers, such as my mother's brothers and my older cousins, were going to work in factories, which had come south to take advantage of low wages and lower unionization rates. The children of small farmers, like my father, were more likely to become skilled or semiskilled blue-collar workers: mechanics, repairmen, and the like. In either case, everyday routines were transitioning from one sort of labor discipline to another, as natural cycles of sunrise, sunset, and seasonal fluctuations gave way to time clocks and punch cards.

Then as now, religious piety provided an important buffer between the "haven" of family life and the whirlwind of a heartless world, a more or less reliable check against profligacy and excess. Members of our small evangelical-fundamentalist denomination (composed mostly of proletari-anizing white and black southern folk) did not drink, dance, play cards, or go to movies. And if in my childhood Hell had seemed more real to me than California, then reckoning with same-sex attraction in my mid-teens had been its own sort of hell—until one evening, when I was sixteen, the pastor of our rural church discretely fondled my knee under the kitchen table and I realized in a flash that I was not alone and that the preachers and Sunday school teachers were as unhappy as I was in the received dogmas.

Luckily for me, the "modern world" (nemesis of religious fundamental-ists everywhere, expressly thundered against from pulpits) was beckoning. Among the generous state-subsidized benefits still available to some poor people at this time was cheap, high-quality public education. And so I left the tobacco fields, piney woods, factories, and textile mills (which were already heading yet farther south in search of cheaper wages) to go study at the state's flagship public university, the first of my family to pursue a col-lege degree. There, during my second semester, I came out of the closet. Higher education, for gay people of working-class origins, is often an inflec-tion point: a moment of opportunity to break from family controls and received ways of thinking, it thus also affords occasion for the crises and predicaments of self-discovery. This is true not only in the United States.

After I had been on the gay scene for a while, I began to wonder at how social class and its nuances swayed life courses. Month after month, year after year, one saw the same faces in bars and clubs; these were gays and lesbians who had managed to put some stable ground beneath their feet. More often than not, they were educated, they possessed "cultural capital" (as the French sociologist Pierre Bourdieu would say of education and related forms of savvy) and were "middle-class" (or at least middle income, to be more accurate).[1] By contrast, lower-working-class kids appeared on the scene—often in a hurry, often in the throes of crisis—and then disappeared after a few weeks or months. Gay kids from working-class backgrounds also encountered obstacles along the way to obtaining higher education: they failed out or stopped out of their studies within a year or two. What happened to them? How did their queer lives unfold or devolve?

Whatever happened to them once they left the scene went on unseen, but of course there were rumors and stories. One was said to be living on the streets in New York City. Another returned to a small-town home to live with his grandmother and haunt truck stops and public restrooms. One was said to have been "reclaimed" by evangelical parents, who locked him up in a mental asylum. Another was said to be in prison. And so on.

I might well have become one of the disappeared, another story of failed self-determination, a negative outcome linked to personal turbulence and economic want. When I came out to my parents, their initial response was to disown me and cut me off, and this lasted for the better part of a year. (Happily, we reconciled; this was not the case for all of my peers.) I stopped out of the university for several months, with no clear plan of return. I was washing dishes in a restaurant, but that didn't pay the bills. At one point, I was homeless for several weeks. I was able to stabilize an increasingly volatile existence because I fell in love, forging a stable relationship with a handsome, educated New Yorker who was ten years older than I. Both lover and mentor, he gave me the foundations of a liberal disputatious education—cultural capital. We spent a year reading and discussing a hundred "great books" from the list he had composed for me. It was an extraordinary, intimate, and mind-expanding experience. We pored over the same texts together, often at the same time, often in bed, sharing a book between us. He taught me a great deal about literature, philosophy, and Marxism—frameworks for thinking about the ongoing changes around me—but more than that, he gave me reason to stay tethered. In my short life, I had never felt closer to anyone. I went back to school, which, after my intimate crash course in the humanities, the social sciences, and logical argumentation, now seemed remarkably easy.

The same search for cultural capital—higher education—is a strong subplot in many of the stories I have been relating. This involves money, of course, but it isn't just about the money: aspirants to higher education strive to participate in a three-dimensional modern cosmopolitan world of enlightened understanding, personal freedom, and material comfort. Today, such participation proves elusive. Under neoliberal practices of retrenchment and privatization, the cost of higher education has risen, wages and salaries have stagnated, and for many, reliable on-ramps into professions are nowhere to be seen. The net result is that working-class people still hear the call of modernity, still aspire to cultural capital and upward mobility, but cannot quite make their personal storylines mesh with those of cosmopolitan liberalism, though they understand these plot lines all too well.

Hypergamy is one of the advantages of gay life—but only so long as minimal conditions for upward mobility remain in place.

In short order, my 1982 senior honors thesis explored, through interviews and questionnaires, working-class gay men's lives. At the time, some of my friends expressed skepticism at the idea that one could be both working-class and gay. Their skepticism conveyed a certain naiveté about the nature of desire and a certain truth about the exposed and precarious position of children of the working class. How, after all, could a working-class homosexual escape family controls and social sanctions to build a stable gay place in the world? Wasn't gayness, with its practices of freedom and independence, essentially tied to middle-classness? And, by this time, it was scarcely a secret that the modern gay style of life was connected to a certain mode of middle-class consumerism, that the gay urban scene had become less a dissident counterculture than a consumerist subculture. Wasn't this lifestyle out of reach for people without disposable income and free time?

I look back in wonder at the naiveté and ambition of my undergraduate project, which worked off a great many hunches and tried to answer deep questions about class and sexuality with a few very rudimentary tools. For better or worse, questions about how the class character of society might shape or constrain our experiences of desire, intimacy, and love have remained vital for me after all these years.

THE CRISIS OF SELF-RECOGNITION

I do not know of any more elegant way to put it than this: at some point in our lives, men who are strongly attracted to other men confront a moment of crisis. This is no less true in Mexico than in the United States. The origins of this climacteric are not mysterious, though the crisis itself is no more a "natural" expression of sexual difference than the length of the working day an expression of the earth's rotation; it occurs only under specific conditions.

We grow up in a social world built around heterosexual institutions and understandings of manhood. These conventions not only presuppose and reinforce heterosexual attraction but also cast aspersions on same-sex attraction or relegate it to the margins and oddities of human experience. Direct and indirect propagandas—sermons, movies, schooling, the prevailing everyday narratives—reinforce the message. Inevitably, then, we confront the question: *Am I that name, which is flung as invective?*[2] (Even in a time of greater toleration, these essential conditions still obtain.) For some of us this moment of truth comes in childhood, for others in adolescence; sometimes it comes much later, and sometimes it is occasioned by other sorts of turmoil. I say "moment," but such a moment may extend over months or years or even a lifetime.

This crisis of self-recognition, along with the forms of introspection, reflexivity, and self-care it supports, is much the same the *modern* world over—and by "modern" I mean those cultures the world over that call upon us to know, to free, and to express ourselves, for without these understandings of the project of selfhood, there can be no crisis or inflection point, only a vague foreboding, a sense of tragedy, a resignation to brute fate. We "moderns" all find ourselves caught in the crossfire between opposed institutional demands ("Conform!" "Be normal!" yet at the same time "Freely express yourself!" "Be yourself!"), but we do not all grapple with the contradictions with the same resources under the same circumstances. The family setting, where the young person debates whether to disclose himself and thus make himself exquisitely vulnerable to rejection, remains the locus classicus of gay self-determination. Erik's, Daniel's, Héctor's, Oscar's, Andrés's, and others' varied life experiences suggest some of the ways a gay life might unfold, or not, under different sorts of circumstances—which hold great sway over the course of events.

Social class figures prominently in how these reckonings play out. We might even say that material conditions—primarily one's class position—"determine" the outcome, if we remember Raymond Williams's discussion

of determination: it is not a divine "external cause" that predicts, prefig-
ures, or controls the course of events; rather, determination is about "setting limits, exerting pressures" within the ensemble of social practices.[3]
Some will deny, minimize, or compartmentalize their attraction, and others will try to build a life around it; in either case, the choices we make and
the actions we take are constrained. Many will strive for gaiety, an imagined world of freedom and abundance, but come up against the hard, cold
class realities of coercion and scarcity. Not only in Mexico is this true.

5 Precarious Lives

Ideas about class differences permeate people's intuitive understanding of the coming-out process—so much so that my friends and subjects would sometimes ask me whether "they" (middle-class gays) experience the same difficulties in claiming a gay identity, have the same experiences of family rejection, as "us" (gays from working-class backgrounds). I want to pursue this line of questioning, the better to try to understand how tolerance and intolerance find placement, intensification, or diminution in class situations. In this inquiry, I try to understand the interplay of directly economic factors (income, resources) and factors indirectly linked to economic standing (education, institutional placement), inasmuch as these can be analytically distinguished, in the shaping of gay people's life chances.

ON MIDDLE-CLASS EXPERIENCES, BY COMPARISON

To be sure, LGBT children of the middle classes can also be subject to coercion and mistreatment. Conservative rhetoric about "family unity" (deployed by Catholic and other religious conservatives in response to gay liberation, feminism, and other "divisive" New Left social movements) and forms of patriarchal authority (deeply anchored in Mexican family law until a series of court decisions and constitutional reforms finally settled the question in favor of gender equality in 2011) are scarcely unheard of among the respectable middle classes. Quite the contrary. The Poblano middle classes are by reputation the keepers of religious piety and family values. Middle-class parents are said to be especially creative in how they withhold approval and extort conformity. One young man related the painful sting of what his father, an ophthalmologist, had said to him many years before when he had gotten into some relatively minor trouble at school: "You were always a good boy, and we always knew that the moment would come when you'd do something stupid. But at least you're not gay." A middle-class mother told her son when he summoned the courage to tell her that he was gay: "I just want you know that I love you, and that will never change, but I will never, ever accept you." Then she went to her room and cried, the nineteen-year-old relates. "What did you do?" I asked. "I went to my room and cried, too."

Such scenes are painful and no doubt damaging, but these mind games, psychological cruelties, and forms of emotional blackmail do not often seem to progress, in the heat of family drama, to physical violence or expulsion. That, I propose, is because middle-class family life is comparatively more "buffered" than working-class life, immersed as it is in middle-class communities where modern forms of cultural capital—education, claims to "modernity," and modern child-rearing—shield one against harsh discipline, patriarchal fiat, and raw expressions of rage and rejection.

When I asked middle-class parents and grandparents whether they knew of cases in their communities in which parents had rejected their LGBT children, the question "But what would the neighbors say?" was a common response. For them, it seemed self-evident that the force of community opinion would cut against ostracism of one's own child. Some volunteered that such family dysfunction was *naco*, a term of disparagement for people or things that are uneducated, uncouth, lower-class ("tacky"). Correlatively, my working-class friends and subjects tended to view this middle-class lifeworld as something of a mystery. They marveled at what they perceived to be the much easier middle-class path to self-expression and acceptance. Many recounted stories like Erik's and Oscar's, involving violent rituals of rejection or expulsion before cooler heads could eventually prevail and family relations reached a point of equilibrium. And the same question "But what would the neighbors say?" they proffered, weighed against gay acceptance in their own communities. (Nosy, opinionated, disapproving neighbors are not an abstraction. Note how the opinions of neighbors figured prominently in Erik's, Oscar's, and others' conflicts with their fathers.)

Raúl's experience is perhaps indicative of how social conservatism and sexual toleration might coexist in an educated, middle-class milieu. Members of Raúl's family over successive generations have almost all been educated professionals: Two of his grandparents were physicians, and his parents are both high school science teachers. But his parents are also Catholic conservatives, and like many Mexican parents, they continued to regulate their son's goings and comings when he was well past the age of eighteen. Thus, all through his undergraduate years, Raúl would wait until parents and siblings were asleep, then sneak out of the house through the bedroom window to join friends at late-night clubs and bars, stealing back into the house at the crack of dawn to greet his parents, sleepily, at breakfast.

His parents found out that he was gay when he became ill with hepatitis in the wake of a series of condom failures. The young man, who was in the process of graduating with a degree in computer science and had been accepted for graduate studies at Monterrey Institute of Technology and Higher Education, was depressed about his health and terrified of family rejection. But his father said nothing; his mother spent several weeks crying and praying the rosary in front of the household altar. "It's depressing," he told me when he was well enough to leave the house and pay me a visit. "They're spending a lot on my treatment, which makes me feel worse, but we can't talk about it." So it went with the three, awkwardly, silently inhabiting the family home, until one day his father eventually mumbled to Raúl that he should take better care of himself, an embarrassed allusion to proper condom use. (In fact, I had already had a conversation with the young man about condom use; he had been under the mistaken impression that prelubricated condoms required no additional lubrication, thus his experience with a series of tears and leaks.)

Raúl recovered; it turned out that he had hepatitis B, not C (which he had initially feared). Although he experienced strategic silences and not-talking-about-it as stressful, Raul's relationships to family remained intact, and his parents continued to support him throughout his graduate studies at Monterrey Tech. Eventually, he received a PhD. Today, as a result, he remains plausibly if not comfortably middle-class. When employed, he applies his mathematical and computing skills in well-remunerated market research, tracking economic fluctuations and projecting consumer demand for Mexican corporate clients while also teaching occasional online university courses part-time as an adjunct professor.

But all the family nurturance and support in the world cannot alter the fact that this is not the same stable, respectable "middle-class" milieu that was once inhabited by his educated parents and grandparents. Firms, especially unstable startup consulting firms of the sort likely to hire a recent graduate, increasingly outsource for the sort of analysis Raúl might provide—or devolve it upon unpaid or poorly paid interns who are eager to try to get a foot on the rungs of the ladder. Meanwhile, tenure-track positions in higher education are virtually unheard of, and universities increasingly assess the performance of their casualized instructors based on student evaluations—without providing them with much in the way of training or guidance. Thus, in the roiling employment markets during the long COVID crisis, Raúl lost and acquired a number of positions, with months-long bouts of unemployment in between. Taking in how fragile his on-ramps to a stable professional middle-class existence are, he contemplates alternatives: perhaps a more "traditional" commercial path. Among other proposals, he has floated the idea of opening, with friends, a small to midsize gay bathhouse in Monterrey, where he has remained since graduating.

I underscore the force of precaritization, which is germane to the wider analysis I am developing here. Under current conditions, both the exploitation of workers and the proletarianization of sectors of the middle class are intensifying. Capitalism's regulatory and disciplinary mechanisms—which include cost cutting, outsourcing, casualization, and other pressures toward downward mobility—traverse class lines and reverberate in economic life, family relations, and sexual matters. In the life of the middle classes, these pressures augur varied forms of cultural conservatism and political reaction but are offset—"buffered"—by educated sensibilities, which imply liberal and cosmopolitan values.

WORKING-CLASS CONSERVATISM

What about the less buffered life of working-class people? Is there something about working-class existence that makes it intrinsically hidebound, narrow, and, by extension, sexually repressive? Many have thought so. Ideas about working-class conservatism typically narrate how a defensive orientation toward a hostile world produces various strands of traditionalism, conventionalism, and fatalism. These notions are deeply embedded in the anthropological and sociological literatures, for almost as soon as social philosophers had trained their sights on the disruptive effects of industrial capitalism, they also perceived workers, peasants, and the popular (nonelite) classes in general as resisting the juggernaut of modernity, as struggling to conserve traditional lifeways amidst the vortex of capitalist "progress."

Max Weber saw popular-class traditionalism, which cordons off certain labor practices and claims ethical sanction for time-honored ways of doing things, as a stubborn barrier against capitalism and its predations.[1] Tracing the social dialectic of capitalist modernity, Karl Polanyi suggested that the popular classes prefer fixed, predictable, and settled ways—"habitation"—over "improvement," which is essentially synonymous with the extension of market rationalities into ever-wider areas of life.[2] E. P. Thompson glossed the popular classes' collective outlook as "customs in common" and held that these are at bottom predicated on a stubborn moral economy.[3] Similar ideas abound in the anthropology of Latin America, where large numbers of people still have one foot in the peasant world. Peasants, perhaps especially indigenous peasants, strive to *conserve* long-standing ways of life, which are menaced by the tempest of capitalist development. (Paradoxically, these conservative strivings can sometimes provide a trampoline for revolutionary movements.)[4]

French sociologist Pierre Bourdieu thought that such customs congealed as ingrained dispositions, unconscious schema; he called these durable ways of doing things *habitus*, a term that encompasses a variety of registers: habit, habituation, habitation.[5] As a conceptual apparatus, habitus leans heavily on interpretive finesse and inventive diagrams, but there is empirical support for some of its component parts. Psychological research finds that working-class people tend to be more empathic than middle-class people, that they tend to embrace norms of interdependence rather than independence. They also tend to be more "fatalistic" than their middle-class counterparts. Broadly put, working-class people are not swept up in the romance of liberalism; they tend to be alert to the myriad ways the world pushes against the individual rather than viewing the world as a field of opportunities for self-making and achievement.[6] Working-class experience thus militates against the modern storyline of the heroic, independent self, a key component of the coming-out narrative.

Bourdieu and his students took this bundle of ideas in a different direction from the socialist celebrants of working-class culture. They tended to view habitus as something like (but more profound than) false consciousness: habitus embeds the rules of the system, more so than resistance to it, in what is self-evident, what goes without saying. They further suggested that lower-class habitus incorporates, naturalizes, and reproduces the sexual order.[7] Is the man manly? Does he know how to comport his body correctly? Has he a "feel" for the rules of the social game? These associations resonate in Didier Eribon's elegiac memoir, *Returning to Reims*, which evokes the economic besiegement of lower-working-class life and describes how gauges of male competence cut against gender and sexual nonconformity. Drawing on his own experiences, Eribon ultimately suggests that working-class homosexuals who wish to have a gay life must escape conservative proletarian conditions, acquiring cultural capital, upgrading their employment niche, and establishing residency in a cosmopolitan middle-class world. The author's trajectory from Reims to Paris is no doubt one of the pathways of gay life, but different insights might have been gained had he returned to the abundant cruising areas, saunas, and gay dive bars of the provincial postindustrial slum. Perhaps more convincingly, Eribon draws out some of the ways the ravages of neoliberalism and deindustrialization have moved the dial on the French working class's political orientation, delivering the socially abandoned working-class vote—which used to go to the Communist Party—to the nativist and anti-immigrant National Rally.[8]

I have no doubt that the classical theorists were onto something. Surely, complex amalgams of popular conservatism do situate sexual understandings and the experiences of sexual minorities in many places. But these tendencies are unevenly distributed across time and space; the content of conservatism varies from place to place; and in practice, it proves difficult to distinguish popular or working-class from middle-class forms of conservatism. I thus lay out four caveats, qualifications to the premise of working-class conservatism, delimitations of its application to questions about gay self-determination.

First, just how much remains of popular traditionalism is an open question. Even as he developed a model for understanding working-class "customs in common," British historian E. P. Thompson doubted that a proletarian moral economy had survived changes of the postwar era (mass media, mass education) in England. Similar doubts logically attach to a long history of upheaval, displacement, development, and mass communication in Mexico. The subjects about whom I write grew up after the dislocations of Mexico's "Lost Decade," triggered by the 1982 financial crisis. They lived through the wrenching years of the mid-1990s' "Tequila Crisis." They came of age with international programing on cable TV, were early adopters of cell phones, cruised the Web in internet cafés from the beginnings of the "information age," and are "digital natives," fluent users of contemporary global social media such as Facebook, Twitter, and TikTok. Given the pervasiveness of such forms of savvy (which we usually think of as "cosmopolitan") among young people of working-class or even peasant origins, "popular conservatism" might best be understood as a generational lag effect rather than a persistent phenomenon. In any case, cultural capital and cosmopolitanism would seem to be far more widely distributed today than they were when models of popular traditionalism and working-class conservatism were drawn up.

Second, and no less germane to the question of sexual repression: religion—which looms large in ideas about conservative reflexes—plays a substantial role in the social and affective life of both the working and the lower-middle classes, but in either case, the connection between, say, religious traditionalism and sexual intolerance is unclear. Veneration of the Virgin of Guadalupe, the national patron saint, is not necessarily inconsistent with gay acceptance. Yuli, the owner of a gay café-bar, keeps an altar to the Santo Niño Jesús Doctor, the infant Jesus dressed as a medical doctor, in her home.[9] She lovingly dresses the child doctor in clothing she makes by hand and pointedly rejects the idea that such forms of popular religiosity imply intolerance. Indeed, altars to patron saints are sometimes stationed near the entryway to gay bathhouses and clubs, where entrants might cross themselves or whisper a prayer before giving themselves over to devotions of the flesh. It is not even clear that small towns—which are often aligned in the public imagination with ideas about the popular classes, rusticity, religiosity, and so on and are collectively stereotyped as being deeply homophobic—are in actual practice more consistently hostile to gay ways of being than big cities, a point noted by Ana Minian, Héctor Carrillo, and others in their studies.[10] Mexico is a large and complex place; religious beliefs, ethnic cultures, and local traditions might be tolerant in one village and intolerant in another, easygoing in one family and repressive in another.

Third, too much talk about working-class *social* conservatism tends to leave unexamined elite forms of *economic* conservatism, which are about the preservation of oppressive class relations. This seems especially true in the era of Trump and other avatars of right-wing, pseudo-populist politics. We scrutinize less educated sectors of the population for signs of intolerance and chauvinism (which are no doubt present) while giving educated and elite sectors a free pass, despite their record of support for policies that have depressed wages to disastrous effects, not only in Mexico and the United States—provided they make token gestures at goals of liberal toleration and inclusion. This is a recurring narrative among the liberal professoriate, a subset of the professional upper-middle classes that, having betrayed the working class for the past forty years, now feign anguish that the working class has betrayed them. So much the worse for the academic habitus, with its prevailing storylines and dispositions, its inability to contemplate its own role in the regulation of class relations.

Fourth and last, the train of thoughts involved in theoretical models of popular traditionalism, which attempt to induce a distinctive culture or worldview from a class position, replicates a timeworn path: the working class is seen as a discretely bounded group, that is, as a subculture or an identity, and is depicted as either an object of pity (for its backwardness) or of praise (for its salt-of-the-earth traits) or of condemnation (for its bad habits). One might be excused for thinking that the concept of habitus replicates, with bells and whistles, Oscar Lewis's or even Daniel Patrick Moynihan's "culture of poverty" paradigm, which contemplated the lifeways of the poor with pity and consternation.[11] We are not far from J. D. Vance's *Hillbilly Elegy* here, which tells readers that the poor of Appalachia and the eastern midlands are trapped in poverty not because of deindustrialization and deliberate policies of offshoring and social abandonment but because of their supposedly maladaptive cultural traits.[12] We are also uncomfortably close to what Adorno called "identitarian thinking," which reduces qualities to categories and things to concepts; it "says what something comes under, what it exemplifies or represents," not what it *is*—which, dialectically understood, is also "to be what it is not yet."[13]

In *The Class Matrix*, Vivek Chibber suggests a different tack, a promising starting point for thinking about culture, consciousness, and habit in relation to working-class existence. Theories of what forms of consciousness tend to follow from class position might be better grounded if they began with the simple fact that the worker needs a job and thus needs the capitalist more than the capitalist needs the worker. The brute facts of economic coercion, the constant pressures of the marketplace, the threat of downward mobility, ultimately steer workers toward individual rather than collective concerns and action.[14] This reality perhaps explains why working-class solidarity and organization are almost everywhere the exception rather than the rule. It implies that workers' spontaneous consciousness, far from being discretely bounded or oriented toward group identity, collectivism, and the past, typically exemplifies the atomizing and serializing characteristics of capitalist modernity.

Chibber's framework has two implications that are especially relevant here. First, it makes working-class social conservatism, when it occurs, a less mysterious phenomenon than it might appear to be under other models. Under the frequently exposed and atomizing conditions that are forced on them (in the present instance, the destruction of social safety nets), workers come to rely on conservative social institutions to get by, both in everyday life and also in times of dearth: the family, kinship, religious institutions, local networks, and so on. If working-class people have sometimes tended to cherish these institutions (and correlatively to reject disruptive forces perceived to undermine them), it is because they are lifelines, material ballasts, and means of psychological support. Absent stronger traditions of the sort sketched in classical social theory—or, alternatively, without strong unions and a redistributive welfare state—these are the only "buffers" working people have against the dislocations of the marketplace and the forms of personal dissolution that follow in their wake. Viewed this way, a tendency toward "social conservatism" is a more or less direct consequence of the economic force of class and the way it steers, constrains, or limits people's options in a class-stratified world.

Second, as I have been showing across various life stories, meager resources limit working-class people's "exit options" from conservative settings and hobble their ability to find safer spaces to exercise their sexuality. Many resort instead to strategies of closeting, masking, covering, and dissimulation. Contrast these limited options with forms of recourse available to members of the middle class and elites, whose resources enable them to find more spaces—and above all to plant themselves in "enlightened" social circles less beholden to conservative institutions.

All to say that class is at once a social position, an economic relation, and a dynamic process. It is defined narrowly by nonownership and structured broadly by tendencies that might wax or wane under sped-up or slowed-down versions of capitalism. And if social conservatism is a strong tendency among working-class people, not an essential trait, then its actual distribution and content remain to be mapped against the outcomes of class struggles over pay, time, and working conditions, but also to be understood with a view of the everyday institutional surround that embeds working-class people's experience of personal life. These caveats and pointers ward us away from models that give us preformed, eternal workers with durable cultural values (Marx chided Proudhon for just such ahistorical categorial thinking). We are reminded to start again at the granular level where Marx started in *The German Ideology*: from "real premises," not dogmas or abstractions; from "real individuals, their activity and the material conditions under which they live, both those which they find already existing and those produced by their activity."[15]

THE EXPOSED AND PRECARIOUS CONDITION OF
THE MEXICAN WORKING CLASS

I trust that, in describing forces and tendencies, I have not oversimplified matters. Not all members of the working class are socially conservative. Some—like Héctor's mother and sister—are quite liberal, and a few are militantly anticlerical. And to reinvoke my modest advice given to Erik more than a decade ago: social norms are not set in stone; they are rapidly changing, part of a veritable avalanche of transformations in the wake of political liberalization and cultural globalization. Oscar's father, a case in point, went from violently intolerant to accepting over the course of a few weeks—as though he had already seen his role scripted in problem-of-the-week series episodes on Televisa or TV Azteca.

But stubborn structures remain in place, some inherited from the past and others revivified in reaction to that very avalanche of sped-up capitalist modernity. The question, then, is not so much whether working-class people are on balance more socially conservative than middle-class people as it is how changing conditions breathe new life into repressive structures and institutions.

So let me paint a changing picture in broad strokes, providing a wide-angle snapshot of the volatile condition of family life in working-class settings under actual neoliberal conditions—in Mexico, for example.

Disorders of anomie and despair, such as alcoholism, as well as sundry forms of interpersonal violence, including domestic violence and lynchings, are concentrated in pueblos and lower-income barrios. This is not a new story, and parts of it have been well documented.[16] But with the neoliberal dismantling of state subsidies for agriculture, small businesses, and local industry, these conditions have worsened—and violent-crime rates, which were already concentrated in low-income neighborhoods, have soared in the wake of the narco wars. Nationwide, the homicide rate rose from 8 per 100,000 in 2007 (following newly elected president Felipe Calderón's declaration of war against the drug cartels) to 29 per 100,000 in 2018, with wide differences among regions.[17] Kidnapping and extortion rackets spread, with the result that life has become less secure for everyone. Robberies are commonplace. I do not know anyone in Puebla who has not been threatened or assaulted and robbed: some on darkened streets at night, some in broad daylight, many along bus routes—and inside buses—to and from work. Robbers sometimes even set up illicit checkpoints along roads on the outskirts of town to stop and rob hapless drivers in the wee hours of the morning. Upticks in reports and perceptions of horrific homophobic violence can be seen in part as a subset of the violence that has engulfed barrios and pueblos across the country. My working-class friends' and subjects' desires to "come out" and be transparent about their desires are checked not only by the possibility of family rejection but also by fear of assault, extortion, and kidnapping.

Under such dire circumstances, varied forms of religious conservatism and popular piety find reliable purchase. These include not just the received forms of Catholic conservatism, amped up by traditional family values rhetoric. Newer salvation religions provide total programs for personal reformation. As Andrés's experience suggests, they lay out rules and practices that support individual stability and self-discipline in an unstable world. They also expressly portray same-sex attraction as a symptom of social disorder and personal dissolution. Nearly 15 percent of Mexicans are members of evangelical Protestant denominations (mostly variants of Pentecostalism) or millenarian religions (such as the Jehovah's Witnesses), and these numbers are concentrated in lower-working-class barrios and indigenous communities.[18] Charismatic versions of Catholicism take on the logics of these religious currents, and these beliefs and practices, too, are skewed to low-income sectors.

Inverse proportions hold for education, a key conduit of liberal, secular, and tolerant values. Today, about half of Mexicans finish high school and 23 percent of young Mexicans (ages 23–35) hold university degrees (putting the country at the back of the OECD pack), but class barriers to education are high, and these figures are far lower than the national average for the children of low-income and working-class people.[19]

In tandem, these factors *tend*, like a series of dominoes falling, to propel repressive sexual norms, coercive gender roles, blunt varieties of personal domination, and patriarchal forms of family authority in lower- and working-class communities. Sexual tolerance and gay acceptance find comparatively fewer sturdy supports there; checks on interpersonal violence are looser; and there are comparatively fewer buffers against paternal caprice.

All of this to say that working-class intolerance is uneven, inconsistent, situationally dependent, and generationally skewed: it is a contingent, not a necessary, feature of working-class life. But it is also persistent, recurring, and thus widely perceived to be characteristic of working-class life.

DISPOSABILITY

I return to the salience of a negative sanction, a constant pressure, that is built into the logic of social class. Disposability, as Michael Denning has shown in his rereading of Marx's texts on wage labor and unemployment, is the essential condition of the working class, precarity its ever-present reality. "It is already contained in the concept of the free *laborer*," wrote Marx, "that he is a *pauper*: a virtual pauper."[20] In other words, the worker is always already unemployable, subject to dismissal—one accident, misstep, or market fluctuation away from joining the ranks of "surplus labor." Working-class life is always under a Sword of Damocles. (I add: middle-class life, too, to the extent that it is being proletarianized.)

Now to spell out the obvious (and perhaps to risk abusing the concept of disposability): gays, especially working-class gays, in Mexico live out stories of precarity, expulsion, and homelessness much like those experienced by working-class gays in the United States. Their crises of self-recognition, their struggles for self-determination, their conflicts with families and communities cannot be reduced to a sort of class crisis—they involve sexual shame, emotional extortion, and moral rules rather than economic calculations—nor can they be boiled down to the specificities of a class position (others in other classes feel much the same psychic tug-of-war), but neither can they be understood apart from the wider dynamics of social class. For, on the one hand, the disciplinary mechanisms applied against LGBT youth in their critical moments of reckoning are the self-same cudgels and bludgeons that regulate the class system under capitalism: the prospect of downward mobility, the threat of unemployability, the fear that one might fall, or rather that one might be pushed, into the ranks of utterly abject and economically superfluous people. And, on the other hand, gay life is never more precarious than when and where working-class existence is stressed, unstable, and precarious.

Disposability, abandonment, homelessness—these form the suspended sentence, the Sword of Damocles that hangs over LGBT people's heads during their crises of self-recognition. Save for brute physical violence, most of the forms of discipline associated with homophobia essentially come down to this blunt social and economic threat. This, the specter of "wageless"—or at least economically degraded—life,[21] is part of what puts the spark in hellfire religion and fortifies other forms of coercion and control. The threat of ostracism is all the more violent because it is wielded by parents, families, and those who supposedly love and protect us, often in the name of the sanctity of family.

DETERMINATION WITHOUT REDUCTION

When I say, then, that one's class condition "determines" one's life chances, that we cannot understand gay people's experiences with predicament and crisis without taking class dynamics into account, I refer not to an external cause or a secret code for spelling out both one's individual fate and the singular trajectory of history. That would be divine law, against which human beings would struggle in vain. Determination in a strictly Marxist sense does not predict, prefigure, or control the course of events; rather, it sets limits and exerts pressures within the wider ensemble of social relations. We aspire, we struggle, we choose, but the choices we make and the actions we take are constrained.[22] And when, under certain circumstances, these constraints are sufficiently binding, they raise the probability of certain outcomes sufficiently to approach the force of determinism in the stronger sense.

In piecing together pictures of how the logic of class expresses itself in changing institutional ensembles, I seek to disentangle three distinct but interrelated elements: class position (one's location in the system of economic inequality), the class condition of society (the way economic inequality structures social relations generally), and pressures that cut across class distinctions (essentially, these are capitalism's regulatory mechanisms, including cost-cutting and casualization). I strive for a dynamic accounting. Nothing is to be gained by putting forward a static and circumscribed model of class wherein the working class exists as an ethnos fully equipped with its own distinct institutions and outlooks, as against a static and enclosed model of identity that prevails today—which, after all, was modeled as a corrective to closed and reductive understandings of class. Class dynamics vary according to changing modes of capitalist accumulation and social conditions. Classes have neither ontologies nor essences, but interests.

Thus, there is no such thing as a working-class family structure, only family forms adapted to changing demands of working-class socialization and conditions of scarcity. There is no specifically working-class social conservatism, only skewings and distributions of forms of conservatism that are common throughout the popular, middle, and even elite classes. Nor is there a distinctly working-class experience of homophobia, family rejection, and so on; rather, there are disproportionalities and concentrations of widely distributed institutional effects. What *is* consistent across time and place are economic pressures. We might productively invert F. Scott Fitzgerald and Ernest Hemingway's canonical repartee (about the rich and their money):[23] What distinguishes working-class families from other kinds of families is primarily their lack of money and resources. A lot follows from this lack. A good deal of what makes for "conservatism" among working-class families is exposure to economic upheaval and social brutality.

Class, then, explains a great deal of what happens in gay life, not only in Mexico. The economic pressures and disciplinary mechanisms of class society *skew* things in a certain direction. Class dynamics *divide* the experiences of gays. And under prevailing conditions, the mesh of religious institutions, gender norms, and family structures closes around working-class life in specific ways and exposes working-class youth to acute forms of repression and intolerance. Precarity, the gist of working-class life, leaves working-class gays doubly exposed.

I come back to truisms, which at least have the virtue of being true. The factors described above and the ways they variously interdigitate under different circumstances—here spelling out relative tolerance and acceptance, there spelling out rejection and shunning—are widely understood by aspirants to gay communities everywhere. If the interplays of these factors have often been overlooked, even in scholarly works that purport to treat the question of precarity in the domain of sexual politics,[24] they might serve as guide rails for new lines of inquiry into the relationship between sexuality and political economy. And, if the logic of the class system, and with it the internal dynamics of capitalism, has been elided by, buried under, or effectively reduced to other terms of inequality (race, ethnicity, gender, sexuality), even in works that purport to be materialist, then perhaps new trains of thought might yield synthetic rather than additive accountings of how identities surge into being and flicker on the stage of history.

So far, I have mostly attended to the ways social class pushes against gay life "from without," limiting, circumscribing, and constraining gay men's options. A more vexing line of inquiry remains; it involves how class works on us "from within," structuring our symbolic worlds and shaping our needs, wants, and aspirations.

Let me sketch something of those symbolic worlds here, connecting them with what has already been shown and anticipating themes to be developed in part II. The worker, the peasant, and the indigenous person are collectively viewed as being intrinsically traditional, conservative, and "backward," and not only by theorists. Something sometimes appears to be "out of joint" about the time of the now, such that we don't all coexist there synchronously.[25] This is a common motif in Mexican vernaculars and literatures. Needless to say, the popular classes—and all of their component sections—are as much products of changing political-economic conditions as are the educated, urban middle classes. In that sense, all are equally "modern"; all are contemporary subjects fabricated on the lathe of history. But this is cold comfort for those who experience their poverty and social exclusion as a form of exile from modernity.[26]

Now let's cut to the chase: How do sexual identity formations exist in this perceived out-of-joint world? Is there something intrinsic in the prevailing definitions of modernity, gayness, and subculture that also tends to sort and reject working-class people? And how might people make do and imagine the possibilities of their lives under conditions that beckon and refuse them at the same time? Desiring, yearning, and aspiring are key here, and what the Italian anarchist Errico Malatesta said a hundred years ago remains apposite: "Everything depends on what the people are capable of wanting."[27]

PART II *Ambiente* and Ambiguity
THE STRUGGLE FOR WHAT ELUDES US

The periphery is where the future reveals itself.

—misattributed to J. G. Ballard

Nothing, of course, begins at the time you think it did.

—Lillian Hellman, *Unfinished Woman*

Everything is bad, everything is good.

—wisdom of Mexican taxi drivers

We know what we are, but know not what we may be.

—William Shakespeare, *Hamlet*

6 Fable of Rapport

Anthropologists often tell a "fable of rapport" early on in ethnographic works, sometimes revealing bits and pieces of the ethnographer's personal life and sometimes using spouses or partners as props.[1] Such stories typically serve to situate the researcher in the field and to establish his or her connection to his or her subjects of study. This one comes late in the course of this work and turns in part on a certain homophobic slur.

I was settling into Puebla for my first yearlong research stay (2006–7), when I would transition from being a frequent visitor (since the mid-1990s) to becoming a visiting scholar by day and a resident alien by night. Almost immediately, like a thunderbolt from the blue, my relationship of eighteen years disintegrated, and I found myself alone and forlorn in a city where no one knew me.

A straight woman who was undergoing a divorce in the United States asked me: Did you ever figure out why you broke up? The answer was (and remains) no. I spent the first months in a brooding funk, examining my pain and solitude. I was forty-seven and had spent virtually my entire adult life coupled up. (My first relationship had lasted for ten years.) My social skills were minimal, in part because I had met my personal needs for both romance and friendship in the relationship, and in part because I was not a naturally gregarious person. My Spanish was still rusty and halting from disuse, so that it required effort to sustain complex conversations. Overwhelmed by grief and homesickness, I contemplated bailing out—resigning my fellowship and returning home—but what awaited me back in the United States was only more loneliness in an apartment that my partner and I had shared. Instead, I withdrew and nursed my wounds and then slowly forced myself to go out, to talk to people. My early goals were embarrassingly modest: I would try to have a conversation for at least a few minutes with one person per day.

I had to relearn everything: how to sleep alone (this was more difficult than it might sound), how to make friends on my own, then later, how to flirt, how to cruise—all dubbed awkwardly into a second language. Awkwardness may have been my ally, since it slowed everything down and provided excuses for any missteps, but more than that, historical circumstances facilitated my learning process. Public, visible gay life in Puebla and other cities was still on the upswing as the Fox *sexenio* (this is how Mexicans refer to a president's six-year term) turned into the Calderón period, and even I had no trouble finding it.

Had I arrived a few years before—or for that matter a few years after—I'm not sure I could have found my place in a city with a reputation for stodginess and conservatism. I doubt that I would have had the patience to play detective, to discreetly search for clues as to the whereabouts of an evasive ambiente. But, for the time being, downtown Puebla was dotted with clearly marked gay cafés, bars, *antros* (nightclubs), and other hangouts where, for the price of a drink (or coffee) and the minimal effort of being interested in other people's lives (which eventually turned out to be no effort at all), one might pass the afternoon or the evening in pleasant conversation. My favorite haunt would become Luciérnaga (Firefly), the gay café-bar that catered to students and young people. It was owned and operated by Yuli, a middle-aged straight woman and mother. Her straight sister Margarita ran the kitchen. Ricardo, Margarita's straight son, and Yamil—a well-built, outgoing, irascible gay man—ran the bar and waited tables.

It was Yamil who insisted, in his way, that I become not an onlooker but an active participant in the gay scene. The garrulous bartender was kind and solicitous with most of the café's clients but would wax playfully churl-ish and aggressive with others—if he thought they could take it.

"*¡Puto!*" he shouted at me from the bar early one evening as I entered the café, using a harsh, offensive term meaning "fag" or "queer." Dozens of cli-ents, distributed across tables and sofas, froze. I was twice Yamil's age, and most of the bar's young clients were still politely calling me *señor* and *usted* out of deference to age and status distinctions. I, too, froze, uncertain as to whether it was I who was being so rudely interpellated. But the brawny bartender was staring mischievously at me and in a heartbeat, I assessed the situation and knew how to respond, how to match Yamil's coarse greet-ing. "Maricón de mi vida," I replied loudly in my best baritone, "te quiero un chingo" (Fairy of my life, I love you fuckloads). There was another pause, as the audience absorbed our performances and verified that we were not on the brink of fighting; then the tension broke and there were ripples of laughter. After this exchange, people at the bar put aside their Poblano ges-tures of respect and distance and began addressing me as *tú*.

Walking home that evening in November, I ambled through a scenic plaza where sixteenth-century buildings faced off against one another and I thought to myself, *This isn't so bad after all.* After this epiphany, I warmed to my surroundings. The staff and regular clients at Luciérnaga became my friends, my extended family, even. The wider ambiente took me in, tolerated my eccentricities, occasionally made fun of my accent or cluelessness, and threw me together with an abundance of kind men, women, and others. Little by little, I wove myself into the life of the place. Indeed, after a little time had passed, my new problem was that I could not stroll across the centro en route to a site or meeting without being greeted and stopped by various friends and acquaintances. (This was, as they say, a good problem to have.) A pair of short-term romances over the coming months helped convince me that perhaps my life was not yet over.

By the time my stay was over, I had made the city my home and did not want to leave it.[2]

There were other epiphanies, as well. For the first time in my life, I really understood the value of the gay scene—the subculture—and the impor-tance of the kinds of connections it fosters. However, I had to forget much of what I thought I knew about such subcultures.

7 Identity and Its Discontents

In modern times, the drama of identity has unfolded in three acts. A shifting cast of protagonists takes center stage to deliver soliloquies on the struggle to be modern, its reverberation in systems of economic inequality, its intended and unintended effects. Across scenes redolent with irony and pathos, themes repeat alternately as tragedy and farce.

I step back here to give a wide-angle view of this ongoing drama: to sketch a very brief history of Mexico's changing political-economic panorama, to outline how evolving ethnic-class formations took shape there, and to suggest how contemporary gay scenes developed within these horizons.

LIBERAL DREAMS AND WAKING NIGHTMARES

The first act begins with independence (1821), when idealists among Mexico's elites dreamed of freedom, democracy, and progress, and culminates with the Liberal dictatorship of Porfirio Díaz. During the Porfiriato (the period of Díaz's rule, from 1876 to 1911), foreign capital drove rapid economic growth, infrastructural development, and modernization.

Continuous economic revolutions produced an incipient proletariat as well as a small urban, educated middle class. Cities began their hundred-year boom.[1]

But despite the rapid expansion of production, Mexico still remained overwhelmingly rural, and conditions in the countryside were becoming increasingly desperate. Thanks to laws that encouraged the taking of indigenous and peasant lands, by 1910 roughly 1 percent of the population owned 97 percent of the arable land, while around 96 percent of rural families were landless—and the dispossessed masses, reduced to debt peonage or worse, were without any bargaining power on resulting labor markets.[2] Such devastation was not an accidental feature of the Liberal regime's policies. Díaz's *cientificos* (scientific planners) viewed the pueblos—indigenous and sometimes mestizo (mixed-race, Spanish-speaking) rural communities that often lived on communal lands—as hopelessly backward, as intransigent obstacles to modernization, and the planners therefore established policies to dislodge them from the land, to liquidate the indigenous peasantry as a class.

The regime was all too successful at dispossessing the rural masses. But there were also unintended consequences, dominoes whose fall the planners had failed to take into account. The new owners of the land produced for export, as intended. Corn crops declined and the price of basic foodstuffs inevitably rose. In short order, the glories of commerce, transportation, and progress had reduced the landless peasantry to the brink of starvation. Mexican society would eventually explode.

It was against this backdrop of capital accumulation and class warfare that homosexuality entered into public discourse. In the nineteenth century, male same-sex intimacies had been largely unmarked and were probably widespread. Carlos Monsiváis notes that stories about men bedding down together could be related without causing controversy or consternation.[3] This would change in 1901 when police raided an upscale party in Mexico City, arresting forty-one revelers, nineteen of them in drag. Contributors to a symposium held on the centennial of the raid have shown how the press sensationally and extensively covered the arrests and their aftermath.[4] Robert McKee Irwin writes that the "scandal of 'the famous 41' was so far-reaching that scenes of male-male intimacy would never again pass unnoticed in Mexico."[5] Robert Buffington aptly compares the social effects of the raid in Mexico to those of Oscar Wilde's trial in England, six years before.[6] Even today, the number 41 looms large with ominous associations: it is an unlucky number, a sign of danger, a warning not to ask too many questions.

As Irwin adumbrates, this story of the 41 provided a vivid blueprint for the hegemonic sexual culture's understanding and treatment of homosexuality in the twentieth century. First, the police raid on the drag ball was illegal under Mexican law, as were the men's humiliations and punishments: they were made to sweep the streets of Mexico City, some still in drag, then many of them were shipped off to Yucatán to perform hard labor in the military. But the press applauded the authorities' unlawful actions against such deplorable men. *Maricones* were not subject to legal protections: they were "criminals," even though their actions were not actually unlawful.[7]

Second, it is well known that historically, across large parts of Latin America, masculine men who sexually penetrated receptive men largely escaped stigmatized labels, at least so long as they maintained a respectable public profile in "straight" society.[8] They were "machos," and their partners were "maricones." By contrast to such popular sexual imaginaries, the case of the infamous 41 inaugurated a distinctly "modern" public discourse on sexuality, consistent with medical and psychiatric models of deviance at the time. Under this emergent model, men who had sex with men were deemed fit for stigma and punishment, without regard to role, dress, or demeanor. Scandalous reporting still identified homosexuality with effeminacy and transvestism, of course, but blurred distinctions between "male" and "female," active and passive roles at the ball. In practice, pronounced active-passive role distinctions would persist in a variety of locales—especially among the lower classes and in indigenous communities—but for the literate national public, it was the 41, not just the nineteen who were in drag, who were ridiculed and condemned.[9]

Third, the story of the 41 was crosshatched with class struggles and class anxieties. The figure of the dissolute dandy, too refined for his own good, provided an ample target for bourgeois moralizing, of course, but the debauchery of the 41 was sometimes characterized as being "low class." Meanwhile, in the penny press, the homosexual revelers were the object of working-class scorn and mockery, their ignominy enlisted in a broad contestation of bourgeois legitimacy. Part of what seemed to inspire such florid reproof in the press, etchings, and even a novel, was the intimation of class mixing between upper-class dandies and lower-class servants and hustlers. Taboos against class mixing were strong in Mexico. In the colonial era, elaborate classificatory schemes based on bloodlines and their admixtures had kept racialized hereditary groups (*castas*) socially separated, at least in theory, and had assigned them different rights and responsibilities; this logic of definition and separation was reconfigured and reinforced in nineteenth- and twentieth-century class divisions. By dint of this logic, homosexuality was a moral menace, in part because it crossed class lines in unauthorized ways and enjoined men of different standing in social and sexual encounters.[10]

Fourth, the story of the infamous 41 contains an important subplot about political power and influence. The original number of arrests reported in the press was forty-two. This may have been a reporting error, but it was widely rumored that one of the arrestees was Porfirio Díaz's son-in-law, who leveraged political connections to escape punishment. (A recent Mexican film, *El Baile de los 41*, relates the story from his point of view.)

REVOLUTIONARY FUTURISM AND THE PEOPLE IT IMAGINED

The second act begins in the throes of the Mexican Revolution, the first "peasant war" of the twentieth century.[11] This was a multisided upheaval that lasted from 1910 to 1920. Leaving as many as 1.5 million people dead in a country of 15 million, it utterly destroyed the old regime. When the killing was mostly over, the Partido Revolucionario Institucional (PRI) gradually emerged from the chaos, constructed a system of one-party rule, and reconstructed the nation. From its formal founding in 1929 (under the name Partido Nacional Revolucionario) until some point when the term "revolutionary" would serve as nothing more than a historical ornament, the ruling party would portray itself as *the* guardian of the revolution.

Freedom, democracy, progress—in a word, modernity—remained the aspirational ideals of the political class, but those terms' meanings shifted.

Under the transformational presidency of Lázaro Cárdenas (1934–40), the PRI took a socialist turn, nationalizing the subsoil (oil, gas, and minerals), expropriating foreign owners, and implementing aggressive policies of land redistribution, agrarian reform, and labor reforms. Although Cárdenas's expressly socialist slogan—"For a Workers' Democracy"—would prove too much for subsequent leaders, the era's reforms established broad legitimacy for the Party and set the stage for a model of managed, redistributive, and internally directed capitalist development under conditions of peace and stability. This model produced the "Mexican Miracle": some thirty-five years of robust, uninterrupted economic growth.[12]

Under the PRI, the state embarked on an ambitious project that would reconstruct, in tandem, Mexican national identity and conceptions of modernity. The rhetoric of indigenous monumentalism was a prominent feature of this project, and that rhetoric prevailed in nationalist political discourse from the Cárdenas years through the 1960s. Modernist public works, expansive murals, household calendars, and so on conspicuously referenced Mesoamerican antiquity, especially the Aztecs, whose empire had spanned much of the territory of contemporary Mexico. Buttressed by artists, architects, intellectuals, and not least of all, anthropologists, the ruling party thus staged the modern nation as an extension of antecedent indigenous civilizations. These moves allowed the PRI to claim a distinctly Mesoamerican and resolutely anti-imperialist genealogy in order to assert a modernity set against both the Spanish colonialism of the past and the US imperialism of the present.

But for all the government's pageantry involving indigenous antiquity, the state's approach to *modern* indigenous communities—still a majority of the country at the end of the Revolution—was another matter. On the one hand, the 1917 constitution had proclaimed Mexico an officially "pluricultural" nation, and some state practices reflected real redistributive aims. Indigenous (and mestizo) communities received title to communal lands under Cárdenas and his immediate successors, a stark reversal of the Liberal land thefts and liquidationist policies under Díaz. Even remote indigenous villages were incorporated for the first time into the national polity, albeit imperfectly. On the other hand, government policies toward rural communities alternated between periods of attention and neglect, while overall, the state took an assimilationist approach to indigenous peoples. If indigenous peoples were poor, perceived to be unmodern and trapped in the past, then the only way forward could be for them to learn Spanish, shed their archaic customs, and assimilate, more or less, into mainstream mestizo ("mixed," Euro-indigenous) society.

This path had been marked in 1925 by the philosopher and intellectual kingpin of the revolution, José Vasconcelos, whose classic work *La Raza Cósmica* (The Cosmic Race) reversed the usual eugenicist notions of the time, with their ideals of racial purity. In Mexico (and Ibero-America generally), a fifth, *hybrid* race—a universal race—was being born through race mixture (*mestizaje*). It was Mexico's (and Ibero-America's) destiny to bring about this universalist future civilization.[13] Vasconcelos, who became rector of the National University and secretary of public education, took note of Anatoly Lunacharsky's work in Soviet education and steered the entire system of schooling toward the construction of this Mexican version of the New Man.[14]

First Interlude: Identity Politics

Now we are accustomed to thinking of "identity politics" in terms of post–New Left projects, when marginalized racial, ethnic, and sexual groups embraced stigmatized identities and revalorized them, creating political blocs based on shared attributes and rallying for either autonomy or rights and recognitions under the banner of identity. The gay movement is paradigmatic of these developments, and some version of it developed wherever conditions (urbanization, prevailing liberal political views, mass education, and a decline in the authority of kin networks over young adults) permitted. But in a wider sense, the conscious and intentional construction of political identity inaugurates the modern world, as Benedict Anderson shows in his study of the origins and spread of nationalism, *Imagined Communities*. After Gutenberg's printing revolution, books, newspapers, dictionaries, schools, and other emergent institutions undermined ancient axioms, coaxed people to join new kinds of communities based on language or ethnicity, and thus prepared the ground for the spread of nationalism and the rise of nation-states. Anderson takes converging political-economic factors—the rise of the bourgeoisie and the spread of print capitalism—into meticulous account.[15]

New, globally interconnected social movements from the 1960s on only retraced in micro steps what was already well established in the macro: they asserted more or less unified identities with coherent interests, and they rallied for rights and protections based on these imagined communities. In either case, the stanchions of alternation are on the one side *state scripts*—expressly drafted for the production and management of populations—and on the other *mass media*, whose markets and propagandistics foster conditions for the creation or dissolution of publics of various sorts, for struggles around identity and its meanings.

From this wider perspective, we might understand the long sweep of Mexican history as the story of the rise and fall of various identity formations. First were the convoluted schema of the aforementioned colonial-era caste system, whose meticulous designations based on the persistence and admixture of racial lineages never actually seem to have been scrupulously followed.[16] But classifications nonetheless multiplied with each generation until eventually the conceptual system became impracticable and fell apart under the weight of its own complexity. Then came the struggles of the nineteenth-century Conservatives, who strove to shore up the institutions of *hispanidad* and *criollo* privilege in what was still an overwhelmingly indigenous territory. But the Conservatives, who looked to Europe, were on both the wrong side of history and the wrong side of the Atlantic Ocean. The next big experiment was the project of the late-nineteenth-century Liberals, who sought to put Mexico on the path to progress and modernity by eradicating the indigenous peasantry and "whitening" the nation through liberal immigration policies. Their class war against Mexican society ended in fire and blood. As against this succession of failed projects, the PRI refounded the nation by planting it for the first time in identifications available, at least hypothetically, to all. The Party's postrevolutionary exercise in nation building was essentially a protracted experiment in identity, with the redistributive and developmentalist state defined externally by its refusal of yanqui hegemony and internally by its embrace of mestizaje.

The Indigenous Face in the Mirror

As that nationalist project was rapidly unraveling in the protracted economic crises of the 1980s, Guillermo Bonfil Batalla offered an alternative vision, amping up the postrevolutionary regime's *indigenismo*, rewriting the terms of its mestizaje, and turning on their head basic premises in the usual desire for modernity. Mesoamerica, the Mexican anthropologist showed in *México Profundo*, is one of the world's handful of "original civilizations": an extended territory where agriculture, cities, and writing had autochthonous origins and where a coherent cosmology and culture developed over millennia among the region's different ethnolinguistic groups. "This . . . Mesoamerican civilization, from which derives all that is 'Indian' in Mexico, . . . is the starting point and indeed the most profound aspect of our country."[17] Among this civilization's deep elements are foodways and ethnobotanical knowledge; an orientation to nature, time, and work; and an expectation of public service. Mestizaje, Bonfil went on to argue, actually has more in common with the liquidationist policies of the Liberals than with any semblance of a racial democracy (its purported aim). Happy talk about hybridity notwithstanding, in practice mestizaje has involved not a "mixing" of peoples or cultures but rather the imposition of European over Mesoamerican values, a "deindianizing" of Indians: in a word, ethnocide.[18]

México Profundo thus offered a belated retort to the imaginary futuristic Mexico of *La Raza Cósmica*: "[The] national project resulting from the Mexican Revolution . . . denies Mesoamerican civilization. It is a replacement project that does not propose the development of the existing culture of the majority, but its disappearance, as the only path for generalizing the culture of the imaginary Mexico. It is a project that ideologically affirms mestizaje, but in reality allies itself completely with only one of the components, the Western one."[19] In Bonfil's accounting, the authentically Mexican path to modernity goes through the village, customs, traditions, not around them. (The details of how this might happen are largely left for others to work out.)

Bonfil's important book mobilized identity politics of the second, post–New Left sort (revalorizing stigmatized identities) to bolster identity politics of the first sort (asserting an ethno-national community). His premise—that silently, persistently at work, not only in indigenous communities but also beneath the façade of mestizo modernity, lie millennia-old cultural structures that resist colonial domination and are capable of sorting and selectively metabolizing new elements, taking in what is useful and rejecting what is not—is seductive and I do not dispute it. If we can entertain the existence of something like working-class culture, nurtured over generations of proletarian struggles with capital over wages, working conditions, and the length of the workday, then we can certainly consider the notion that deep elements of Mesoamerican civilization persist, reproducing themselves in opposition to the culture of the colonizers and the domination of class elites. This is perhaps especially clear for people who still have one foot in the peasant world, which is implicitly indigenous in Mexico. Some of my subjects speak Spanish but name in Nahuatl all the parts of the corn plant at different stages of the organism's life cycle. These are distinctive designations for which I have no corresponding words in English except through generic modifiers (green, dry, rotten) or analogous borrowed terms (root, stalk, tassel, ear, silk), though I, too, grew up cultivating corn. Such indigenous vocabularies distill a millennial history of people and maize, as Bonfil shows. Similar arguments about the depth and resiliency of Mesoamerican civilization can be developed around the quintessentially Mexican (and only superficially Catholic) holiday the Day of the Dead,[20] the persistence of *mayordomías* (civil-religious structures that institutionalize the expectation of public service) in small towns and even in big cities, and so on, as Bonfil notes.

Bonfil tapped a pervasive uneasiness with the balance of forces involved in hybridity, a sense that internalized relations between tradition and modernity, indigenous and European, are fraught and unjust. He was right. Little spectacles of this imbalance play out in everyday life. Preparing for an outing, a young man combs his hair in my mirror and complains, embarrassedly and in a confessional mode, about his "rebellious Indian hair," as though I have just seen something shameful about him. Another refers to his dark skin color as "dirty" (*sucio*) compared to others in his family whose skin tones are "cleaner" (*más limpio*). Another tells me with pride one day that he is mestizo, Mexican—*not* Latino or Hispanic, terms that I have introduced into the conversation—and then a few days later suggests that race mixing has concentrated the worst features of indigenous and African people (among them laziness) in the Mexican gene pool. Some of my subjects think they have to give up one identification (indigeneity) in order to claim another (modern gayness).

I have no doubt that if more people viewed their collective patrimony more positively—if they stopped using the word *indio* as shorthand for all that is ugly or stupid or inferior—that this perspective would buttress them in facing the challenges of the future. But I also suggest that an enhanced sense of pride and self-esteem would still not be enough to break working-class Mexicans out of the discontents of mestizo modernism. Let me briskly outline some of the limitations of Bonfil's approach to identity.

First, the idea of reclaiming an authentic identity potentially opens up the path to purifying projects about which history has little good to say. It offers the one lure, "Are we authentic yet?" in place of the other, "Are we modern yet?" The answer to either query will always be "no."[21]

Second, Bonfil no doubt underestimates the success of the official ideology of mestizaje, which fell in line with the turn of the wheel—industrialization, urbanization, mass education—to produce the modern Mexican working class. This mestizaje was so successful that one seldom hears the word "mestizo" anymore: it is implied, it is all but synonymous with the Mexican popular classes.

Third, and in consequence, one has to look increasingly hard to see autochthonous depths and profound structural elements resonating in everyday experiences. They are still there, of course, and perhaps they always will be, but the majority of the descendants of Mesoamerican civilization, the working class, now live in cities and are employed in maquilas and foreign factories and chain restaurants owned by Carlos Slim; they shop for imported or reimported goods at Walmart and Home Depot; they eat pizza and hamburgers as well as corn tortillas. Mesoamerican cultural nationalism, by itself, has less to say about their condition in 2023 than what Bonfil's 1987 work suggests.

Fourth, I underscore what Marxist anthropologists and historians have always said about the place of the village in the wider political-economic system. Mesoamerican civilization, no less than European civilization, was organized in terms of hierarchy, rank, and caste—and in this context, communitarian and redistributive practices in the villages helped facilitate the extraction of surpluses from the laboring masses and, at base, amounted to "shared poverty."[22] Thus, while the Spanish *conquistadores* conducted a brutal, relentless war against Mesoamerican cosmology and religious beliefs, their initial approach to Aztec political-economic structures was more circumspect. Essentially, they lopped off the feathered head and replaced it with the Spanish crown, preserving intact the system of interethnic domination that the Aztecs had built while intermarrying with indigenous elites to produce the new governing bloodlines.

Fifth, a scrupulous examination of the social terrain necessarily prioritizes the logic of class in explaining present-day inequalities, even while acknowledging the continued placement of an indigenous minority in the nation and internalized racisms in mestizo culture. To crib the logic of a passage from Cedric Johnson's discussion of race and class in the United States: indigeneity is still derogated and the mestizoized descendants of pre-Columbian civilization are still lumped near the bottom of the economic heap, but anti-indigenous racism and forms of oppression based on the hacienda system (whose division of labor reproduced ethnic identities) are no longer the primary determinants of material conditions and social mobility for most dark-skinned Mexicans.[23] In fact, after disaggregating class, ethnicity, and color, a careful sociological study found surprisingly little in the way of evidence that active discrimination steers Mexican labor markets and keeps phenotypic hierarchies in place.[24] Instead, contemporary forms of *class* oppression steer the fates of a growing mass of Mexicans who disproportionately (but not exclusively) have indigenous roots. Their labor has been degraded or even made obsolete by "hyper-industrialization, the large-scale introduction of automation and cybernetic command, just-in-time production, and other strategies of flexible accumulation" in Mexican farms and factories.[25] They were born into poverty and remain there because the conditions for upward economic mobility among less skilled and less connected workers have stagnated.

In any case, recuperative attempts in the wake of Bonfil's classic have taken relatively restrained forms: the compilation of new indigenous dictionaries; scattered panethnic movements based on language rather than village; laudable attempts to preserve or teach indigenous languages in elementary schools; and most notable, the Zapatista uprising, which instead of igniting a national or even wider regional rebellion quickly retreated into localism. The modesty of these efforts would seem to show that affirmative indigeneity alone—the embrace of Mesoamericanness, even in its most politicized version—provides a poor blueprint for reimagining the nation as a whole under contemporary conditions.

The Mexican anthropologist sets his reading public in front of a mirror and asks them to contemplate what they have been trained to deny or disparage: brown skin, black hair, indigenous features. "The clear and undeniable evidence of our Indian ancestry is a mirror in which we do not wish to see our own reflection."[26]

Most working-class Mexicans understand very well that an indigenous face stares back at them in the mirror but receive the idea of reclaiming their authentic selves with some alarm, as though it would pull them back into the past. Maybe the more productive tack for the theorist of such scenes would be to take up analytical positions from inside the antinomies and discontents, rather than to banish the unpleasantness right away, and to try to understand how the one framework for identity work (mestizaje) provides a template for other kinds of identity work—gay identity, for example. Maybe there are discontents that we can resolve and discontents that we endure, live with, and work through. Maybe epochal sadness forms the substrate of the present, without which no happy meanings could be had.

NEOLIBERALISM, TOLERANCE, AND THE DEMOCRATIC OPENING

The third and final act in our didactic production begins in the slow breakdown of the center-left dictatorship, a redistributive but increasingly corrupt regime, and its transmutation into a neoliberal regime.

Start in boom times: The oil shocks of the 1970s initially benefited Mexico, pushing annual economic growth rates well above 6 percent by the close of the decade. Flush with petrodollars—derived from public ownership of oil and a state monopoly on its extraction—the country's leaders leveraged international loans. They used this money to subsidize industrialization and the nationalization of floundering industries, which were protected from foreign competition under nationalist economic policies, no doubt lining the pockets of politicians and cronies in the process. So far, all of these steps followed the script of centralized and dirigiste practices that had produced the Mexican Miracle. But the party-state proved ill-equipped to deal with what came next.

Economic Disasters, Political Repression

In 1981, Paul Volcker, chair of the US Federal Reserve, fought oil-shock inflation by hiking interest rates to 20 percent. This move also raised the rates on Mexico's variable-interest loans at a time when deepening recession in the United States (the intended consequence of the Fed's tight money policies) was contracting demand for Mexico's exports. In 1982, as the price of oil was coming down, Mexico's leaders found themselves unable to service a rapidly growing foreign debt, and the country defaulted, setting off the wider Latin American debt crisis. Unintended dominoes fell once again, but the International Monetary Fund (IMF) was there to steer outcomes. Rather than arranging debt relief, the IMF rolled out yet more loans—with requirements for "structural adjustment" attached. By these means, the IMF progressively coaxed Mexico (and all of Latin America) to privatize state-owned industries and utilities and to abandon economic nationalism and centralist planning in favor of free trade and deregulated markets. In the name of this new wave of "modernization," a series of Harvard-trained Mexican presidents oversaw the dismantling of the import substitution regime (which had taxed imports to foster the growth of local industry and agriculture) and the implantation of a neoliberal globalized regime.

There were abundant horrors and intensifying scandals all along the way. The regime's increasingly coercive and undemocratic character had already come to the fore in the 1960s. In 1968, the military killed hundreds of peacefully protesting university and high school students in the Tlatelolco section of Mexico City. Waves of brutal repression against student activists, New Left social movements, and youth countercultures continued well into the 1970s. Then the 1985 earthquake in Mexico City put the Party's incompetence and cruelty on full display. Bribing inspectors and officials, builders had skirted Mexico City's tough construction codes, resulting in some ten thousand deaths during the seismic event. And in the wake of the earthquake's destruction, authorities began bulldozing buildings with people still trapped inside.

Three years later, the presidential election was purloined in plain view. Cuauhtémoc Cárdenas, son of the beloved Lázaro, had split with the PRI to run on a fusion ticket of small left-wing parties. On the evening of the vote, early returns showed Cárdenas ahead. Then the results disappeared from TV screens, and the government abruptly announced that the computer system used to tabulate the votes had "crashed." When the system was eventually "restored," the results showed Carlos Salinas de Gortari winning 50 percent of the vote as against 31 percent for Cárdenas. But no one believed those results, and the parallel tabulation had shown Cárdenas winning.

Over the course of the 1980s, the GDP contracted, real wages sank, the informal economy expanded, and infant mortality spiked. Modernization, for those who still believed in such a thing, was running in reverse. Worse, the country's economic travails would not let up. Barely recovered from the monetary crises of the 1980s—the "Lost Decade"—Mexico entered yet another currency crisis at the end of 1994, the so-called Tequila Crisis. The causes of this crisis were complex, and they had nothing to do with tequila. The Zapatista Uprising in Chiapas—timed with the launching of the North American Free Trade Agreement—had made investors wonder whether Mexico was really a safe bet after all. Then the 1994 elections had been a bloody, expensive mess. The PRI's initial candidate for president, Luis Donaldo Colosio, gave a galvanizing speech about the need for political reform. Colosio's aims were modest: he envisioned a PRI that would meld "economic modernization" with the well-being of Mexican families and a strengthened democracy. But his speech upset powerful factions in the Party hierarchy, old-school political bosses who wanted to hear nothing about enhancing democracy. When the candidate was assassinated on the campaign trail, rumors and surmises flew. (Rumors intensified when the PRI's party head was assassinated later the same year.) Replacing Colosio with Ernesto Zedillo, the PRI ramped up election-year government spending and extorted its business supporters for large, under-the-table campaign contributions to fund the usual vote buying. Sensing instability, people moved their money out of Mexico if they could—and they could, precisely because neoliberal Mexico no longer had regulatory controls on capital flight.

Years later, my friends from various settings recount how they survived the ensuing economic catastrophe. One tells how, when he was a child, his father, a schoolteacher, sold the family's furniture piece by piece to keep food on the table. Still, before the crisis was over, the house was bare and the children were hungry. Another relates that when he was seven, he and his sprawling family fled economic collapse in the countryside and arrived in Puebla to sleep outdoors on the earth in a makeshift family camp. Another tells how she, a creative and informed young mother, bought large bags of soybeans to produce soymilk and tofu for her three children's alimentation. Her children thus had protein at a time when meat, cheese, and milk had disappeared from poor and middle-income diets. Of course, many headed north, and Mexico's emigration trickle became an avalanche. Millions relocated to the United States, mostly without visas.

Second Interlude: Material Foundations

I have not forgotten the subject of this inquiry, nor have I strayed from its logic. One can scarcely understand the architectonics of sexual cultures without taking into account the material foundations on which they rest. The Liberal-era construction of the "modern" homosexual, crisscrossed with class struggles and status anxieties, laid the groundwork for later developments in sexual identity. The dynamics of mestizaje, with their recursive appeals to tradition as a springboard for modernity, their per-petually frustrated aspirations, form a durable template for varied kinds of identity work in Mexico, including the kinds of "mixing" involved in contemporary gay identity. And, closer to the present, the decline of authoritarianism, histories of economic hardship, the rise of new kinds of modernism to replace old versions of the same: these are necessary parts of the story. Each of the three above storytellers—the boy seated on the floor in the bare home, the boy who slept on the ground, the industrious young mother—belongs in one fashion or another to the ambiente, the amorphous gay scene. Shared experiences of economic crisis and material privation mark their life stories, their yearnings, their imagination of same-sex relations, and their entry into gay life.

Florescence

It was against this backdrop or, better yet, within these changes and devel-opments, that modern globalized gay identities took shape. I exercise some caution about how I say this. It is true that homosexual scenes, more or less stably planted, had existed in Mexico City since the early twentieth century. These scenes have been well documented by Víctor Macías-González and others.[27] During the late 1960s and early 1970s, internationally connected sexual communities in the capital megacity and in Guadalajara expanded and consolidated. But outside the megacities (Mexico City and Guadalajara) or tourist-heavy cities (like Acapulco and Tijuana), homosexuals for the most part kept a low profile. Local authorities vigorously repressed suspect youth subcultures and specifically discouraged the development of gay scenes and nightlife. This made for discretion and indirection—even, to some extent, in the megacities. Enter, stage left, the bumbling American anthropologist.

The gay scene in Cuernavaca was invisible to me when I spent summers there in 1983 and 1984, taking Spanish lessons at one of the city's many language schools. I am not saying it wasn't there; North American gay tourists were already calling the place Queernavaca, I am told. I am saying that it resisted casual detection. (I did, however, see a band of prepubescent schoolboys mocking and tormenting an old queen on the streets of the neighborhood where I stayed.) I couldn't even find gay nightlife on my visit to Mexico City's Zona Rosa in 1984, after having read scandalous stories in a local newspaper describing the neighborhood as the center of homosexual life in Mexico. No doubt my gaydar was deficient, and in any case, I didn't know exactly where to look. I didn't know which peripheral streets had bars, much less which other districts in the city hosted gay nightlife. Tellingly, there were no "bar rags" to consult—weekly or monthly publications supported by ads for gay establishments, distributed in and around bars and clubs. And so I wandered quaint streets named for European cities, searching in vain for signs of gay bars and clubs. Old-timers express surprise when I tell them this; they insist that the Zona was quite lively by this time and rattle off a list of their favorite haunts—then surmise that I must have happened into it during one of the periodic *limpiezas* (cleanups). President Miguel de la Madrid's wife was said to have complained to the police chief that there were too many homosexuals in the Zona Rosa, and police responded for a few weeks by shutting down bars in the thick of the Zona and discouraging cruising on the sidewalks. (Indeed, my late-evening hookup attempt in the near-empty plaza of the Insurgentes metro stop was pointedly interrupted when a policeman approached us; my intended made a fast beeline to one of the exits and disappeared.) This was not the first, nor would it be the last, such limpieza.

For most of the dictatorship's duration, the state's forms of social control had depended on a restricted media environment dominated by two compliant TV channels (one of them state owned). Control over information and entertainment began to erode as the state intensified neoliberal reforms, and through the 1990s, a different sort of media ecosystem was rapidly evolving. Satellite dishes, connected to the world by pilfered access codes, and cable TV were bringing uncensored international programming to the masses. Internet cafés, present almost from the very beginning of the desktop computer revolution, connected students and young people to the World Wide Web. Mexican pop music expressed new forms of youth rebelliousness. (Singer-songwriter Gloria Trevi's storied and scandalous career tracked this cultural opening.)

As the PRI inevitably relaxed censorship and curbs on some forms of expression, local TV programing began to take up themes of sexual tolerance. Some informants describe how even homophobic parents and siblings wept while viewing Mexican problem-of-the-week shows that depicted the rejection of gay and lesbian youth by their families. One said that such TV programming had curbed previously unchecked fear and hatred, noting how, early on in the HIV/AIDS epidemic, neighbors had lynched a gay man in their *vecindad* and burned his body and possessions. In addition to their manifest messages, themes of sexual tolerance on Televisa and TV Azteca served multiple purposes: they reassured audiences that Mexico was indeed a "modern" society, with liberal, up-to-date sensibilities, and was sensitive to the plights of misunderstood minorities. These themes also substituted for broad expressions of *political* dissent against the PRI, which were still controlled in broadcast media.

And if it had seemed that the gay world had been hiding from me in the 1980s, the ambiente would make itself more visible over the course of the 1990s. Or perhaps it had been hiding in plain sight all along, and I just didn't know how to see it. Only a couple of gay bars had established themselves in downtown Puebla by the late 1990s, and these felt like speakeasies: you knocked on an unmarked door, and someone peered at you through a slot to decide whether to let you in. But in the zócalos, the most public of spaces in Mexican cities, it was on full display, at least for those who knew how to see what was happening. There, in the central plazas, in the background of left-wing political rallies, family outings, tourist jaunts, and *plantones* (protester occupations, typically condemning waves of assassination in the pueblos)—or rather, one might think, tactically in the midst of these multiple rhythms of everyday public life undergoing chaotic amalgams of liberalization and repression—cruising and other forms of gay socializing were becoming increasingly visible. These less formalized zones of gay life took advantage of the degrees of freedom and latitude that had historically been permitted in the public square. Michel de Certeau, the Jesuit scholar and the master theorist of "poaching," would have smiled: for there, in scenic green tracts lodged between Church and State (always the same plan: the cathedral on one side of the square and the municipal or governmental palace on the other), plural usages of the public space were allowing for the emergence of counter–public spaces; these operated contrary to all intended usages but nonetheless were subtended by the prevailing usufructuary customs.

These floating scenes were organized according to rules and proxemics that I instantly understood. Cruising rarely happens in highly visible areas or where people cluster in dense groups. So in Oaxaca, men sat or ambled singly in the less trafficked sections of the zócalo, out of view of the restaurants, or in the adjacent square (a dimly lit extension of the zócalo). When strictures begin to relax in small-to-medium town settings, young people invariably engage in public expressions of affection, but these are at first circumspect. So in Jalisco, university students were bold enough to stroll sections of the plaza holding hands—but only late at night, when crowds had considerably thinned. Codes and understandings would sort matters more or less efficiently at busier times in the evening. Thus, in Puebla the collective will inscribed itself on space and time according to certain norms of usage: a gaggle of young gay men occupied the eastern side of the zócalo on certain nights of the week where they socialized in boisterous gatherings. Cruising, however, occurred more discreetly: it was distributed along the less populated south to southwestern side of the square, or concentrated in isolated sections, lest the uninvolved public be scandalized. Sometimes, these little islands of freedom dilated dramatically.

Mérida's zócalo put on display an astonishing spectacle whose scale and audacity boggled the imagination: scores, sometimes hundreds, of well-groomed young men with nothing to do took over the entire zócalo on certain nights of the week, spacing themselves over the wide square and calibrating distances so as not to impede hookups.

As attitudes shifted, policing, too, became more tolerant. The mere suspicion that gay men were conducting assignations in public places might have once drawn law enforcement to the scene, but now the police took little official notice of cruising—and at least some were actively participating in it, in or out of uniform.

Meanwhile, on the political front, tightly controlled elections were giving way to genuinely contested elections. During the 1990s, the two main opposition parties were vigorously contesting (and sometimes winning) local elections. These were the PRD (Partido de la Revolución Democrática, the center-left party founded by Cuauhtémoc Cárdenas and others after the 1988 electoral theft) and the PAN (Partido Acción Nacional, a much older, conservative party). Blood was often shed in the election process, especially during campaigns in the pueblos where local PRI chapters unleashed paramilitary violence against leftist peasant and labor movements aligned with the PRD. Democratizing trends culminated in 2000 with the election of the PAN's Vicente Fox to the presidency.

Leftists dourly compared 2000 with 1988 and observed that the PRI would hand over the reins of government to a conservative but not to a leftist. Feminists and gay activists fretted, and logically so, over what the election of a social conservative might mean for women's and gay rights. Despite its secular stance, the PAN is understood to be a center-right Catholic party, originating in part in conflicts with the PRI's socialist and adamantly laical elements in the 1930s and 1940s. Then, there was the question of tone. During the campaign, Fox had roused audiences with wrestling-match rhetoric, distinctly and repeatedly referring to his opponent, the PRI candidate, Francisco Labastida, as "La Vestida," the drag queen. (Such displays of disrespect likely motivated voters. As one informant put it, "He openly expressed the contempt that we had been swallowing for years.")

Low comedy notwithstanding, Fox had campaigned in part on a promise to respect the autonomy of civil society, and this was a promise he kept.

Under Fox, from 2000 to 2006, the state first took a hands-off approach and then a decidedly warm approach to the "third sector" of civic organizations—voluntary associations, nongovernmental organizations, and social movements. Feminism, gay rights, disability rights, and other new social movements flourished under Fox, who passed antidiscrimination laws and established CONAPRED (Consejo Nacional para Prevenir La Discriminación), the National Council to Prevent Discrimination, in 2003. The next year, the Federal Law for the Promotion of Activities Undertaken by Civil Society Organizations was passed, providing a legal framework for NGOs and nonprofits to contribute to social development.

Activist observers express two strong currents of opinion about such developments. Some point out with pride that CONAPRED did not just suddenly appear, a gift from the state, but that decades of agitation and organizing had laid the groundwork for it. Others are more skeptical of the council, viewing it as more form than substance, or suggesting that discrimination is less pressing than other issues—or sometimes even observing that the council fosters nuisance complaints, sometimes against gay establishments (which, nestled into cramped spaces up narrow stairways, might be unable to accommodate the needs of disabled people, for example). But there can be no doubt that a national council to prevent discrimination changed the public conversation about matters related to gender, sexuality, ethnicity, and disability.

Denouement

I arrive at a series of difficult points on governance, changing political-economic relations, and sexual repression. These points are difficult not because they are complicated but because they challenge New Left orthodoxies, which tend to associate capitalism unambiguously with sexual repression.[28] Neither the classic liberationist literature nor trending taglines like "capitalist cis-hetero-patriarchy" are helpful here; suggestions that neoliberalism intensifies various forms of discrimination and personal subordination miss the mark entirely.

The form of governance that the PRI implemented over much of its history was both quasi–social democratic (the PRI maintained observer status with the Socialist International and eventually was admitted as a full member in 2003) and culturally conservative. Even a butcher like Luis Echeverría (secretary of the interior from 1963 until 1969, and thus an architect of the Tlatelolco massacre, and then president of the republic from 1970 to 1976) could deploy anti-imperialist rhetoric, invoke labor solidarity, and entertain close relations with Cuba, China, Allende's Chile, and the Palestine Liberation Organization (PLO) while depicting New Left movements and countercultural trends as symptoms of cultural decadence, immorality, and failed masculinity. Echeverría thus presided over a harsh, protracted crackdown on youth subcultures and most forms of rock music in the wake of the 1971 Avándaro Rock Festival ("Mexico's Woodstock"). Attempting to deflect, absorb, and neutralize youth subcultures, the regime instead promoted *nueva trova*, the neofolkloric music that was Cuba's main cultural export, and *nueva canción*, associated with Allende's Chile.[29] This was no paradox. The polemic against cultural imperialism tightly condensed economic Leftism with cultural reaction. It traded in the received ideas about masculinity, femininity, and the family, repurposing them and making them central to conceptions of the nation. In taking this tack, the PRI's approach reflected the style of many other early- to mid-twentieth century political movements on the Left, perhaps especially those with revolutionary origins and nationalist bearings. Hippy bashing, insinuations about sexual predilections of long-haired men, and retrograde gender politics were all part of the package.

By contrast, trends toward openness and gay visibility accelerated dramatically under Fox, who advanced a genuinely neoliberal political vision characterized by deregulation, free trade, and laissez-faire economic policies on the one side of the ledger and tolerant, anti-discriminatory, pro-diversity social policies on the other. This, too, was no paradox. Anti-discrimination, as Walter Benn Michaels has cogently argued, is the neoliberal utopia: it brings both economic and social policies under the rule of deregulated markets; it disallows irrational forms of animus that would interfere with the way markets distribute gains and losses; and the embrace of diversity provides a new source of legitimation at a time of rapidly expanding social inequalities. Diversity is neoliberalism with a human face.[30] Nancy Fraser draws out a parallel argument: if the old political-economic regime (Fordism and the welfare state in the North, redistributive corporatism and dirigisme in the South) was associated with what New Left social movements tilted against (traditional forms of patriarchal authority and personal subordination), then the post–New Left would embrace the "flexible teams," the "horizontal networks," and the personally empowering entrepreneurship of neoliberalism.[31] NGOs, nonprofits, and voluntary associations, carefully cultivated by the Fox administration, occupied spaces vacated by the shrinking state and provided some semblance of aid and relief in the absence of robust welfare programs. In expressly forwarding this progressive version of neoliberal modernity, Mexico was well ahead of the United States.

The Fox sexenio was thus a time of heightened economic precarity and personal liberation.

There were no major economic meltdowns, but the economy was stagnant, real wages declined, and the informal sector—street vending, CD and DVD piracy, smuggling and contraband—expanded rapidly. Small businesses went under, and empty storefronts abounded everywhere. Such signs of distress normally would have triggered ameliorative social spending, but budgets for social services and anti-poverty programs were kept lean. Employment markets were characterized by casualization (irregular or impermanent work), informalization (work in the "informal" sector, without regulation or protections), and black marketization (clandestine or illicit activities). Modernization, marching under the banner of neoliberalism, once again took a detour.

At the same time, modernization found its métier on the cultural front. Gay nightlife exploded in Mexico City, and local authorities liberally granted liquor licenses to LGBT bars and cafés, permitting the expansion of gay establishments in second-tier cities. Although Puebla (like many other previously resistant cities) was still under PRI control, assorted gay commercial ventures proliferated, marked by nameplates and see-through windows. Gay couples strolled the streets holding hands. Pride parades arrived in small towns like Tlaxcala. Rainbow flags unfurled.

The Gay Dialectic

Mexican aphorisms sometimes express a folksy, dialectical approach to events: "No todo lo malo es malo, ni todo lo bueno es bueno" (Not all bad is bad, not all good is good). Some reduce this sentiment to a paradoxical version, as an old taxi driver once told me when I complained about the rainy weather: "Todo es malo, todo es bueno" (Everything is bad, everything is good). The trick, of course, is to take in the messiness of history and to see the "good" in the "bad" and vice versa.

Marx and Engels did this rigorously, magnificently, in the *Manifesto*. There, Marx "manages to praise the bourgeoisie more powerfully and profoundly than its members have ever known how to praise themselves," observes Marshall Berman in *All That Is Solid Melts into Air*. But, "if his dialectic works out, it will be the virtues for which he praised the bourgeoisie that will bury it in the end."[32] John D'Emilio encapsulates an ancillary version of this perspective in his classic essay "Capitalism and Gay Identity," which hinges on capitalism's contradictory relationship to the family and personal life. Taking the historian's view, D'Emilio shows on the one hand how capitalism needs and enshrines the institution of the family—for social reproduction and for the fulfillment of personal needs—and on the other how urbanization and the development of the free labor system effectively released men and women from family control, thereby liberating sex from reproduction and ultimately paving the way for the construction of gay identities. A certain "dialectic—the constant interplay between exploitation and some measure of autonomy—informs all of the history of those who have lived under capitalism." Socialism, then, can push forward the wheel of history, not by developing programs that seek to buttress the flagging structures of the heterosexual nuclear family under male authority—for that would be a reactionary, backward-looking agenda—but by providing the material conditions that support personal autonomy and new kinds of interpersonal bonds.[33]

Neoliberalism in Mexico retraced the steps of earlier waves of capitalist development and intensification: in pursuit of its bottom line, it eviscerated the social contract and destroyed customary rights and protections for workers and peasants, piling up huge fortunes for some and reducing others to penury. The verdict of history is not ambiguous on these points. But it also replicated a certain dialectic of capitalist modernity: It undermined the old regime, with its forms of authority vested in political party and family. Its deregulatory ethos prodded local authorities to reduce their heavy-handed suppression of gay scenes in many cities, at least for a time. In reducing the masses to a monadic existence, neoliberalism capacitated individuals—or some of them—with new needs, new freedoms, and stimulated them to organize their activities in new ways.

We live these changes in ambiguity. The meaning of gay life cannot be grasped without understanding both sides of this dialectic.

8 *They* Lived in a Different Time from *Us*

Sometime in 2007, my friends and connections at Luciérnaga were discussing *Secreto en la Montaña* and asked me what I thought of the movie. Secret in the mountain? I turned the phrase over a couple of times, trying to deduce the English-language title of what everyone understood to be a film of great significance. "*Brokeback Mountain*," someone offered in English. "Oh!" I exclaimed and began making excuses: I don't see many movies; it's been a while since I've been to the theater. From behind the bar, a cheerful, rotund lesbian in her early thirties aired her astonishment while mixing a cheap version of Sex on the Beach and assorted clients expressed surprise that I, a gay North American, had not seen the movie.

And so a showing was quickly arranged for my benefit. The film would be screened the following evening in my downtown apartment around the corner from the café-bar. Yamil, the bartender and waiter, would secure a copy of the movie from one of the many small, backstreet shops that sold pirated DVDs and CDs. Ricardo, the cook's straight son, would bring beer. "I'll bring popcorn," piped up a regular client. "I'll come, too," beamed others.

The following night, nearly a dozen people showed up for the special showing after the bar closed at 10 p.m.: waiters and cooks, a factory

worker, university students, a couple of recent graduates seeking work . . .
We rearranged my apartment's rustic furniture and squeezed into chairs,
settling in to watch the movie on my oversized laptop, which was strategi-
cally positioned on the dining table within view of everyone. At the time,
pirated videos were ubiquitous in Mexico—I am not sure I ever saw a
"genuine" DVD there—and they never seemed to work quite right on my
laptop, so I periodically leaned in to rejigger the settings. Such were modern media in much of the global south at this time: a make-do version,
often involving black market copies and trademark or copyright infringe-
ments. (The culture industry treated these practices as losses to its bottom
line, as "piracy" and theft, but there are good reasons to view them as
gains: they extended the reach and prestige of brand names and media
products into markets where consumers could never have afforded regular
box office admissions or album purchases.)[1] Other than a couple of freeze-
ups, the movie aired without interruption, and as viewers became
absorbed in the film, sidebar commentary gradually diminished.

About fifteen minutes before the end of the movie, Jack and Ennis are
together for what, unbeknownst to them, will be their final meeting. Over
a campfire, the protagonists vent anger, then talk about their lives apart,
their frustrated feelings. The dialogue makes clear how homophobia,
apartness, and discontent have been internalized: Ennis wonders whether
strangers on the street can "see" his secret desires, and he blames Jack for
his unhappy condition. "Why don't you let me be?" he implores. "It's
because of you, Jack, that I'm like this—nothing, and nobody." Ennis, who
was born poor and has become poorer, attributes his downward mobility,
his degraded life chances, to homosexuality—specifically to his relationship with Jack.

Even though I had read reviews and thus knew something of the plot
and of this scene in particular, I was unprepared for the moment's emotional effect. I began to sniffle. And as the movie careened to its conclusion, I tried to suppress my responses but continued to quietly sniffle.
Then came the final scene, with the two men's shirts hanging on a nail in
Ennis's subproletarian abode, the one inside the other, and the surviving
cowboy mumbling a posthumous vow to his departed lover, "Jack, I
swear. . . ." I began to weep. (I'm not sure whether I wept over Jack's and
Ennis's broken lives or over my own.)

At which point Diego, a twenty-year-old, leaned in, put his arm around my shoulder and said in his best avuncular voice: "Don't cry, Róger. You have to remember, *they* lived in a different time from *us*. *We* have more chances to build a better life. *We* don't have to live like *that* anymore."

THE YOUNG MAN'S COUNSEL

Now if this were a certain kind of work, I would reflect at length on the globalized object of the movie as it ultimately presented itself in the field: a revisionist Western, a cosmopolitan Hollywood reflection on rustic life, set in the recent US past and filmed in Canada, imported and disseminated for Mexican viewerships largely via black market circuits, at a propitious moment in the development of sexual subcultures. But I have just told you, in uncluttered thumbnail form, much of what you need to know about the political economy of media circuits. Instead, I focus on the young man's counsel, which contains an amalgam of theoretical premises and claims. Some are related to temporality, of course, and others to solidarity: I was touched by Diego's emphatic use of "we," by the location of "us" in a definitely shared time, and by his openhearted willingness to include *me*, an outsider and foreigner, in his imagined modern community. His assertions open lines of inquiry into the making of a gay community and the conditions for citizenship in it, specifically under current economic and social conditions. How does this "we" take shape, and what might it have to do with the regime of neoliberal globalization that fostered in Mexico, on the one hand, the breakdown of one-party rule, the diffusion of Hollywood cinema, and the spread of gay establishments and, on the other, the destruction of rural economies, declining industrial wages, and a sequence of economic shocks that battered the working and middle classes?

A closer examination of the contours of the young man's life gives his optimistic proclamation richer resonance, throws light on how different identities interweave or unravel under the flag of gay internationalism, and suggests some of the ways these complicated circumstances are actually lived.

THE WARPS AND KINKS OF MODERN LIFE

Whatever Diego might make of the cosmopolitan present, his past was rural and indigenous. His mother was from a Mazatec village in the state of Oaxaca; his father was a Nahuatl-speaker from a small town across the border in the state of Puebla. His parents separated shortly after his birth, and Diego grew up in his mother's pueblo.

These facts came out during conversation one afternoon while we were watching an *India María* movie, of all things, on the wall-hung TV at Luciérnaga. La India María is the fictional protagonist of a series of popular, low-budget Mexican films; the character was created and acted by María Elena Velasco, a Poblana actress who died in 2015. People still argue about whether Velasco's comic persona demeans or lauds indigenous people, but her character's perpetual condition—good-hearted country bumpkin surviving the challenges of the big city, doing good deeds, and coming out well despite the odds—still resonates with wide audiences some fifty years after the series' first movie aired in 1972. (A camp internet meme superimposes India María's face on the Virgin of Guadalupe, as if to say that both are iconic of Mexico: backward, perhaps, but our own and lovable.)

"Oh," I said, naively, "I didn't know that you are indigenous." "I'm not," the young man replied. Confusedly, I said: "But your mother is indigenous, and your father is indigenous." "That's right." "And you grew up in a village where everyone speaks Mazatec." "That is correct." "Then aren't you indigenous?"

Diego answered my question with a question: "Did it stick to me?" To my puzzlement, he then elaborated: "Do I speak Spanish with an accent? Do I dress like a rustic? Do you hear me whistling?" At first, I thought his last reference was to the low-class whistling of porters or car parkers on the streets. In fact, he was referring to a specific marker of indigenousness: some members of his mother's ethnic group, the Mazatecos, conduct extensive conversations across hillsides in an elaborate form of "whistle speech."[2]

I did not know whether indigenousness had clung to him or not. His narrative was consistent with the findings of long-standing scholarly analyses of mestizaje ("race-mixing" but, in this context, cultural mixing: the taking on of a mestizo—that is to say, a "mixed" Euro-indigenous—identity) in Mesoamerica. American readers will immediately think of racial "passing," but the analogy distorts important differences between the construction of race in the United States and the definition of indigenous ethnicities in Mexico. In the United States, under the Jim Crow system of hypodescent, the one-drop rule defined people as "black" if they had *any* African ancestors, but light-skinned people could sometimes move to places where their family history was unknown and present themselves as "white." In Mexico, where virtually everyone has at least some native antecedents (mestizo is not "white" or Spanish; it is "mixed"), indigeneity is less a question of ancestry than of institutional attachments. Being indigenous means being formally and legally tied to the land in certain ways. In its most pronounced form, this implies membership in a pueblo that collectively owns the surrounding farmlands and is organized as a "closed corporate community," granting agricultural usufruct rights to members.[3] This is to say that ethnic identities are locally based: one's ethnos is vested in the village, not in the ethno-linguistic group. When an indigenous person leaves the community, moves to the city, abandons characteristic forms of indigenous dress, and ceases to speak a minority language, she or he sheds identities that are locally based. She or he ceases to be indigenous—at least according to formal rules and understandings.

And this is the long trajectory of mestizaje in Mexican history. Over time, a declining percentage of the nation has spoken an indigenous language, been tied to the land, or viewed themselves as indigenous. Thus, at the time of the Mexican Revolution (1910), 85 percent of the population was rural; a similar percentage of Mexicans consisted of peasants, farmers, or agricultural workers; and a majority of the population undoubtedly still spoke an indigenous language at home and in the village. By the 2020 census, 21 percent of the population was rural (36 percent by some ways of accounting). And, although 21.5 percent of the population described themselves to census takers as culturally indigenous, only 6.6 percent (of those three years of age or older) were found to speak an indigenous language (with a great deal of variation among states and regions).[4]

These numbers no doubt undercount the speakers of indigenous languages. Diego, who speaks two indigenous languages, might very well dissimulate to a census taker. "It is well known," writes Guillermo Bonfil Batalla, "that many people who speak an indigenous language as their maternal tongue hide and deny that fact."[5] Even so, the age structure among those reported to speak an indigenous language reveals something of the durability of language use at home, especially in low-income rural areas, where birth rates are comparatively high: 29 percent of small children (ages five to nine) are recorded as speaking *only* an indigenous language, meaning that Spanish is still not the first language learned by nearly a third of Mexicans. But the main trends are clear. Indigenous languages and self-identification are closely correlated with a shrinking rural sector. "Deindianization," to use Bonfil's term for mestizaje,[6] has happened across wide terrains in the wake of personal mobility, urbanization, and mass education. Yesterday's Indians compose the bulk of today's working class, especially its less skilled, lower-paid sectors.

Diego retraces the steps of others who have walked away from indigenous identity, a process that involves push and pull, coercion and consent, receptivity and resistance. But this is not quite the end of the story, for the sweep of "modernization" is not uniform and indigenousness does invariably "stick" to those who ever once inhabited it (or whose parents or grandparents were indigenous).

Some of the signs of indigeneity are stamped on the body. When middle-class Poblanos directly refer to someone's short stature (a trait frequently associated with a rural, corn-based diet) or dark skin (which may not actually be darker than the speaker's), or a body marked by physical labor in the sun, what they most often are saying, indirectly, is that the person is, or may be, or once may have been, indigenous. Immigrants recently arrived from rural or highland areas are marked by an implicit or presumptive indigenousness, whether they (or their parents) once spoke a "dialect" (as Mexicans refer to indigenous languages) or not. Whole geographic regions thus connote ethnicity. Ahuitzol, another of Luciérnaga's habitués, relates how his university classmates correctly deduced his ethnic identity from his hometown in the Sierra Mixteca, which straddles the border between Puebla and Oaxaca and is the homeland of the Mixtecos. He was distinctly unhappy with his classmates' deductions, which he equated with racist taunts.

"You can't talk about him that way!" someone once interjected when I referred to a mutual acquaintance as indigenous. In fact, I was saying nothing bad about the person, nor was I demeaning indigenous people. In fact, my absent friend spoke Nahuatl at home with his parents and siblings. But direct references to a person's indigeneity can be a touchy business, precisely because indigenousness is both stigmatized and "sticky." Implicit indigeneity "sticks" to a very large percentage of people because indigenous origins are ubiquitous, especially for members of the broad working class. People have often disclosed to me that their parents speak or spoke Nahuatl, which was once widely spoken in Puebla and other states in Central Mexico, or Zapotec, or some other indigenous language—but usually only after months or even years of establishing friendship and trust. One may be, under different circumstances and at different moments, both mestizo and indigenous or, at any rate, implicitly indigenous.

Nor is this quite the end of the story, either, for the swirl of things said and unsaid embraces contradictory attitudes, and these complexities infuse everyday practices in sexual subcultures in metropolitan settings.

On the one hand, then, Diego's affirmation of cosmopolitanism, his claim to sexual citizenship in the international gay world, seems linked to his rejection of a marked ethnicity. Now in actual practice, some native communities are more accepting of sexual and gender diversity than are mestizo communities; this point is well established in the ethnographic literature and by recent waves of activism, and I brought it up in our conversations.[7] But Diego pointedly described the Mazatecos as "*homofóbicos*" and "*machistas*," traits he linked to their "backwardness." In his mind, rural and indigenous meant backward and homophobic.

On the other hand, he also understood something of the interplay between stigma and fetish, the not-so-secret appeal of prohibited things and rebuffed people. That is, he knew how to parlay elements of an implicit indigenousness—a well-formed, lean frame; dark features; rural origins and a certain outward toughness—as "currency" on the sexual marketplace. Diego presented, at least at first impression, as a *chacal* (literally, jackal), loosely translated as "rough trade," a term that attaches to desirable, sexually opportunistic, dark-skinned young men of the lower classes. Mexican writer Carlos Monsiváis gives a sense of how this term circulates in gay cultures—of how, in a socially stratified setting, the chacal's desirability is amped up and supercharged by prevailing ideas about physicality, work, and ethnic origins: "In the argot of those who are in the know, the chacal is a young proletarian with an indigenous or recently mestizoized appearance. . . . [His] is proletarian sensuality, a pleasure that the experts in racist indulgences widely decipher, a body that comes from the gym of life, from hard work, from the dust clouds of amateur or dirt-field soccer, from exhaustive walks, from running for hours singing war cries."[8] He is unlike us, the writer goes on to say, throwing his voice into the thoughts of bar-hopping middle-class gays. Or perhaps, on second thought, he is like us but without money.

The ability to navigate such warps and kinks implies some acumen, and Diego was world savvy long before his arrival in the big city. He had discovered gay life while still living in the pueblo. A progressive mayor had brought two computers to his remote village as part of an educational project, and Diego had learned to surf the satellite-connected internet in his mid-teens. He recounts the absurdity of his original exchanges: internet chat with a friend at the other terminal across the room. But soon he was conducting conversations with interlocutors in far-flung cities. He quickly discovered gay websites and chat rooms, and not long after that, he was arranging weekend trips to the city of Oaxaca for dates and liaisons. The men with whom he was hooking up—American and Canadian tourists, upper-middle-class Mexican professionals—desired in him a certain kind of young, authentic masculinity, an authenticity that was enhanced by his autochthonous rural origins.

Early on, the boy's intelligence called attention to itself. He had been encouraged by alert schoolteachers to pursue higher education. Here, too, Diego navigated kinks and warps. His strategy, as I understand it, took shrewd advantage of a quirk in the public university's admissions process, which requires prospective students to apply to a given *major*: he had taken the entrance exam for admission to study mathematics. Popular majors such as history, literature, communication, or business routinely turn away qualified applicants. There simply are not enough seats in classrooms to meet demand for enrollment. Statistically, then, one's chances are better applying in less popular fields. And so, with excellent scores, Diego was admitted to Puebla's large state university, BUAP (Benemérita Universidad Autónoma de Puebla), with a fellowship to study mathematics.

But gay life in the big city had proved more engaging than the study of math. (This is a recurring story: I recall how my own grades had tanked the semester I came out of the closet.) By the time I met him, Diego had lost his fellowship and had withdrawn from the university. He could be found nightly at one of the downtown internet cafés, where he maintained a personal website (rumored to feature nude or seminude photos of him), chatting with scattered friends and lovers; then later, at one of the gay bars in the centro; or perhaps, failing that, in the zócalo, where one goes to pass time, to meet friends, or to cruise.

Many of us live a discrepancy between how the world sees us and how we see ourselves; the discrepancy for Diego was extreme. I do not remember how it came up; I had used the word "effeminate" in one of our conversations, and Diego understood me to be deprecating unmasculine men. "But Róger, I'm effeminate," he interjected. I was skeptical, having already noted how some of my interlocutors sometimes misused less familiar terms. (A twenty-year-old worker at the Volkswagen plant surprised me by describing himself as a "pedophile." It turned out that he meant that he was attracted to slim young men his own age or slightly younger. I introduced him to the term "twink.") And so I told Diego that most of us would describe him as "butch" (a word I also used in English). Diego persisted: "When I was a boy, I used to wish that I was a girl so that I could marry a man when I grew up. OK, so I look tough. The other kids called me names, so I got tough. And I can make that work for me. But all this that you see is an act. My preferred role is bottom [*pasivo*], a hundred percent bottom. Men want me to fuck them, and I do, but when they find out I want to be fucked, they lose interest." I protested that there's plenty of demand out there for butch bottoms. "That's not been my experience," he sighed.

As we became friends, we sometimes discussed his life plans and goals. He contemplated a return to university studies in a field that held more interest for him—literature, perhaps. But such plans always seemed vague to my ears. If I have listened to what he said and to the desires he expressed, Diego's first priority in life was romantic: before planning a career, before undertaking further study, before any other goal, he wanted a boyfriend, a partner, a husband. He enthused when the subject of marriage equality came up, even though legal recognition of same-sex marriages (as opposed to civil unions) seemed a distant proposition at the time: Here was a gay political aim that spoke directly to his understanding of a good life. I used to try to cajole him out of such talk: "You're young! You should be studying!" But as I have come to reflect on the realities of economic life in the service sector of a low-wage economy, and the relatively low return on a university education for lower-class people without family connections, it has seemed less and less clear to me that Diego's priorities were entirely misplaced. Of course, gay relationships are, arguably, unstable, especially those forged in youth, so perhaps either option was equidistant from the probability of failure and disappointment.

When Diego gave me his lesson on the open possibilities of modern gay life, he was working as an all-purpose cook, dishwasher, waiter, deliverer, and errand runner in a *fonda*, a hole-in-the-wall restaurant that catered to market people and downtown salesclerks. The optimism of his narrative about gay life contrasted with the precariousness of his economic existence. He had recently lost his tiny, one-room apartment—which, against all odds, he was trying to maintain on his own. Single, unattached working-class people in Puebla normally share the costs of a cramped apartment with multiple roommates, sometimes sleeping four or five to a room, but Diego had had a string of roommates who failed to pay their share of the rent: a Bible-carrying, evangelical cook whose straight boyfriend beat him up when he failed to fork over his earnings; a young college student who spent all of his meager allowance on bars and nightlife and thus came up perpetually short when rent came due; a young middle-class lesbian who was going through troubled times and was ultimately reclaimed by her family . . .

So now Diego was sleeping in the back of the fonda. The two sisters who owned the eatery adored him, fawned over him, and were happy to help him out—with the added benefit of having him serve as a night guard for free. But by this time, business was going into steep decline. A hepatitis scare didn't help. Although the doctor who examined him said that Diego was not ill, he certainly had had the visible signs of the illness—yellow eyes and jaundiced skin—for the better part of two weeks. Word went around and food orders declined precipitously. Within a few more weeks, and despite the sisters' best efforts, the eatery went under.

Unemployed and now homeless, the young man shuffled between friends' couches, lovers' apartments, and other impromptu arrangements. Displaced from the safer neighborhoods in the centro, he was twice mugged on unlit streets in a lower-working-class suburb; the muggers roughed him up and got his all-important identification cards, without which it is all but impossible to apply for work, to receive health care, or to conduct any kind of routine business. He was spotted, periodically, loitering in a park frequented by hustlers, prostitutes, and sex workers.

BECOMING MODERN

A young man like Diego, who struck a public pose of "rough trade"—a guise belied by his "effeminate," romantic inner nature—might have said at this stage in life that he was only passing time, that being with men was just a phase, that he was actually "straight," that his primary motives were monetary, and so on. The tug of history, the hold of local traditions and identities, and the coexistence of varied sexual constructs do give such men such options, at least for a while, perhaps especially in countries like Mexico. Instead, and from an early age, he had claimed a gay identity, a way of being that he understood to fit him personally and at the same time to be contemporary, global, and universal. How Diego navigates these ideas and their crosscurrents is instructive. His claim on gay identity, mediated by old and new communications media, locates *us*, by contrast to *them*, in a world of open possibilities: "*They* lived in a different time from *us*." This is to say that *they* were rustics, trapped in the past; *we* are fortunate to live in modern times, when our desires can express themselves freely. All that stands in the way of our happiness can be relegated to the past, offloaded onto unfortunate others. A series of transpositions makes this doubly intelligible in Diego's view, with the American cowboys of *Brokeback Mountain* standing in much the same relationship to the time of now as Mexican indigenous people in remote villages.

If we listen only to what people say when they speak this way, we might think that a cosmopolitan international gay identity has already arrived in Mexico, that indeed it arrived long ago. Of course, it has, replete with the

ideological distinctions and machinations to sustain it, which include ethnic and class logics—but any examination of just what this might mean,
how it calibrates with the imagination of time, and how it might work
for most people undermines a complacent view of this "arrival." First,
there is the matter of all those unfortunate people who are still today
trapped in the past: cowboys, indigenous people, rustics, poor people
in general. Then there is also the matter of all those social forces (small
minds, political reaction, economic collapse) that threaten to pull us
back into the past—or something worse, since those who actually lived
in the past had never tasted sexual freedom. Lastly, there is a necessary
uneasiness about the way we inhabit this fabulous, precarious present.
For once one sets foot inside the portal of modernity, the work of identity
can never be finished; one must perpetually introspect and work on
oneself: Have I truly understood and correctly embraced my desires? Is
my gayness informed and up to date? Am I modern, truly modern, yet?
And if I think of this sexual moment in quintessentially modern terms, as
a "marketplace," have I attended to my own product placement? Am I
toned, fit, well dressed, and savvy about sexual arrangements? (Before
such infotainment went online, gay weekly or monthly "bar rags" were
there to help. I once encountered Diego in Luciérnaga poring over the
advice column to update himself on terms like "polyamory" and "ménage
à trois.")

Like Erik's declaration, "I am gay," Diego's counsel, his rejection of an
indigenous identity, and the way he imagines time can all be understood
as speech in the optative mode, that is, as expressions of a desire or wish.
By contrast, his actual life experiences not only show how material circumstances and class predicaments can undermine even the most transparent aims and desires, but also suggest some of the ways ambiguity and
contradiction haunt the supposedly open field of gay possibilities. For the
very physical traits that made Diego attractive in the ambiente were the
qualities that he strove to reject: indigeneity. And the secret of his personal charm lay in part in guarded dispositions that he developed in the
face of homophobic bullying: toughness. His gay life itself thus was shaped
by a sort of closeting, an inverted closeting, if you will: a gap between his
secret, inner desires and his public, manifest persona.

CRUEL OPTIMISM?

I am tempted to invoke Lauren Berlant's *Cruel Optimism* here, a book that marks the advent of post–queer theory's "turn to affect." The recurring tagline for (and the first line from) this influential work is straightforward enough: "A relation of cruel optimism exists when something you desire is actually an obstacle to your flourishing." The book turns on the idea that we construct the object of desire as "a cluster of promises we want someone or something to make to us and make possible for us." That is, we project our wishes onto, and we confuse them with, persons or things in the world. Berlant admits that, understood this way, all optimism is cruel, but she insists that some optimisms are crueler than others—specifically, she means those that undermine or diminish our well-being.[9] Now to apply Berlant's readymade notions to Diego's (and others') dilemmas: Perhaps if what one expects from citizenship in gay modernity is *happiness*, then one is attached to the wrong expectation and thus doomed to a life of perpetual frustration. Or better put: Perhaps gay identity is something ill-fitted to the circumstances of poor and working-class queers in Mexico (and other places). Like a mirage in the desert, this gaiety disappears as we approach it. The harder we chase after it, the faster it recedes.

I held these very thoughts as my trump card as my ideas gestated over several years. I discussed this framing via email with Berlant, and even today these ideas seem to constitute a plausible working hypothesis. But, in the end, I am not satisfied with this approach. For who said that desire was supposed to be good for us? What experts would be the arbiters of what is beneficial and what is detrimental to our "flourishing"? And if we apply Berlant's wry and knowing take to Diego's situation, where exactly was his original error? Was it in his desire to be clear about his desires? His disidentification with indigenousness, to support his identification as gay? His longing for a rather old-fashioned kind of intimacy? His belief that the present is a time of freedom? Or in the way that all these identifications and attachments hang together within an intelligible frame of references for him? Or was the original misstep his willingness to convert himself into a bundle of promises for other men's enjoyment? If so, how could he have avoided the placement of his own embodiment in a social world populated by others and shaped by their desires? One might just as well say that his struggle to be gay was a distraction from the class struggle, for all the good that such an insight might do. Or one might wax sour about the possibilities of modern life, which condemns us all, one way or another, to the pursuit of happiness. In this pursuit, we miss our mark as often as not; we stage and restage various kinds of identities; we engage in sham or fakery rather than expose our vulnerabilities; and we are sometimes mistaken about the nature of our desires. This is the human condition today, not only in Mexico.

Although the explicit backdrop of her analyses is the breakdown of the New Deal version of the good life and the formation of a neoliberal subjectivity in the United States, Berlant avoids terms like "commodity fetishism" and "reification" in favor of the language of object relations and affect, prolix extensions of a very thin limb derived from Raymond Williams's short chapter about "structures of feeling."[10] All very well and good, but perhaps her arguments actually would be stronger if they were planted more clearly in a diagnostic of discourse, ideology, and hegemony. We could then get down to specific claims about either institutional shifts and their shaping of subject positions or consumer culture and its production of feelings, needs, and wants. We might even want to "test" these premises against the experiences and accounts of real human subjects, who might account for themselves in other terms. (This—essentially "method," in the parlance of the interpretive social sciences—still eludes most humanists of the affective turn.) Perhaps we would then be in a better position to contemplate the unfinished, unfixed nature of human practices and sentiments in changing social formations—which was, as I understand it, Williams's real aim in broaching the notion "structures of feeling."

Much of what is cruel about the optimism that Berlant purports to describe seems to be a continued attachment to the expectations of a good life wrapped up in the postwar bundles. These have to do with unionized wages and stable family life. But, to put things bluntly, it is not nostalgic feelings or retrograde expectations that are obstacles to anyone's flourishing; it is the machinations of the ruling class, whose representatives and managers have clawed back the social and economic gains of the postwar working class, putting ever-greater numbers of people in an exposed and precarious position. Substitute "culture" for "affect" here, and the core premise of the affective turn sounds a lot like the thesis of the culture of poverty.

Berlant's exhibits of objects toward which optimism might be deemed cruel seem calculated to appeal primarily to liberal humanities professors. Such depictions are basically about the existential positioning of members of the academic class, who rarely reflect on their own habitus and can thus construe dissent and subversion broadly in their own analytical speech acts and critical declamations. Eve Sedgwick once described these forms of academic grandstanding as "dreary and routine forms of good dog/bad dog criticism by which, like good late-capitalist consumers, we persuade ourselves that deciding what we like or don't like about what's happening is the same thing as actually intervening in its production."[11]

Meanwhile, other longings go uncommented on or appear to be as cryptic and as mysterious as hieroglyphs to the chattering classes. These mundane yearnings of ordinary people—who are immersed in humdrum problems and who often desire decidedly old-fashioned things like gay-ness, dignity, equality, or marriage—are dismissed, classed essentially as retrograde errors or forms of false consciousness. One scarcely need underscore the class dynamics that unfold, either silently or with great fanfare, in these academic practices.

I am trying to define a space here where individual longings, collective identifications, and personal frustrations might be understood in global political-economic and historical contexts. I am also urging an approach that suspends judgments based on what we academics think we already know: a series of pat positions, moral declarations about what is good and bad, and claims about false consciousness. The task is a difficult one, for the individual person is not an instance or example but his own unique being who demands to be understood on his own terms. Like other unique beings, he makes choices under circumstances not of his choosing. He replies to questions about his choices not with answers but with more questions.

In Diego's case, is it fair to say that he was too busy attending to his imaginary gay life to notice that his real material life was falling apart around him? Perhaps, but saying so seems distinctly unhelpful. He scarcely needed to be reminded of his material conditions. Or should we chide him for wanting constancy, connection, and an old-fashioned (het- ero- or perhaps homo-normative) version of intimacy in an inconstant world? Such chastisements would seem presumptuous, not to say coun- terproductive. Shall we summon his ancestors, who still haunt mountain- sides and valleys, to shame him for shedding one identity, indigeneity, for another, gayness? My own modest attempts along these lines did not impress; he wanted forms of freedom and access that were not available in the remote village. Or would it be more accurate to say that his actual class position has come to the fore, and that it proved a feeble support for the creative development of any of his longings, romantic, material, or spirit- ual? That much seems indisputable, although we might take a page from Williams's "structures of feeling" to refrain from reducing a person's lived experience to a set of fixed forms.

DIEGO'S RETREAT

With his world falling apart around him, Diego beat a hasty retreat back to his pueblo in the remote highlands. I wondered whether he had gone back home for good, but it turned out that he was biding time, visiting with family, regrouping, and making plans. A year or so later, he returned to the city to begin taking classes, eventually enrolling in BUAP to study accounting. When he graduated five years later, he began working as an accountant for a midsize manufacturing firm. He has continued in this line of office work until the present.

After a season of turmoil, Diego now has the material things of this world more or less in hand: a steady job, a reliable good income, his own home. He is the *only* working-class person I know whose life has, after a short detour, followed the desired economic path of upward mobility. His is a rags-to-riches story, so long as we count "riches" narrowly and define "middle class" as salaried white-collar employees. I wish I could also report that the finer, more spiritual things also have been added to him— that he has found his desired happiness in an intimate conjugal relation- ship. What better demonstration of my working premise, that class posi- tion shapes one's experiences of homosexuality and one's life chances in the gay world? But life seldom simply enacts the sociological script, much less our own preferred fairy tales. Invariably, there are quirks and kinks along the way.

In Diego's case, the gifts of nature proved fleeting. By his mid-twenties, he was rapidly thickening and broadening, his features coarsening, so that he scarcely resembled his former lean, defined, athletic self. These physical changes accelerated as he approached thirty. No longer a beautiful young tough, he had aged out of his niche in the sexual marketplace. Accustomed to having been the desired, he seems unable to accommodate these changes and to cultivate a new niche for himself. (On the gay scene in the United States, we used to have cynical apothegms for the kind of switchover that eludes him: "Today's trade is tomorrow's competition," which means, among other things, that today's desired attractive youth will be tomorrow's desirer of attractive youth.)

Now in his mid-thirties, the not-so-young man reports that he spends twelve hours a day at the office, pushing numbers from column to column, monitoring compliance with federal regulations, and performing other administrative tasks. "This doesn't leave me much time for romantic adventures," he claims. "Plus," he adds, perhaps expressing nervousness that the hustler would become the hustled, "I've bought all my own furniture and don't want people coming in here stealing things." He tells me that for sexual release, he visits a bathhouse from time to time, a far cry from his earlier dream of connubial domestic bliss. He socializes, but infrequently, with a small network of gay friends. Matters that in his youth seemed of vital importance now seem all but forgotten.

But he still talks about an affair he had fifteen years earlier with a handsome French visitor. The two could often be seen together strolling in the zócalo, immersed in conversation in cafés, or dining out in the centro. Their relationship lasted for two or three months, with the adoring thirty-something-year-old man murmuring French obscenities to Diego in intimate moments, lavishing wet kisses on the young man's tightly yoked ass, and always asserting without hesitation the "active," dominating, penetrative role in bed. Diego seemed to be swept away in the relationship, and many observers thought that he would live happily ever after with his exotic foreigner, but the young man's romantic longings proved more than what the romance could bear. It was Diego who ended the relationship when the Frenchman would not commit to a permanent and exclusive relationship—a "marriage," as it were, though gay civil union arrangements had not yet resolved into formal marriage rights, either in Mexico or in France.

"Many things change with time," Diego tells me, waxing philosophical and perhaps reflecting on his own corporeal changes, "but memories do not. These memories I keep." And so, for Diego, the time of the now, the modern time of open possibilities, has been swallowed up by the past, sealed into remembrances bitter and sweet, left behind with the march of time.

9 Putos

In Mexico, the relationship between sexual identity and class position is no secret, nor is how this relationship fits with a wider storyline about tradition and modernity. People tell and retell a joke that succinctly captures the logic of these relationships. This jest has retained its currency over many years, and I have lost track of the number of times I have heard it.

"Father," begins an earnest young man from a working-class barrio, "I have something to tell you . . . I'm gay." "My son," the father replies, "I didn't know. But let me ask you a few questions: Do you shop at high-end boutiques and wear name-brand clothing? Do you rent an apartment in the fashionable part of town? Can you even get into posh clubs that charge 100 pesos at the door?" Expert raconteurs will play out each of the queries with minor variations, and the boy's answer to all three questions in sequence is, basically, "Why, no, papá, of course not. You know that I can't afford such things."

Then comes the punch line, the father's flat-footed response to the boy's earnest self-disclosure: "Well, my son, I love you very much and I'm sorry to tell you this, but you're confused, you're mistaken. *No eres gay, eres solo un pinche puto:* You're not gay, you're just a fucking fag."

A word on words here: I have rendered *pinche puto* as "fucking fag," and this will do. *Pinche*, a strong but frequently used adjective in Mexico, is used to augment insults (e.g., *pinche gringo*) and is often translated this way, parallel to the way English speakers use the participial adjective "fucking" to emphasize a sense of annoyance or surprise. But the Mexican modifier has nothing to do with sex; rather, it connotes concepts that are readily scaled onto class hierarchy. It might be more accurately translated "insignificant," "worthless," "cheap," "lousy," or "miserable." *Puto* is the masculine form for *puta*, whore or prostitute. A pejorative term for male homosexual ("fag," or perhaps "queer"), it trades on both promiscuity and (arguably) lower-class standing (for what class of person would take money for sex?), sometimes connoting cowardice. Almost anything that provokes rage or annoyance can be "puto" and the noun is readily converted into an adjective (e.g., *mi puto trabajo*, my shitty job; *el puto carro*, the fucking car; *puto sol*, damned sun). Mexicans freely fling the homophobic term in both friendly banter and angry insults, not unlike the way P. J. Pascoe's subjects trade pejoratives in *Dude, You're a Fag.*[1]

Tellers, gay or straight, seem to relish the cruelty of this joke, the sting of its punch line, which gives a rather straightforward description of the material obstacles that stand in the way of the young aspirant's path to a modern, destigmatized sexual identity. The jest tells us, in so many words, that being poor, working-class, or even lower-middle-class makes it extremely difficult to claim a gay identity or to assert membership in a modern gay community. If we add that these difficulties multiply for dark-skinned, indigenous, and rural queers, for manual laborers, and for recent immigrants to the city, we say the obvious, but we are also saying essentially the same thing. "Gay" is understood to be an affluent, cosmopolitan, up-to-date identity. "Puto" are all those who come up short: rustics, poor people, indigenous people, anyone without money in his pocket: the broadly defined working class.

The fictional father's mention of a 100-peso admission fee and other lifestyle costs is no joke; he is merely enumerating the high barriers to full participation in a modern, cosmopolitan identity. The minimum wage in 2018 was MXN$88.36 (US$4.72) per day, not enough to meet the minimum basic needs of a single worker, much less to afford a night on the town. As Mexican labor and human rights advocates have pointed out, this low standard violates the 1917 constitution's mandate for a living minimum wage (which includes provisions for the material, social, cultural, and educational needs not only of an individual but for a family).[2] A quarter of the population is supported by the equivalent of either one or two minimum-wage jobs. To make matters worse, or certainly more precarious, nearly 60 percent of the workforce is paid off the books or gains its income in the informal sector—in either case without benefits or protections.[3] This large reserve of surplus labor (workers not integrated into the formal economy), in combination with the low minimum wage, exerts a drag on wages and working conditions across the spectrum. Mexican laborers thus work the most hours of countries tracked in OECD data (2,128 hours per year) and pull the lowest average wage: US$16,429 per year.[4]

Such conditions discipline labor and bolster profits, making Mexico an attractive site for export-oriented investments in the neoliberal globalized world, obviously, but they also keep the economy in a rut. Low wages weigh down the national economy by suppressing consumer demand, stifling the development of internal markets, and fostering high levels of social inequality. Mexico ranks near the bottom of OECD countries on income inequality, no matter how this is measured.[5] The World Bank calculates that 42 percent of Mexicans live in poverty, per national definitions of the term.[6]

An even greater share of the population lives with the sense that modern life is eluding them. For most people, being "modern" means, above all, being able to afford modern amenities, labor-saving appliances, quality wares, creature comforts. For a substantial subset, it means just being able to keep one's head above water. The grubby facts—limited purchasing power and wide social inequalities—contribute to Mexicans' sense that modernity is eluding them.

The story's father is being cruel, but he is not only being cruel. What if we take his words literally? He tells us, first, how class limits and steers the boy's options by way of brute economic logic (limited resources); then, consequently, how class dynamics mark social spaces, coding "gay" as "middle class"; and, finally, how these conditions consign the boy to the unhappy role of frustrated aspirant.

FAKING IT

Mexicans bluntly depict the difference between modern gay identity and customary stigmatized identities as a *class* distinction linked to education and purchasing power. In conversation, I once referred to a certain urban park, frequented by working-class and low-income people, as a "gay zone." (I was sketching the contours of gay life in the city, mapping sexual geographies—a common technique in LGBT studies.) My interlocutor, a closeted gay man recently graduated with a master's degree in sociology, immediately corrected me: "No, Róger, only the putos go there. The gays are in the centro. Or they are in scattered clubs in the city's outskirts."

Yamil, who was always telling me that I did not really understand things, pressed a literal understanding of all of this to me one evening at Luciérnaga, after I had commented innocently on how the gay scene was flourishing in Puebla. Yamil's response was distinctly disapproving; he was angry. Gayness, he insisted, was essentially a consumer culture. It involved the exhibition of certain outward signs of wealth: wearing designer labels, going to expensive clubs, indulging in the latest designer drugs, showing off a second language. "But most people can't afford designer labels," he went on, "so they buy imitations." After a pause, he continued: "Look around you. Every Lacoste and Polo in here was bought at the Fayuca," Puebla's expansive black and gray marketplace, where contraband items, knockoffs, and stolen goods are sold. "Or they lie."

I thought about some of my friends' petty deceptions and tried to see the point that Yamil was making. One contact was trying to master basic discriminations involved in wine tasting. He had memorized certain perceptual measures (dryness, acidity, body, balance) and frequently dropped these references into conversation at the bar—although everyone knew that he lacked the budget for even a minimal vinous sampling. (Admittedly, this is a common domain for class and status simulations everywhere.) Another posted elaborate Facebook messages simulating travels to foreign countries, sometimes clipping and reposting other people's photos of faraway places to authenticate his fictions. (I was surprised to find some of my own photos on his account: "Just back from a quick trip to Washington, DC—Georgetown was beautiful!") And I recalled the young man at the bar a few weeks before who had pretended to speak English with me, perhaps too drunk to realize that we were not actually communicating—or perhaps hoping that I would play along with his penny ante deception.

"But," I protested, "look at Juan-José." I referred to the man who made rounds every evening selling gum, candies, and churritos out of a box strapped to his trunk. "He's obviously poor. He doesn't wear designer labels. And he's gay." The ambulatory vendor often passed time with us at the café-bar, trading stories and sharing laughter before continuing on his rounds to other bars and clubs in the centro. Yamil scoffed at my example, underscoring the theme of wanting what you cannot have. "Yes, but do you know what Juan-José wants above all? He wants a white, blond, blue-eyed man. And he's never going to have one. He's always going to be frustrated and alone and unhappy."

No doubt I had caught Yamil—who made his living in a gay establishment, after all—in a foul mood, perhaps coming down after a cocaine binge. "Well," I finally offered, "you and I are gay, and we don't do any of those things. There's never been an expensive designer label on either of us!" Yamil might have retorted that by dint of the fact that I was a professional, had a decent income, and was traveling, I was, in fact, quite gay, even if decidedly unstylish. ("Your whiteness is your calling card," I was once told after criticizing a friend's unsustainably expensive wardrobe. "People will make inferences about your education and salary no matter what you wear. I have to dress the part.") Instead, he suggested that I was making a category mistake and broached another opposition, more clinical and less class-freighted than puto versus gay. "No, Róger," he gently corrected, "you and I are *homosexuals.*"

FRUSTRATED LONGINGS

Yamil was being cruel, certainly, but was he only being cruel? He pivots from a description of how class imposes limits to how it shapes gay aspirations and defines a symbolic world. What he tells us is that themes of consumerism and social climbing closely track with the markers of modern, cosmopolitan gay identity. Attempts at displaying this identity frequently come down to inauthentic performances (fake designer labels, pretending to be something one is not) and failed attempts at staging a cosmopolitan identity (speaking a second language badly, getting caught making false claims). Such performances and the scripts on which they are based are scarcely unheard of in the United States (or other countries), nor are they unique to the gay scene, but they do have a specific placement in Mexico.

The sorts of status-marking commodities that display gay identity in Mexico are closely connected with trade liberalization and the dissolution of the closed, protected national market that had clothed, shod, and equipped Mexicans for decades under the import substitution regime—that is, with the opening of the economy to US and other international name brands. One might surmise that the desperation of the association between gayness and elusive merchandise was spurred and intensified in the popular imagination by the intense economic hardships that accompanied Mexico's economic and cultural opening. But the association itself was not invented out of whole cloth. Desires for designer labels and foreign name brands predate neoliberalism. *Gringophilia*, the love of all things gringo, specifically, was a strong cultural undercurrent even under closed economic and media markets. Carlos Monsiváis thus recounts how youth subcultures from the 1950s on appropriated American forms of music and dress to strive for an international "look" (a word that many now use in English).[7] Such performances asserted, as against what Octavio Paz described as a national inferiority complex with Mexicans understood to be trapped in the past, that Mexicans were in fact modern, "contemporary with all men [and women]."[8] These longings, these assertions, play out over changing conditions.

Later, in the 1980s, after the crackdowns on youth subcultures had waned, young people who aspired to a modern, cosmopolitan image would ask me to bring them down a pair of Levi's on my next visit—or, better yet, to sell them a used pair out of my suitcase. A simple thing, a pair of Levi's, but the ardor of the craving was anything but simple. Jeans made for the national market were deemed unstylish and of lower quality, while the "Levi's" that were sold on the black market were of questionable provenance. A pair of authentic Levi's jeans was a statement to the world about one's worldliness, especially when combined with a modish haircut. (Variants of the mullet were then in fashion: hair long enough to signify freedom, yet short and kempt enough to not draw the attention of the local police.)

Today, the situation is different, although the unfulfilled longing remains the same. Ironies abound. Designer labels—some of them on clothing fabricated in Mexican maquiladoras, exported to the United States for labeling, then reimported to Mexico for sale at high prices—are ubiquitous but unaffordable.

Consider now the intrinsically frustrating predicament of the cultural present. Neoliberal globalization in countries like Mexico tempts, teases, and tantalizes; it stokes tastes and desires that cannot be satisfied. Unobtainable material objects are proffered together with unobtainable cultural goods, status markers, ways of being, forms of freedom, and personal goals—and these are unobtainable, at least for members of the broad working class. Perhaps in saying this, I owe more to Lauren Berlant's *Cruel Optimism* than I care to admit.[9] But I am not unlocking some secret of gay life or working-class culture here, and I claim no interpretive finesse. The discernment of cruelty and frustration in these optimistic longings is not my discovery, derived from an objective view over and above the scenes of pretense and simulation. I am simply recording, quite literally, what my friends, contacts, and subjects tell me. Everybody knows this, in some fashion or other.

Nor am I even asserting that this desire for a gay modernity is *bad* (as opposed to frustrating) for working-class aspirants. We all long for all manner of things that we cannot obtain (contentment, happiness, perfection), and the fact that these longings frustrate us is not necessarily an index of their unhealthiness. What if people are at their most authentic when they long to be something else, something other than what they are? And what if we push the point even further? Maggie Nelson's recent book *On Freedom* and Tim Dean's earlier work *Unlimited Intimacy* are finely attuned to the experience of feeling liberated, fulfilled, and connected to others by way of engagements and entanglements (drugs, risky sex) that many see as condemnable, pitiable, or self-destructive.[10] Either way, there's not much point in moralizing.

FETISHISM?

Marxist thinkers have long queried how the fetishization of commodities acts on people's consciousness. For Marx, this effect involves a conceptual somersault: the more the exploited worker gives up of his or her life and agency in the production of commodities, the more those products of labor appear to be imbued with life, agency, and other human attributes.[11] The main intellectual tradition that follows from Marx's piercing insight sees commodity fetishism as the nucleus of reification ("thingification") and false consciousness (not being aware of one's true class interests) in culture at large, and this understanding animates members of the Frankfurt School's approach to the culture industry (mass entertainment media) and consumer culture.[12] However, in the wake of youth rebellions of the 1960s, populistic work by cultural studies scholars flipped the script and tried to imagine consumption, especially consumption of mass media products, not as the site where workers deliberately give up their freedom but as a politically empowering act. Thus, captains of the culture industry *encode* conformist messages in a variety of products, but consumers might "read" texts, images, and objects differently and against the grain, subversively *recoding* them.[13]

These opposed approaches, it seems to me, miss the mark. On the one hand, the people about whom I write are not unwitting dupes. They are exquisitely aware of the labor power that goes into the production of the objects they desire. Some have worked in maquilas, sewing together the cloth that goes abroad to be labeled before it comes back to Mexico to confront them in shops as unaffordable clothing. Few are under any illusions about how capitalists dig a profit out of labor, and all tell stories about pilfered wages, unpaid overtime, and cruel or coercive management. On the other hand, there is no mystery to be decoded here, no conformist message to be subversively recoded. In the global south as in the global north, advertising campaigns—some of them no doubt drawn up by publicists who took classes in cultural studies or queer theory—selectively target gay consumer niches and stoke connections between gay identity and acts of consumption. Buyers, consumers, people on the scene like Yamil—or any joke teller—can assert an ironic or critical or even chastising distance between the mere object itself (expensive wares) and its "fetish" (the attributes and qualities it is held to magically embody). They discern the calculations of the hawkers who are keen to affix rainbow flags to their merchandise in the month of June, the better to cultivate brand loyalty, the better to augment their bottom line. Yet this heightened critical awareness does little to quench anyone's uncritical desires, either for the politically minded or for the apolitical.

When I ran into a local political organizer at one of Puebla's Walmart stores, I joked that we could convene a socialist caucus meeting on the site. (I had just run into other Left activists at Walmart the same day.) Unfazed by my implied criticism of us all, he replied: "Everybody wants quality goods at low prices." So they do, and so it is with the striving for gayness in a world of commodified objects—though the desired goods in the latter case are of presumably higher quality and undeniably higher prestige than what one might typically encounter at Walmart. They belong instead to the status-bearing consumables ("status symbols") linked to an affluent lifestyle whose analysis was inaugurated by Thorstein Veblen and whose implications later set Jean Baudrillard down the path of rethinking the relationship between economics and semiotics.[14] Or, at any rate, they belong to a mass-produced, middle-class version of the same.

What might productively be said here is that everybody wants dignity, respect, personal freedom, and higher social standing. Under the redistributive corporatist regime of the mid-twentieth century, these were to be found in meaningful work, labor unions or peasant associations, paths to a modicum of social mobility, and scripted forms of family life. "Putos" were by definition excluded—unless they concealed their sex lives. Under the newer consumer economy, the symbolic and material rewards for collective working-class projects have declined, reliable on-ramps to social mobility have collapsed, and the desired social goods circulate at a remove from working people in elusive, unaffordable commodities. Meanwhile, some of the received scripts, however fragile, remain intact. "Putos," seeking to escape stigma, then, aspire to "gayness" via status symbols and attempts at conspicuous consumption.

Our usual Left-academic interpretive stratagems, which over time have become moral injunctions, fail us here. The jinx that traces the movement of these products is different from the ghost of labor that clings to the commodity's fetish.

The problem is not not knowing (the locus classicus of theories of false consciousness) but, rather, not having. People know what they want. They very often understand why they want what they want. They might even have a self-conscious or ironic sense of what this wanting *does*. They certainly understand the frustration it entails. None of this knowledge deters the spirals of longing, because no contemplative critique, no savvy media literacy, can interrupt the real economic circuits that devalue labor and inflate commodity prices. The ache provoked by not having is real: not having the basic necessities, not having the intangibles associated with personal freedom, not having social standing.

Sumptuary rituals and conspicuous consumption are older than capital: they serve not to conceal or falsify relations of production but to index status groups and mark identities of various sorts. They find special placement in late-capitalist consumer culture, especially in its peripheral versions, where they have been retrofitted for the masses. There, they direct the flow of traffic between "tradition" and "modernity," low and high status, and so on, delineating the distinction between "puto" and "gay" (among other things) according to these wider logics. Consequently, they serve as a densely trafficked transfer point between want and imagination.

In their real lives, working-class gay men experience material privation, social disapprobation, and restrictions on their sexual freedom. These experiences of want raise the relative value of the subcultures and accoutrements of more elite gay circles. Anyone can see that men of means have more freedom than men of want; anyone can see that it is better to be perceived as "gay" than as a "puto." Working-class men aspire to this world of affluence and freedom, attempting to access it through largely imaginary means. Symbolic camouflage, opulent theatrics, and sartorial simulation provide aspirants with a modicum of protection against the harshest forms of homophobia, perhaps, and with a sense, however fleeting, of being better off than they are. And just as everyone looks better in a nice suit or fashionable attire, everyone likes the feeling of being better off. But anyone can also see that these sumptuary rituals ultimately fail to work their magic: they can no more change a puto into a gay man than they can change a worker into a middle-class person.

What, then? Again, moralizing (about bad personal choices or misguided beliefs) misses the point, which ought to be to understand how the changing system in its totality produces subjects for whom freedom and dignity are constricted to consumer choices, fakery, and simulation. In practice, these conditions amount to a predicament; they *test* us. We light a candle at the altar of aguante: such frustrations are to be suffered and endured, not transcended.

APPEARANCES

Distinctions tracked in gay settings are not unrelated to those mapped in wider society. These distinctions invariably take in colonial histories, traditional forms of domination, and modern capitalist relations. Raiment, coiffure, accessories—all the commodities and services that go into a person's look—are important because appearances are where the strands of inequality come together, reveal themselves, or unravel.

Erik recounts the story of how he and two straight friends had initially been refused entry into one of Puebla's upscale antros. Like other establishments along Avenida Juárez, the straight nightclub posted notice of a nondiscriminatory policy at the door: "In this establishment, we do not discriminate on the basis of race, religion, sexual orientation, socioeconomic condition, or for any other reason." The bouncer was polite but told the group that this was a private club, with admission by membership or invitation. Now, this is an old trick everywhere: clubs keep out people deemed undesirable or less desirable by citing membership policies. But Erik could see that people were entering without presenting any membership cards, so he asked a pair of well-dressed, lighter-skinned strangers if his group could enter with them. The pair assented, and the bouncer relented. Eric reports that later that evening, from inside a bathroom stall, he could overhear the conversation of his group's sponsors: "Who were those Indians and what pueblo did they come from?"

I have never heard of anyone being denied entry to a *gay* club based on appearances, but surmises made at a glance about a person's material condition—his class, his ethnicity, or the relative proportions of his mixed ethnic origins—certainly do happen in gay settings. Put-downs, jests, and insults frequently refer to the colonial history marked on a person's face. Raúl, whose skin is dark, relates that when he "tapped" a prospect on Grindr, the object of his interests curtly rebuffed his attentions and called him *"pinche indio de mierda,"* shitty worthless Indian. Racist slurs of this general sort provide the backdrop for commonplace banter and petty squabbling. *"Cara de nopal"* (prickly-pear cactus face) is one of many ways of referring, playfully or insultingly, to a person's autochthonous looks. Such banter goes on until someone feels genuinely insulted and his feelings are hurt, then apologies are made and relations are patched up, until the banter eventually resumes along the familiar tracks again. Indeed, so frequent were my acquaintances' complaints about everyday insults based on complexion that I began asking them: "Do you feel more oppressed because of your class position or because of your skin color?" I had almost expected my subjects to argue that, in practice, these were much the same thing. One scarcely need conduct a large-sample survey to see that darker-skinned Mexicans *tend* to be poorer, and lighter-skinned Mexicans richer. But, to a person, every one of my working-class informants said that *class* weighed more heavily in his everyday experiences of privation and insult than did race or color.

"Look, if I had money, I'd dress the part and I'd pull up in a fancy car," Erik said. "It's unlikely that some poorly paid bouncer would give me grief over the color of my skin—and even if he did, what's it to me? I'd complain to the manager, or I'd wave some money around, or I'd buy something." My working-class acquaintances viewed money as the great solvent of prejudice, even if they acknowledged the inevitability of being viewed as "indigenous." Darker-skinned middle-class informants, by contrast, tended to weigh color discriminations more heavily in the scheme of things—which is to say that slights and bruises involving presumed ethnic origins could loom larger among their concerns precisely because brute economic privation had been taken out of the picture.

Now the sorts of color distinctions that I am writing about here are different from the kinds of animus and suspicion that structure experiences of racism in the United States. The former distinctions and derogations occur *among* mestizo or mixed-race people (a very large majority of Mexicans), whereas the latter are interactions *between* corporate races: legally defined groups whose status is ascribed on birth certificates, official paperwork, and census data. Still, we might draw out broad parallels. Adolph Reed Jr. has written extensively about the class basis for contemporary anti-racist politics in the United States at a time of intensifying economic inequalities that cut across race and ethnic lines: this politics is driven largely by members of the professional managerial middle classes who feel the sting of racial animus but not class exploitation, and serves as an alternative to broad, multiethnic, working-class politics.[15]

Grant Farred succinctly and convincingly—though perhaps inadvertently—demonstrates the salience of class over race and how upper-middle-class elites come to be the bearers of modern race consciousness in his description of the incident that motivated him to write a short philosophical treatise, *Martin Heidegger Saved My Life*. While the South African–born black philosopher was raking leaves outside his spacious home in Ithaca, New York, dressed down for the part, a white woman passing by mistook him for hired help and asked, "Would you like another job?" Farred retorted, "Only if you can match my Cornell faculty salary." That is to say, the academic puts the woman, who was presumably *not* an Ivy League professor, in her place and asserts the real hierarchy, based on income and cultural capital—although the inevitability of being viewed as a manual laborer still stings enough that he was motivated to unpack the encounter with a short, ruminating academic text.[16]

Was Erik's group initially rebuffed because of the way its members were dressed or because of their skin color? More than likely, it was the way the two came together, the way the one evoked the other, for people look for obvious and subtle cues to make surmises at a glance. Darker skin implies lower socioeconomic standing; shabby or unstylish dress is an even stronger sign of privation. Appearances in the aggregate thus gauge a person's ethnic origins, his relationship to modernity, his savvy about fashion trends, and above all his class standing. The signs of class, status, and power might set up a struggle among themselves in the visage, on the corpus, but in the end when people strive to present a modern, affluent image to the world, their options are ultimately limited by their purchasing power.

ON THE INEVITABILITY OF BEING A PUTO

Yamil and I were riding in a car one evening with Ricardo and other straight friends, on our way to Cholula, the ancient village–cum–university town just outside Puebla, where the antros play house, techno, and other varieties of electronic dance music. Miguel, a twenty-something-year-old straight man, had already had a few beers and was leaning out the window shouting "Putos!" at random passers-by on the streets. (Occasionally, some of his targets of abuse appeared surprised; more often, they were unfazed.) Each time this happened, Yamil would say, "Hey, there are putos here in this car with you," and Miguel would mumble something like, "Oh, I'm sorry, guys, I didn't mean anything by it," and then within seconds returned to shouting "Putos!" at strangers along the way. These comic reenactments continued like a constantly replaying loop for twenty minutes or so as we navigated side streets and looked for parking.

I do not want to minimize the violence of this term. Every homophobic assault is probably prefigured by the flinging of this label—and a great many other assaults are, as well. But harsh banter is common in Mexico, and I am not convinced that Miguel was motivated by animus: he was seated, leg to leg and shoulder to shoulder, after all, in the back seat of a compact car with two gay men. For him at this moment, the term served as a not-altogether-coherent expression of joy and exuberance, the ritual breaking of taboo in giddy moments. I thought of an occasion when a gay acquaintance had received a phone call from his best friend since childhood, a straight man. I could hear the caller's coarse greeting on the speaker: "puto puto puto puto puto puto puto puto. . . ."

Straight people, too, have ideas about their usage of the term, which like *güey* ("dude") or *no mames* (literally, stop sucking, used as an expression of surprise, meaning "no way") serves as a tic utterance, an everyday discursive unguent.

Over the years, FIFA (International Federation of Association Football) has warned and sanctioned the Mexican Football Association for its fans' persistent chants ("*¡Eeeeeeh Puto!*"), meant to heckle opposing teams. In 2014, Mexican sportswriter, podcaster, and media entrepreneur Mauricio Cabrera penned a response to the international organization. Reviewing some of the varied and contradictory ways Mexicans fling the term—in anger, in friendly jest, in envy, in a self-effacing mode—the sports writer argues: "In Mexico, we are all putos, at least in some of the word's meanings":

> The word is ingrained in our culture. We say it without thinking of one man penetrating another. What's more, we don't call homosexuals putos, at least

not to their faces. We have been educated to be respectful when we detect a gay among us. Unless he is our friend, of course, because then it fits. And it is possible that he also calls us puto without it implying the possibility that we might end up in bed together. We live in a country of putos.

Noting the irony of trying to turn the soccer stadium into a Davos Economic Forum, Cabrera concludes:

> Yelling puto is not like throwing a banana at a person of color to make him look like a monkey. [The author refers here to racist taunts in some European stadiums.] Puto is the way the Mexican expresses himself. To greet, to mock, to laugh, and to challenge. If FIFA and [Sepp] Blatter [then president of the organization, later banned from the sport on corruption charges] hear that and imagine with horrified faces two men having sex, it is because they do not understand that in Mexico, being a puto is inevitable.[17]

Perhaps the straight sportswriter's inspired rant gives deeper insight into the place of the puto in Mexican society. It suggests that below and within the cruelty of the joke (*eres solo un pinche puto*) lies an inner empathy with the working-class gay boy's inevitable plight: we are all putos, sometimes, and this is especially true for the masses trapped on the lower rungs of a stagnant economic system, who are not just putos but pinche putos.

Mexican jokes and banter are often harsh, but such jest also contains principles of solidarity. This is the other side, like signified to signifier, of the status-climbing commodities in their social ambits: the consciousness of false consciousness. I underscore key points, some of which are widely understood in Mexico. Davos-style language policing cannot erase the stigma of terms like "puto" because it cannot affect the wider political-economic and institutional structures of repression and subordination. FIFA's enlightened neoliberalism prettifies the sport but has nothing to say about the social structures that generate anti-queer views and feelings. In any event, such enlightenment was nowhere to be seen in 2022, when the World Cup was held in Qatar, an emirate that criminalizes homosexual relations and where 6,500 migrant workers died, many apparently from heat stroke, in the buildup to the sporting event.[18] International bodies often express fine sensibilities about racist or homophobic slurs, but it's fair to say that with few exceptions they care nothing about the economic conditions that broadly immiserate the masses, not only in Mexico—much less how those conditions exacerbate the suffering that derives from discriminatory or demeaning acts motivated by animus.

Lastly, this, then: Some uses of the term "puto" defy easy classification (high or low, positive or negative) and recalibrate the frustrations and accomplishments of everyday life, as when Mexicans say "I hate you" as a form of praise.

"Puto Ares," his own teammate exclaimed when Ares charged gazelle-like across the basketball court, leaping like a dancer at the finish to score the winning point.

Ares beamed. Onlookers applauded.

10 Postcards from the Ambiente

Cuernavaca, 1984: One sunny afternoon, a young man my age approached me on the street to ask, "¿Eres de ambiente?" I did not understand his question: Am I of the atmosphere? What could he mean by that? The boy was persistent, meeting my gaze with a winsome smile and posing the question twice more. We both wanted to make a connection, but in addition to language barriers there were conceptual obstacles. We stood there awkwardly for what seemed like several minutes, as people passed us by. Then the young man gave up and walked away.

Puebla, 2018: "Well, you couldn't have been very bright, then," observed Jorge, an affluent and well-traveled sixty-something-year-old gay Poblano, when I explained to him my difficulties locating a gay scene in the 1980s. "And you certainly didn't do your homework. I mean, all the information you needed was right there in *Spartacus* [a gay men's travel guide, founded in 1970 and circulated broadly during this period]."

Germany, 1932: "Not everyone occupies the same Now." Ernst Bloch's fanciful phrase has been widely quoted in the "queer temporalities" literature, though the main thread of Bloch's ruminations seems to have gone missing: it is, after all, the capitalist mode of production that introduces warps and kinks (or perceptions of them) into the fabric of time. Time out of joint, for Bloch, is related to society out of joint—to the stratification of society into classes.[1] Put less whimsically: owing to their segmented material realities, social needs, and collective dreams, different class strata cannot be said to comfortably cohabit the same sense of "Nowness," which, for want of a better word, we call modernity.

If this is a gambit, I will add that not everyone occupies the same conceptual Here, either, even though we might pass one another on the street.

El Noa Noa, 1980 and 1964: Even during the peak years of cultural repression, there were limits to invisibility and discretion. Over a long career, singer, songwriter, and Mexican pop icon Juan Gabriel took on those limits as an enabling condition: he *flaunted* it. Clad in sequined, frilly, gender-bending attire and dancing in a feminine style, he belted out over-the-top romantic hits that often contained no gender pronouns (an easier feat in Spanish than in English). In 1980, when he was already a superstar and on his way to becoming one of the most successful performers in the history of Mexican popular music, he sent out coded messages to a nascent world. In "El Noa Noa," the singer invites listeners to accompany him to a *lugar de ambiente* (literally, a place with atmosphere) to revel the night away in carefree dance. "Este es un lugar de ambiente donde todo es diferente" (This is an ambient place where everything is different). Named for the club in Ciudad Juárez where Gabriel first performed in the 1960s when he was sixteen years old, the song would have no special meaning for "straight" listeners. But those who were *de ambiente*, "in the life," would know exactly what the phrase "lugar de ambiente" meant.

Perhaps this was the singer's answer to the Village People, whose fame continued to ripple around the world—and who, for the record, never used the word "gay" in any of their songs, either.

"Ambiente" (environment, surroundings, atmosphere, climate, milieu) is a capacious term. If I say "*medio ambiente*," I refer to the natural environment. If I say "*ambiente local*," I refer to local color. Typically, gay people in Mexico and other Latin American settings use the word without modifiers to mean something like the homosexual demimonde: the gay scene or subculture.[2] But this way of speaking, directly, about the sexual milieu obscures important parts of the term's conceptual domain, I suggest, and at any rate scarcely exhausts the term's meanings, which are anything but direct.

No one seems to know how long "ambiente" has been used this way, but this usage certainly predates dissemination of the term "gay," which was not widely circulated in Mexico until after the mid-1970s according to Stephen Murray and Manuel Arboleda,[3] arriving with the Village People according to Jorge. One aging, insiderly source speculated that it was Carlos Monsiváis who originated the term during the cultural surges and upheavals of the 1960s. (Monsiváis was involved from the start in Mexico's gay liberation movement.) This seems doubtful. Monsiváis himself claims that "ambiente" has been in circulation across urban Latin America since the 1930s as an adaptation of the anglophone term "gay."[4] The writer is evasive about his sources, and I am skeptical of his suggestion that the term originated as a translation of "gay." However, I am willing to believe that the term's designation of a sexual underground dates to the early years of the twentieth century, a time of urban expansion and waxing cosmopolitanism in places like Mexico City.

We might take cues from some of the term's ancillary uses. Women prostitutes also sometimes use the same word in the same tone today to refer to the milieu of sex work: the brothel is an ambiente, certain streets are the ambiente.[5] In this sense, the term "ambiente" refers to something not quite aboveboard, a disreputable place or activity, a scene hedged by euphemism and misdirection.

"Gay" has a similar semantic history, at least up to a point.

From its first appearances in English, the term denoted noble, colorful, happy, and excellent. But there was already something happening with the adjective's connotations in the early modern period when it appeared in such combinations as "gay lothario," "gay dog," or "gay abandon." By the nineteenth century, as Howard Richler explains, the modifier "was sometimes applied to a woman deemed to lead an immoral life, such as a prostitute." Around the same time, the term began to populate other sexual scenes. "Hugh Rawson reports in *Wicked Words*," Richler continues, "that in 1889 during 'the Cleveland Street Scandal (involving post office boys in a male brothel in London's West End), a prostitute named John Saul used gay with reference to both male homosexuals and to female prostitutes when giving evidence to the police and in court.' . . . By the turn of the twentieth century, [the] term 'gay cat' was used by hobos to refer to a tramp's companion, usually a young boy, and often his catamite." The word was also used by American ex-patriates in Paris in the 1920s. In one of her plays, Gertrude Stein repeatedly referred to a female same-sex couple as being gay; this was in 1922.[6] Cary Grant used the phrase "gone gay" in the 1938 film *Bringing Up Baby*, an insider reference most viewers would not have understood. Of course, in wider society, the term continued to mean "merry," "happy," and "festive." Its use, in a certain kind of way, with a certain intonation, allowed speakers to communicate with others who were in the know without being overheard to say "homosexual" by nongay listeners. "Gay," like "ambiente," turned on equivocation and misdirection.

An abrupt semantic shift occurred in the 1960s, when a new generation of activists began using the street-savvy term "gay" in preference to off-putting clinical terms like "homophile" or "homosexual." By 1968, Frank Kameny put forward the slogan "Gay is good" after hearing Stokely Carmichael chant "Black is beautiful." In 1969, in the wake of the Stonewall Riots, New York activists founded the Gay Liberation Front; in 1970 Carl Wittman published *A Gay Manifesto*; and so on. These developments mark a turning point. If the term "gay" had originally equivocated, paying deference to intolerance as the price of entry into the subculture, its new politicized use signified the public embrace of a positive identity. As though to underscore the semantic shift, the early broadsides of the period carefully instructed gay readers, as against their own retrograde gay conventions, on how to properly inhabit this new, politicized gayness.[7]

Leningrad, 1930: Words, Valentin Vološinov teaches us, participate in the continuous stream of verbal intercourse, which is in turn party to historical happenings without which words could have no meaning. Intonation, accent, direct and indirect quotation: these are all elements of this participation.[8]

The milieu, the present: Across Mexico, the older term "ambiente" has been joined by the newer word "gay." Up until now, I have been using the two words more or less synonymously. Now I take a different tack. I want to describe some of the ways the two terms designate overlapping but analytically distinct domains, how they parse time and space, and how they track fault lines—warps and kinks in the conceptual here and now.

Today, Mexican (and other Latin American) speakers have two ways of posing the question to you. If they ask you, "¿Eres gay?" they are asking for clarity about your identity. It is a question that presupposes a globalized classificatory apparatus, and you don't have to be gay to understand what is being asked. However, if they ask you, "¿Eres de ambiente?" they have asked something different. Such phrasing of the question still pays tribute to intolerance: the question is rather like the dated English query "Are you in the life?" I stress something that is not always understood here. The latter interrogative makes fewer presuppositions about identity than the former: it is not asking you for your identification papers. It asks instead whether you have fellowship with an amorphous "us." People who might be of (or at least in) the ambiente include putos and gays, of course, and all the varieties of *jotos* and *maricones* implied therein (there are various ways of marking stereotypical effeminacy), but also *mayates* and *chichifos* (straight-identified hustlers), *chacales* (lower-class sexual opportunists who more than likely would not identify as gay), lesbians in all their varieties, drag queens, trans women, bisexuals, and an assortment of fellow travelers and participants who are involved but undeclared. The term works off ambiguity, not clarity, and takes this ambiguity as its enabling condition. It also continues, even now, to function as a secret key to a hidden door: if you are not *of* the ambiente, you probably will not understand the question, and the questioner will not have revealed himself to you.

Lumpers and splitters: If we lump categories, we might say that the ambiente is just another name for amorphous, plural gay scenes. The word "gay," after all, historically traded in broad associations with prostitution, frivolity, and promiscuity; it once functioned as an *avoidance* of dangerous words like "homosexual" or "queer." If we split terms, we might say that the singular gay scene is the ambiente submitted to certain modern, globalized modes of formalization and rationalization, especially the injunction to declare an identity and to take pride in it.

Anachronism: Some might think of the word "ambiente" as an anachronism. No doubt the term marks its user as a tad old-fashioned. It trades in euphemism and indirection, which are products of repression, at a time of open declarations and pride. But, notwithstanding the advent of globalized gay modernity, rainbow flags blazing, the conceptual domain it encompasses continues to have a vital existence. The ambiente exists everywhere something like gay life exceeds the boundaries of formalized gay institutions and identities. The term, then, also signifies something like a real-world and practical alternative to the reified identities and rigid classificatory schemes of modern sexualities. If "gay" is bright modernity, bathed in light and transparency, the ambiente is dark modernity—an opaque, alternative sexual modernity, if you will, no less modern than the hegemonic version but caught up in distinctions that render it by definition "premodern." (Modern and archaic are distinctions internal to modernity, not external to it.)

Might the scene it describes also have a certain class character?

Practices of space: Jorge expresses impatience with the need to label everything and everyone. He doesn't care whether the men he blows identify as "gay" or "straight" or something else altogether.

He waxes nostalgic about the plural sexual scenes in existence in the 1970s and 1980s, naming a dozen or so bars that catered to different tastes and sectors in Mexico City, then mapping an expansive underground scene in Puebla, places where one might reliably cruise, hook up, have sex, or establish connections. These included an abundance of cantinas (women were not allowed entry but drag queens were); a string of working-class dive bars (some of which still exist) where *bugas* (straight men) might be picked up without much effort; a number of bathhouses of the sort that have existed in Mexican cities since the colonial era (these were de ambiente especially at certain times of day); certain public restrooms and parks (especially at certain hours); darkened balconies and standing bars at the back of generic movie theaters (where oral sex was common); and the local Sanborns (a drugstore diner where discreet hookups occurred and where groups of men who were de ambiente met for weekend lunches or dinners). All of this existed, in more or less stable institutionalized form, long before the word "gay" had entered the lexicon. (I am using the word "institution" here in its strictest sense: a relatively stable pattern of collective activity involving rules, values, roles.)

This expansive scene vastly exceeded the "private parties" and closed networks that often appear in the gay studies literature to describe "pregay" scenes.[9] In fact, by Jorge's count there were many more informally designated places for men to meet other men in the past than there are formally designated gay places in the present. The ambiente's wide, flexible map approximated what Gordon Brent Ingram glosses a "queerscape," a subcultural landscape redefined by plural, private, and formally prohibited uses of public and semipublic spaces.[10] This was an interlocking system of winks and nods and bribes, an admixture of public censure and private tolerance. It carved up the formal map of the city into greater or lesser islands of freedom, calibrated according to rhythms of the day and week—this cinema balcony on certain weeknights, that park during late afternoons, these cantinas on weekends. The point of keeping things in motion was to stay a step ahead of the authorities, who might police this cruising area while leaving that one unobserved. The object was to avoid calling too much attention to any particular site lest the authorities undertake a limpieza.

Almost all of these floating scenes had a certain affinity with lower-classness; that is, they were outside the zones of middle-class respectability. Or, alternatively, they translated zones that were respectable during business hours into afterhours places of lowlife pursuits.

Jet lag: It is easy to lose track of time in narrating these landscapes. I describe Jorge's mapping to a younger gay man, contrasting the past sites he recounted with the gay bars and gay bathhouses of the present. "But Róger," the young man says, unimpressed, "these things all still exist today." He then begins to name a series of parks, plazas, public toilets, and (nongay, "traditional") bathhouses where gay life goes on outside the boundaries of gay identity.

Zona Rosa, 1969: Although Monsiváis never openly declared himself, it was never a secret that he was gay. He had even scored an early public reference in *Modisto de Señoras* (*Ladies' Fashion Designer*), the 1969 Mexican spoof that had somehow evaded censorship and anticipated a subplot in Hollywood's *Shampoo* (1975). In it, D'Maurice, Mexico's most successful fashion designer, played by Mauricio Garcés, pretends to be homosexual because it's good for business—and because it provides the perfect cover for seductions of rich clients' beautiful wives. Although no one in the film ever uses the terms "gay" or "de ambiente," the movie's protagonist name-checks personages and places in Mexico City's sexual underground in camp witticisms and inside jokes: "My spots are written by Monsiváis," he crisply quips to a reporter, using "spots" in English, "and my boutique is the Zona Rosa's tattoo parlor." (The reference would have escaped most of the viewing public at the time. Although he had worked as an editor and had held important fellowships, Monsiváis published his first essays in 1969.)

Apotheosis, 1990: Juan Gabriel had two popular nicknames—Juanga, a contraction of his stage name (which always sounds to my ears like a drag name), and El Divo de Juárez, a masculinized version of *diva*. He performed in a variety of popular music genres, including ranchera, mariachi, ballad, pop. And as his fame grew, so did his flamboyance.

In 1990, El Divo performed at the Palacio de Bellas Artes—the first-ever nonclassical performance there: a fund raiser for the strapped museum, slated over the objections of the high-art crowd and homophobic critics. Carlos Monsiváis reviewed the concert, describing it as an "apotheosis," an all-people's triumph over elite taste and narrow opinion:

> Juan Gabriel is the literal vindication of all that is expelled from the television canon or what is never included there: the *nacos* [tasteless lower-class people] and the *traileros* [truck drivers] and the romantic secretaries and the homeless housewives-in-waiting and the "*raritos*" [queers] and the teenagers from the slums. . . . At the center of his success is Juan Gabriel's voice: soft, bellicose, impossible to assimilate according to the vocal orthodoxy, dreamy, emphatic; something that comes from pilgrimages of desire and an eagerness to undertake them, and of sentimental transformations of the province, which are the negation of modernity in the middle of the endless trip to Los Angeles. And this, above all, comes from a coarse insolence that is impossible to conceal and the desire to star in a marginal aesthetics, without any theory or critical reasoning. *I am what I am / and what I am*

needs no excuses. [Monsiváis writes this couplet in English. It is drawn from Gloria Gaynor's single "I Am What I Am," a song from the Broadway musical version of *La Cage aux Folles*, which had had its first run in the mid-1980s.]

In his review, Monsiváis evokes the perpetual scene from Gabriel's concerts, a ritual, hysterical "unlocking" of the "homosexual nucleus" that lies just under the surface of everyday life:

One of the climatic moments of his performances occurs during a ranchera song, when he asks, "Who wants to marry me?" And the answer is predominantly or almost exclusively masculine. And the cockfighting enthusiasts, the mayors, the heads of the press, the fearsome beings to whom are attributed complicity with the local authorities (new definition of narcos), the braggart machos, all rise up and howl with the selfsame sincerity of those who stage the prohibition: "I do, Juanga! Juan Gabriel, you are the only one! Look at me! Here I am, look at me!" . . . And Juan Gabriel, indifferent and pleased, knows in advance the submissive answer to his provocations, that whatever they say will be verbal incense. *Life is a sham / Till I can shout / Hey world! I am what I am.* [Again, here the writer makes recourse in English to the gay anthem.][11]

Juanga never openly declared his homosexuality, but others did so for him, especially in the wake of various scandals, revelations, and extortion attempts. His fans took it all in stride. His late-in-life response to a cloddish journalist who asked him to declare at last his sexuality—was he gay? bisexual? transgender? what?—was evasive but also clear: "What can be seen need not be questioned, my son." In the end, Monsiváis gave more public clarity. The coffin at his 2010 lying-in-state at the Palacio de Bellas Artes was covered by three flags, as tidy as a giftwrapped box: the Mexican national flag, the National University's coat of arms, and across the middle, the gay pride rainbow flag.

Lo popular: The ambiente was produced and reproduced within a zone of strategic silences. It still is. It also has a certain resonance with *lo popular* (the popular, pertaining to the popular classes), and thus with kitsch and lower-class taste, despite the brutal forms sometimes taken by homophobia in *barriadas* (slums) and pueblos. These are paradoxes. Paradoxes contain robust truths, thicker and more entangled than logical propositions. A vibrant scene lurked and continues to lurk just under the radar of respectable society. It nestles in low places, in the lacunae of working-class existence, and in interstitial contact zones where the classes scandalously mix and socialize.

The Mexican lower classes, even the homophobes there, found their voice in a gaudy, obvious, flamboyant singer who admitted nothing and concealed nothing and whose music spoke to them in a language they understood of their own loneliness, marginality, and aspirations.

"Play that record by my *putón novio*," by my big queer boyfriend, was how one subject's homophobic father used to ask his mother to play Juan Gabriel.

More definitions: "Modernity," Anthony Giddens tells us, is about the disembedding and stretching of social relations across time and space. It is "globalizing" from the start. It also involves the Enlightenment idea of a "break with tradition."[12] This break crucially turns on a certain trajectory of selfhood. The self becomes a reflexive project, something that one works on, in dialogue with time, subject to a narrative of self-identity. Above all, in "taking charge of one's life," one must "be true to oneself." It will be obvious that gay self-determination is an exemplary subset of these ideas and practices. No doubt some are dealt a better hand than others in this quest for authenticity. But even the most impoverished and underprivileged today live in a world saturated by the institutions of modernity.[13] Schools, novels, TV shows, pop music, websites, and the buzz in the air all, all call on us to know ourselves, to actualize ourselves, to be what we are, with whatever resources we have.

Time out of joint: "Modern" and "modernity" are ambiguous, troubled terms. Historians and philosophers have wrangled over how to use these words and how to periodize the timespans they purport to describe. Many anthropologists have argued against their use altogether, seeing how they appear to relegate the discipline's subjects to a time of the past.[14] No doubt they do just that. Time runs amok in both scholarly and vernacular narratives.

Typologies: Thirty-five years ago, I described popular-class sexual ideas and practices in Nicaragua and other parts of Latin America as "traditional," the better to understand how they did not conform to the "modern" medical model of homosexuality—which, I made clear, had become the norm for educated and internationally connected middle-class sectors.[15] The basic picture I drew of active and passive roles—with the anally receptive partner in same-sex relationships taking on a stigmatized identity and the phallically active partner largely escaping both stigma and identity—was reproduced by studies in many sites across Latin/Latino America.[16] But, no doubt, my temporalizing dichotomy was awkward, and I had offered an old-fashioned typology at a time when these were increasingly viewed as suspect: to typologize is to dehistoricize, to make one's subjects or their cultures into fast-frozen objects.[17]

Daguerreotype or no, thirty-five years have now passed. History has moved on, the internet happened, everyone has seen *Will and Grace*, and educators and activists have intensified the development of cosmopolitan ideas about sexuality everywhere. Active-passive roles no longer organize clear-cut identities in the sexual imaginaries of most young people in Latin America, even in most working-class settings.

Global sex: Then, later, Dennis Altman used the terms "modern" and "modernity" in connection with evolving sexual scenes across Asia and the global south, lucidly describing the international spread of rainbow-flag-adorned gay bars, rituals of self-disclosure, and core meanings (a man who has sex with other men is a homosexual), which he opposed to variegated "traditional" sexual understandings and subcultures (under whose definitions a man who has sex with other men might or might not have a special identity, depending on role or circumstances).[18] Perhaps the most rigorous criticism of Altman's work on sexualities in globalization is that he took it as self-evident that "modern" meant "Western" (or North Atlantic) and "globalization" meant the spread of Western (or Northern) models of sexuality.[19] The view of evolving sexual scenes is different if we see "modernity" everywhere and understand "globalization" as a two-way street.

But it seems to me that, for the most part, Altman's critics cobbled together hasty responses, as though they couldn't get away fast enough from the implications of inequality and hierarchy contained in the time-lagged paradigm, which they read as negating the creativity and agency of sexual subjects in the global south. In their zeal for celebrating creativity, agency, and diversity, the critics did not always dig very deeply into real-world subjects' understandings of changing subcultures, nor did they think out whether the conceptual inequalities marked in everyday discourse (and in academic models) map onto real material conditions. Precisely what went missing, then, was an accounting for what constrains the agency and creativity of working- and lower-middle-class people across the global south: class dynamics propelled by the uneven development of capitalism on a planetary scale. One influential writer even suggested that Altman and others "unwittingly posit a white gay male gaze" when they describe unequally weighted global forces (which, on a skeptical reading, seems tantamount to dismissing political-economic approaches, tout court).[20]

In actual practice, many of his critics ended up more or less back where Altman started, trying to work out the interplay of continuities and disjunctures in the dense mix of old and new sexual understandings, received and imported notions, local and global identities.[21]

Ethnographic verisimilitude: I use the terms "modern" and "modernity" because they loom so large in Mexican discourses about Mexican experiences, often in the crudest of ways.[22]

Elusive modernity: Octavio Paz mapped the conceptual terrain in 1950 in *Labyrinth of Solitude*.[23] In a series of reflections on (and myth makings about) Mexican identity, Paz sketched some of the ways that a longed-for sense of modernity eludes Mexicans, leaving them alone and trapped in the past. The critical reader might be reflexively suspicious: Paz was one of those revolutionaries who became a domesticated intellectual, arguably a part of the establishment. Perhaps. But Paz's ruminations resonated (and continue to resonate) to broad themes in Mexican culture.

The theft of modernity: A basic storyline about elusive modernity is second nature to broad Mexican publics. It goes like this: Cosmopolitan modernity was born in the Spanish Conquest, then transferred along with the loot to the cities of Europe. Although it flickered insistently among local elites in rich colonial enclaves such as Puebla de los Ángeles (which were globally connected not only to Europe but also to China and India by way of the Philippines, Spain's farthest colonial outpost), it was withheld from the vast majority, the descendants of Mesoamerican civilization, who could participate in transoceanic culture only in indirect, frustrated, or debased ways—and who today see themselves as living in a different modality of time, a time lag, even if they also know fully well that it is really the same time everywhere.

This strange and contradictory bundle of ideas, derived from class formations in the colonial world's extraction economies and reproduced (with modifications) under changing regimes of capital accumulation, continues to shape how Mexicans view themselves in relation to the Colossus of the North. The United States has science, technology, special effects, individual freedom; Mexico has tradition, culture, cuisine, family. North Americans own the future, Mesoamericans the past.[24] And these notions of time out of joint continue to replicate themselves in class schema, ethnic distinctions, and sexual categories, as I have been showing over the course of stories, notes, and observations.

The endless quest: These themes were taken up repeatedly in the prolific writings of that most Mexican of authors, Carlos Monsiváis, who, with an admixture of biting irony and deep affection, contemplated his compatriots' melancholy longing to be "contemporary with all men," to participate in the world culture of the time. Here, Monsiváis reflects on how globalization and modernization are assimilated at local sites. (He casts a withering glance at the knots intellectuals tie themselves up in when they advocate for "premodern" authentic identities.)

> An extraordinary photograph by Graciela Iturbide synthesizes the process: A Tarahumara Indian, showing her back to the camera, climbs up a mountain as she carries in her hand the equipment that will neutralize or defeat solitude: a gigantic radio. The defenders of indigenous identity will censor her for her predilection, but they are not there in the sierra to alleviate the immense monotony. For reasons similar to those of the Tarahumara woman, the youth of ethnic groups abandon their typical dress and urban adolescents adopt punk clothing. The communities remain, affected by or benefitting from (according to who is judging) the need to come closer to the nuclei of modernity, and everything continues to be the same except that it is very different.[25]

Monsiváis tracks this endless quest for modernity—ultimately, people's aspirations for products and freedoms to which they have little or no access, which implies the perpetual posing of the question: "How contemporary am I?"—in a long succession of Mexican youth subcultures: rockers, hippies, punks, goths. "They know that if they are not modern, they will be nothing in their own eyes."[26]

Nuclei: Among the elusive "nuclei of modernity," for some of us, is an elaborate package of ideas and practices associated with gayness—its contemporary version, not its historic version, if you will. The idea at the core of coming out—the notion that we, each of us, ought to align and organize our lives in the light of our desires, and thus must learn to understand and accept our innermost authentic longings—is a relatively recent one, though the picture of the sovereign self-making human being on which it leans is implicit in a long history of the liberal subject whose coming-into-existence defines the experience of modernity. It depends not only on the idea of an autonomous personal life—a space of inalienable self-ownership within which we might pursue our own authentic aims relatively free of interference by the state, kinfolk, or other institutional actors—but also on the preexistence of a cultural apparatus, a set of signs and meanings that defines men, sexual attraction, sameness, and so on.

(I do not want to ignore the latter, "anthropological" element here. Some variants of the ambiente expressly deny this sameness, to some degree or another. Active-passive dualisms still shape perceptions, especially in settings that presuppose the exchange of money: the penetrating, "active" party is not understood to be of the same sexual substance as the penetrated, "passive" party; only the latter is understood to be thoroughly gay, puto, or the like. One still sometimes encounters this idea even at the core of urban, gay settings: "I'm not gay, I'm active"; or, more frequently, "I'm not *completely* gay because I've never been fucked." But these notions today sound quaint, even when uttered by earnest twenty-year-olds, because they are no longer hegemonic: they are residual, not dominant ideas.)

We have always been modern: Men have always found ways to connect with other men, at least under conditions of city life, with its anonymous places out of view of kith, kin, and community. We might be tempted to call these ways of connecting "traditional" or "premodern," but in view of their placement in the currents of urbanization and global connection, the better move would be to call these scenes Modernity 1.0. This was the domain of the ambiente. What was new about the emergence of an explicitly gay scene, organized under rainbow flags (Modernity 2.0), was that furtive cruising had come out of remote unlit parks and seedy cantinas (where it was often framed by elaborate pretexts or drunken alibis) and planted itself, more or less openly, in zones of middle-class respectability (the centro). Gayness is a heroic narrative, a commitment to a coherent storyline, a taking possession of oneself in one's own interests, a refusal to go on living in the shadows: *Your life is a sham 'til you can shout out / I am what I am.* This precise move, this uncoordinated yet concerted claim on public space and personal dignity, could only have occurred under certain conditions—foremost among them, political and economic liberalization.

But as against the notion that one can cross the Rubicon only once, I suggest instead that one crisscrosses it all the time.

Time, gender, class: The gay scene was planted in the ambiente, which continues to exist all around it. The former did not displace or supplant the latter; rather, it established hegemony over the wider terrain. The result is less a hybridization or syncretism, a homogenized blending of all the pregiven and imported elements, than an uneven and irregular landscape mapped along irregular grids and graticules. Built into this social landscape are certain understandings of time, gender, and above all class, understandings that grade and sort participants: How close is one's position to imagined nuclei of modernity? Where does one align on a spectrum of masculine to feminine stereotypes? Has one the economic power to assert a truly independent life?

Sexual geographies, 2022: Distinct cultural and regional variations come into view if one travels outside the urban core. The cowboys of Chipilo, descended from Italian immigrants, are said to view homosexual relations as one of the benefits of friendship. They sometimes undertake trips to the city in search of new friends. They do not think of themselves as gay, or as anything special for that matter; they are, however, part of the ambiente. The famous gender-crossed *muxes* from the Isthmus of Tehuantepec are de ambiente, part of the world of sexual and gender diversity. Indeed, a complete accounting of sexual diversity among Mexico's indigenous groups would be an encyclopedic undertaking. "AC/DC no importa a los Zapotecos" (AC/DC doesn't matter to Zapotecs). I overheard this line at the coffeehouse table next to me in Oaxaca. The speaker, a Zapotec man, was chatting up a strikingly handsome French bohemian, who seemed to be reluctant to sleep with a married man; the suitor expressed an indigenous cosmopolitan theory of modern sexualities in transnational terms.

Across undulating sexual geographies, as broken up as any map of Mexico, there are tangles of local storylines here, dense knots of activities there, condensations of desirings and dreamings spelled out in different idioms and vernaculars.

Tensions: Now, I am not the first to describe the coexistence of multiple sexual imaginaries, or the first to show how these are organized in people's everyday consciousness in terms of binary oppositions involving the concept of modernity. In describing how received concepts and practices commingle and clash with newer ones, I partly retrace moves made by Héctor Carrillo in his lucid and detailed treatment of gay life in Guadalajara. One could scarcely read *The Night Is Young* without learning a great deal about the placement of sexuality in Mexican history and society.[27] But I take a different tack, starting with the salience of social class in the organization of sexual geographies. And I underscore certain persistent tensions in the stretchings-out of social relations across conceptual time and space. My working-class subjects do not tell cheery stories about seamless, fluid navigation across this variegated landscape, and I am not trying to tell a story of happy-go-lucky hybridity. Putos, who aspire to gayness but are denied entry, are perpetually thrown back into the wider ambiente, whose pleasures they typically view as a sort of consolation prize. At the risk of being reductive, we might say that "gay" is a prominent class formation in the world in the evening. Or, to better frame it, we might say that it is a way of dreaming, of trying to align oneself with the kind of economic clout that might underwrite a dignified life, a sort of "imagined cosmopolitanism," to finally use Louisa Schein's unavoidable term.[28]

Citizenship in the gay world has its advantages, and people seek them out. The flexibility of the ambiente also has its rewards, which people also seek out.

Excursions: Some crisscross this terrain on pilgrimages and tours and day trips. Héctor, for instance, goes to gay bars and nightclubs in the evening, where he socializes and gossips with gay friends and affects the signs of middle-classness. He cruises nongay, working-class bathhouses and other places in the afternoons, where he seeks the straight-identifying chacal who will be his lover or husband. His circuits are not terribly unusual, nor are his desirings.

Queer? Some might want to translate ambiente as "queer." The way Mexicans use the word "ambiente" does bear some resemblance to the way North Americans began using the word queer after the 1980s: both terms evade the specificity of spelling out L-G-B-T. But whereas North American activists repurposed a word redolent with stigma, the word "ambiente" is about atmospherics: it floats above both identities and stigmas. Whereas "queer" is already an in-your-face, militant word, "ambiente" is softer, more pleasing, and quite decidedly apolitical: it benevolently encompasses varied scenes; it subtends the marvels of an ecosystem. And whereas "queer" strikes a lumpen or downscale pose, relishing the frisson of transgression, its true history derives from the desires of urban, educated, upper-middle-class people to put some distance between themselves and other (lower-middle- and working-class) sectors, which had by this time embraced the term "gay." The ambiente, by contrast, is unavoidably associated with the popular classes, with unlit, unfashionable places, with practical solutions to the urgency of desire.

Revolving door: I come back to overlapping and nonreciprocal framings. Perhaps the ambiente might be not only a token of the past but a harbinger of the future. After all, the stable middle-classness to which gayness aspires seems to be an increasingly elusive thing; more and more people experience economic precarity or are downwardly mobile. Or maybe the ambiente is a resigned portion of everyone's life: what is left over when we lose faith in heroic self-narration and accept the limitations of our placement in the material world. It is there, always, in the circular movement of our lives, to be entered and exited (to borrow Nestor García Canclini's turn of phrase) the way we might crisscross the threshold of modernity.[29] In any case, the ambiente can be experienced only as a fallen world.

Oaxaca, 2015: It is sometimes easy to lose track of gradation and ranking in this circular motion between a beautiful fallen world and an imagined middle-class scene. Some of the muxes with whom I've spoken move, mostly without contradiction, across such conceptual platforms as "gay," "de ambiente," "queer," or "transgender" and are world-savvy connoisseurs of transcultural traditions of drag and camp. At least one puts on her men's clothes and poses as a *cholo*—a lower-class street tough—when she cruises Oaxaca's zócalo. It was in such impressively butch form that I met her one evening, and we talked for several hours in deep conversation about the ambiguities of identities and the kinky trajectories of desire.

Ambiente and ambiguity: I am aware of the precariousness of some of my claims here, how they might seem to set back the clock on studies of sexual cultures. Academics, activists, and social workers today tend to belabor airtight distinctions among concepts such as "gay," "bisexual," "straight," "drag," "transgenderism," and the like, even if they give lip service to the umbrella of queerness. There are good reasons to make such distinctions, but they have not always been apparent to inhabitants of gay scenes (and were not rigidly elaborated in early classics of gay studies). The difference between drag queens and trans women, for instance, was not so clearly marked in the gay bars of my youth, and David Valentine suggests how much work it takes to maintain distinctions today: social workers in New York strive to "correct" transgender youth who identity as gay—as though they were casting their vote in the wrong ballot box.[30] As against this approach, which constructs classificatory schemes in order to produce finely delineated political or social subjects fit for modern identity politics, it seems worthwhile to reiterate that the ambiente—which is an environment or ecosystem, after all—hosts different forms of life, varied ways of being, that are bound together not by identity but by modalities of interest and different sorts of fellow feeling.

Marked and unmarked: This demimonde the ambiente, where no one has to explain himself and no one checks ID papers at the door, has no fixed address. I find myself thinking with it, using it as a conceptual placeholder—and I sometimes think it has sprawled across unanticipated landscapes, creeping across the borders of place and time and stealing into my memories. Certain American discotheques of the 1970s, for instance, now seem to me like the ambiente: they were ambiguous, sexually charged, and perhaps a tad dangerous. No doubt this conceptual domain is an imaginary place, a fever dream, an idea that beckons us—not only Mexicans but all of us who now encounter the concept. Or could it be that it is actually more real than our reified city districts, with their rectilinear streets, unambiguous signposts, and clearly posted neighborhoods?

Critique: Sometimes, the view from other scenes gives us leverage for thinking critically about durable analytical problems, especially if we remember that far-flung social formations and the conceptual oppositions they produce are interconnected in the long history of the world system. In that spirit, I venture a few propositions:

Getting subcultures right: What British cultural studies misunderstood about subcultures in the 1970s was amplified by American queer theory in the 1990s, leaving us with poor conceptual models almost everywhere.[31] The tendency has been to think about subcultures, especially sexual subcultures, as sites of rebellion, resistance, nonconformity: spaces where identities proclaim their radicalism through forms of consumption and rituals of resistance. This approach gets almost everything wrong. Subcultures are first and foremost zones of sociability, places where human beings seek connection, not sites of resistance or subversion. They are creative social spaces where people try to make lives with one another, often in ways that are forbidden or are not readily accommodated by the usual institutions (family, kinship, school, and the like). But they are more about getting laid (or getting high or having a good time) than about making a statement or staging a politics. They can be mobilized for political purposes, of course, and some do morph into subcultures of rebellion for a time. But this is not their default mode.

Getting identities right: The idea that identity is essentially about negation and that communities coalesce around defiance was for a long time the crack cocaine of academics who desperately wanted to believe that their writing about these subjects, their critiques of the norms that subcultures supposedly resist, represented "interventions" of some sort in the social world. This illusion led the theorists to experience great puzzlement over what it turned out that gay men and lesbians, or at least large numbers of them, really wanted: supposedly conservative things like dignity, respect, acceptance, marriage, kinship, stable connections, middle-classness—desires that cut against the existential outlaw queer version of identity that the theorists had imaginatively fashioned, often in the name of a heroic presentism. This way of thinking about identity has not quite died with queer theory, which, according to Michael Warner, officially gave up the ghost sometime in the 2000s.[32] It comes down to us today as what socialist critics call "left-identitarianism," a form of expressive politics that actually has little to do with the communities it purports to represent but that thrives on grandstanding and declamations in their names. There's no joy there, in language policing and online call-out culture, but only acrimony and recrimination. Like the worst apparatchiks and hacks of the Stalinoid Old Left, we spend most of our time sniffing out deviations from a shifting party line—except that today, there is no party (which, even in its most devolved form, still won real gains for the working class), but only a shifting cast of academic and online activist opinion-makers. We are all but one misstep away from being purged and shunned, and so we wear our grievances on our sleeve and redouble our efforts at purging and shunning others. Just as one once encountered everywhere the word "power" but nowhere the word "love," today one encounters accusations and ultimatums everywhere but little generosity anywhere—and almost nothing in the way of realizable demands that might actually make our lives freer, easier, better, happier.

Postqueer: And so we postqueers could take a page from old-school zones of toleration, from the sensibility of the ambiente. Not everything is political, and we should not strive to make every question a litmus test. But I will not tie myself up in knots advocating for the "premodern" version of subculture, or doing battle with the postmodern version of identity. I offer instead two cheers for the middle term, "modern gayness," which affords aspirants a sense of dignity and self-possession. It makes politics possible. For all its consumerist entanglements, it makes demands on society for respect and on the state for rights. It confronts stigma and attempts to transcend it. Its imagined future is a *happy* one, not a make-do or get-by one, not fleeting moments snatched from a reluctant world.

The persistence of tactics: The ambiente, however, cannot be banished or swept away, for aspirants to this gayness are often frustrated—frustrated by their real class positions, their lack of resources, by racisms and intolerances on the gay scene; that is, by the elusiveness of the very thing that they seek. Even those closest in class position and purchasing power to the nuclei of modernity might come to feel left out: "It's stressful being gay," an educated, middle-class professional just into his thirties told me. "You have to dress *de moda* [fashionably], you have to go out to the *right* bars, you have to work out and keep a tight stomach. And don't gain a kilo [2 pounds] in the wrong place!" The ambiente today exists in relation to such frustrations. It takes in all those tactics past and present that attempt to experience gaiety in the here-and-now by *evading* identity, stigma, detection, and regulation but also self-regulation, conspicuous consumption, displays of middle-classness.

And even if you don't have the 100-peso cover for entry into the club, and even if you are not, strictly speaking, "one of us," you can make merry with us on the sidewalks, there, on the geographic or conceptual fringes of the gay scene.

11 Urban Tribes

Flashback, 2008: Mexican cities were roiled when punks, goths, metalheads, *darketos* (devotees of the night or the dark side), and assorted urban tribes attacked the newest rock subculture, the *emos*. The young, willowy, androgynous emos—short for *emotivos*, emotionals—were defined by a long fleck of hair over one eye, an enthusiasm for anime and manga, and emotional expressiveness, though in practice they seemed to register sullenness more consistently than any other feeling.

Perhaps it was their devotion to nonviolence and pacifism that made them inviting targets for pent-up frustration and indiscriminate rage. Or maybe it was their supposed middle-class status that drew the ire of other subcultures. Class inflects every imagined community, and rock subcultures were based primarily in working-class slums. Subcultural practices tended to ossify participants' subproletarian standing: members of some tribes were committed to programs of piercing, tattooing, and body modification so extreme that no matter what their class origins, they no longer had the option of a normal workaday life and could subsist only in a shadowy world as ambulatory vendors, selling candy, trinkets, or drugs in the streets. Emos, by contrast, were at least presentable in public and were *said* to be from respectable, middle-class families. Some were, but my queries with them usually turned up mundane working- or lower-middle-class origins. Of course, social standing is always relative, and the emos' reliance on police protection in the riots further inflamed groups accustomed to being harassed by the police.[1]

After the first riot in Querétaro, social media—YouTube, other websites—crackled with anti-emo messages and calls for their murder. Goths said that they attacked emos because the latter had stolen elements of the formers' style. Metalheads and others called the emos maricones (faggots), and there can be no doubt that homophobia played a key role in the swirling street violence. The "Movimiento Anti Emosexual" ("*emo*sexual" plays off "*homo*sexual") posted expressly homophobic messages on its website.[2] Some of the repugnance directed at the emos seemed ad hoc but expressed the seriousness with which urban tribes invested in identity. The activist, journalist, and nonacademic Mexicanist John Ross quotes a twenty-year-old punk's philosophical revulsion: "The emos don't stand for anything. They don't have a philosophy or an ideology. They are not a tribe—they're just a style." And then this: "Actually, I think the emos want to be beat up."[3] Perhaps. But a fleck-haired, black-clad acquaintance at Luciérnaga pulled a knife out of his pocket to show me and said, "I'm a pacifist but I believe in self-defense. If they come after me or my friends, I'm going to cut them."

I asked Francisco—a darketo whose tattoos and piercings had spread like kudzu vines across the visible surfaces of his body and whose investment in the accoutrements of identity had recently culminated in a pair of horns at the top of his forehead—whether he had participated in the communal violence. "No man, I don't hate nobody," he told me. The fear-inspiring darketos, it turns out, played a key role in lowering the rhetoric and reducing tensions among the urban tribes.

The violence passed in a few days, lasting long enough to make international news before a peace treaty was hammered out. Savvy commentators referenced 1960s conflicts between Mods and Rockers in the United Kingdom, or Hell's Angels and hippies in the United States—or even similar events playing out in the postindustrial US Midwest at the same time. Mexican journalists took the opportunity to explore ancillary themes: youth violence, homophobia, bullying (an English word that was then entering into Spanish), depression, cutting, anorexia, suicide . . .

But more than opening a window onto given themes, events demand a recap of historical developments. In the 1950s and 1960s, youth subcultures, many of them based on imported rock genres closely connected with the United States, proliferated in urban Mexico, capturing young people's desires for freedom and modernity, for participation in the culture of the times, of course, but also recruiting them into the culture industry's version of "youth."[4] For a good part of its history, the evolving gay scene coexisted symbiotically in this youth-oriented social landscape, one subculture among others. Urban coteries persisted, intensified, and multiplied over the long decline of the dictatorship and the transition to neoliberal democracy, much as Carlos Monsiváis foresaw when he quipped: "Will the day arrive when there are more youth subcultures than young people?"[5]

The merest of facts here challenge complacent trending narratives in the decolonial mode. The children of Mesoamerican civilization were not taking on neoindigenous identities (as Guillermo Bonfil Batalla had hoped in *México Profundo*) but instead were joining different sorts of urban tribes, often accompanied by musical soundtracks with English lyrics. Over time, subcultures marked off, populated, and struggled over the borders of an increasing number of conceptual niches.

Of course, time has continued to pass, and today, rock seems a comparatively quaint font for identity. For better or worse, reggaeton and varieties of narcoculture music, which includes mashups of trap, norteño, and other genres, have taken the place of waning rock genres and subcultures in many venues. These are arguably more "authentic" sites for experiments in identity, but also more violent.

There are many detours in the struggle for modernity, freedom, gaiety, and a rich personal life. These twists and turns might draw participants into a dark undercurrent of the dialectic. People have to invest their agency somewhere. Trapped in a stagnant economy and deprived of outlets for social or political efficacy, they absorb themselves in youth, identity, body modification, and fantastically improbable imagined communities. Deprived of purpose, the work of identity redoubles itself. What cannot develop, involutes. What cannot express itself creatively in the world turns against itself and comes to violence.

But, at the same time, even the most prefabricated of subcultures are sites of dreaming, aspiring, socializing. Youth subcultures are like toy versions of identity, if you will: toy in the sense that most people grow out of them, for the most part, but also in the sense that they model mechanisms of identity formation that are relatively transparent, so that savvy participants learn something in the process of taking on and putting off tribal costumes. And what is true of working-class desire in the gay scene (which most of us will *not* think of as a toy version of identity) is also true of straight people's dreaming in other subcultural scenes: people want what they want, not what we might wish for them to want. Beneath it all, they yearn for an escape from boredom, lack, and solitude.

And if we still believe in the eternal fecundity of the human condition, we can wonder: Might the same dark undertow take those whom it carries along to outcomes that are ultimately creative and life affirming? Might the work of identity, toy models and all, even if mediated through melodramatic plot lines, borrowed soundtracks, hackneyed clichés, and culture industry pastiche, even if piled up in incomprehensible heaps, lead subjects willy-nilly to an eventual disenchantment with the contrived and flimsy enjoyments permitted under consumer capitalism, to a tender awareness not of our uniqueness but of our universal needs and predicaments?

12 A Tale of Two Cities

The florescence of gay nightlife did not last very long. By 2011, municipal authorities in Mexico City and Puebla were shutting down gay bars and curbing the flow of LGBT people on public sidewalks. Some referred to these developments as a new limpieza. Although the bar closures and enhanced policing did resemble old-style cleanups of the past, the logics supporting the new restrictions came from opposite ends of the political spectrum and reflected new social and political-economic conditions. These events caution against a typological or categorical approach to identity formations: they remind us that sexual geographies fluctuate, that identity is a moving target. They show that what neoliberal reforms give with one hand they can take away with the other. They might make us wonder about what role, if any, old-style homophobic animus played in the unfolding of new concerns and moral panics about alcohol, sex, and minors. Not surprisingly, there was a class content to the new social hygienics.

LIMPIEZA

In Mexico City, under the center-left PRD (Partido de la Revolución Democrática), authorities began shutting down megabars in the Zona

Rosa. Diminished floor space drew diminished foot traffic, and reliable participants on the scene reported that police were harassing and even arresting sidewalk congregants and revelers on flimsy pretexts. But suppression of gay nightlife was not uniform. Smaller venues—a string of lively one-room bars—were left open. Sex clubs, bathhouses, and private sex parties continued operating as usual in other, far-flung precincts. New clusters of medium-sized bars opened, mostly on rundown streets, as gay nightlife, previously concentrated in the Zona, was channeled and dispersed into other parts of the city.

These closures came in the wake of the passage of the city's gay civil union and marriage laws, and the proximate timing is important to note. The city had recognized same-sex civil unions in 2007 and passed the marriage law at the end of 2009 to take effect in 2010, putting Mexico City near the forefront of Latin American marriage equality trends and well ahead of other Mexican states and cities. In fact, Mexico City's marriage law catalyzed changes nationwide, leading to a series of legal cases. Early on, in 2010, the Supreme Court ruled that gay marriages performed in Mexico City had legal standing across the country. In 2015, the Court ruled that state bans on same-sex marriage were unconstitutional and guaranteed gay couples the right to seek injunctions against such bans, paving the way for same-sex marriages across the country. The approach of organized gay civil society to these synchronous developments was telling. Gay NGOs, which receive their funding and thus their agendas from US foundations, spent years engaging in public campaigns and litigation for marriage equality, to be sure. Their response to events in the Zona was muted. Although some activists spoke privately with city officials or tried to mediate between the bar owners and elected politicians, activist groups staged no protests and published no broadsides on the struggles over public space.

Now, at the beginning, *very* few people took advantage of new marriage rights in Mexico City, with only a few hundred same-sex couples getting married over the first couple of years.[1] Mostly, according to local gay academic observers (some of whom were among those getting married), these were upper-middle-class professionals with property or children or both. Without property to inherit or children to benefit from custodial rights, even long-established couples from other social strata had few incentives to marry. "Why disclose yourself," an academic colleague explained, "when families and neighbors are unaccepting or unenthusiastic?" At the same time, hundreds of thousands lost access to the expansive nightlife of the Zona, which now seemed like a ghost town. As anyone could see, these were mostly younger, less affluent gays. The gain of new rights (for a few) as against the loss of public space (for many others) did not escape local observers' attention. "I'd gladly give up gay marriage," Oscar quipped, "if we could have the Zona back."

The connection between the one thing and the other was never spelled out in so many words. What seems incontrovertible is that so long as the civil union and marriage laws were kept bottled up in a legislative committee, the Zona was allowed to boom—and moving against the scene there would have invited accusations of official homophobia. (The city's head of government, Andrés Manuel López Obrador [AMLO], emphatically had *not* wanted same-sex marriage or liberalized abortion laws passed on his watch [2000–2006] as he prepared for his first presidential run in 2006.) The new civil union and marriage laws removed the presumption of homophobia and drove administrative logics toward a privatized and domesticated understanding of gay life. Under the new understanding, then, gay people, like everybody else, now had the right to marry; why would they also need to festively occupy so much public space?

The public space in question was viewed as prime real estate, and the closures were happening at a time when municipal authorities and commercial interests were attempting to upscale and gentrify the Zona. Private developers were in the process of launching new high-end housing, hotel, and commercial projects; the city, meanwhile, was promoting an anodyne profile of the Zona as a historical site for arts and literature. One expects private enterprise to do what private enterprise does, but there was something especially galling about the city's publicity campaigns. By the mid-twentieth century, the Zona had been dubbed "pink" (*rosa*) because it was neither completely "red" (for prostitution) nor "white" (for respectability) but an admixture of both. It became an important site for arts, culture, and literature precisely to the extent that it was ground zero for the development of lively bohemian and sexual subcultures from the 1950s on. The district's real historical profile, then, was more that of a *zona de tolerancia*, where laws against prostitution and norms regulating "public order" were not enforced, than that of a staid arts district. Yamil underscored his perception of the city's hypocrisy: fast-food chains, including two VIPS, which were hardly consistent with the image of an artsy district, were left open—as were table dancer clubs aimed at male heterosexual audiences.

In the escalating tensions over the use of public space, some neighborhood groups complained about noise and nuisance. They claimed, among other things, that patrons at one of the bars were having sex behind the bushes in the wee hours of the morning. The claim that this was a regular occurrence seemed implausible to anyone familiar with the scene: the bushes in question were skimpy and at the time barely knee high.

I puzzled over these developments with friends, informants, and passersby on the forlorn sidewalks of the depopulated district. Many expressed initial puzzlement: "Gays have always voted for the PRD. Why are they repressing the ambiente?" Some gestured at cozy arrangements between real estate interests and city government, the same old circuits of the same old corruption. Gay observers scoffed at city officials' sometimes-stated aims: child protection and liquor law violations. These were new concerns for Mexican governments, which had long turned a blind eye to underage drinking (to say nothing of underage working), and their implementation would reshape bars, cantinas, and nightlife in many settings. "The clubs were checking IDs at the door," noted one. "I don't see how minors were getting past security." Another said, "It's easy enough to fine establishments if they sell alcohol to minors. They'll get the message and stop doing it. But closing down *all* the large bars? It's obvious that the city has other aims in mind." One added, in response to periodic claims that the Zona had become a site for teen prostitution: "That wasn't the issue. The real issue, what the authorities were freaked out about, was gay high school kids on the sidewalks, sometimes in large numbers. But those kids came to the Zona because they wanted to, not because somebody made them. And what are you going to tell gay kids? That they can't go out and socialize in groups with their friends? That they're forbidden to use public space?"

Finally, one insisted:

> Oh, I can tell you why they repressed the scene. The PRD calls itself "revolutionary," but its leaders and elected officials come from the elites, like any other political party. They have the same outlook and sensibilities as other

elites. They looked at the Zona Rosa, and what did they see happening there? Throngs of people from different social classes were socializing together. That's not allowed in Mexico. You have to remember that we have a caste system of sorts. [This interlocutor probably references the colonial-era system of *castas*.] Throw in wide age ranges and it's doubly alarming. Why, the bad habits of the lower classes might rub off on the children of the middle class! Class mixing, not homosexuality, was the real taboo.

Some of the elements of the cleanup replicated the logic of Rudolph Giuliani's quality-of-life campaigns in New York City in the 1990s, which aimed to revitalize Times Square and close porn shops and other venues frequented by gay men. The similarity to New York City's practices was not entirely coincidental. Mexico City's center-left government had hoped to reproduce the Big Apple's crime decline, which, rightly or wrongly, was being attributed to Giuliani's innovations. It also seemed prudent for López Obrador, a leftist, to open a channel of communication with conservative Republicans in the United States. So, starting in 2002, Mexico City began paying millions of dollars to Giuliani's consulting firm to advise the government on community policing, zero tolerance law enforcement, and how to improve quality of life.[2] (The first wave of quality-of-life enforcement had begun under the prior administration of AMLO's mentor Cuauhtémoc Cárdenas, and involved the removal of hundreds of thousands of unlicensed street vendors scattered across scores of blocks in the historic center.[3])

Propositions about quality of life, of course, beg the question: Quality, defined how? For whom? My interlocutors emphasized that *their* quality of life had been adversely affected by the closures. Their views often echoed those of Lauren Berlant and Michael Warner, who wrote about the New York City cleanup and advocated for what they called "queer counterpublics." Begin with the place of the local in the wider urban ecosystem: "A district like Christopher Street [or the Zona Rosa] is not just a neighborhood affair. The local character of the neighborhood depends on the daily presence of thousands of nonresidents."[4] Gay commentators also aired sentiments similar to those expressed by Samuel R. Delany, who, reflecting on the seedy pornographic theaters that had defined Times Square before the cleanup, inverted the usual quality-of-life arguments, with their assumption of an agoraphobic heterosexual middle-class public whose members seek to avoid contact with people from other walks of life: "Given the mode of capitalism under which we live, life is at its most rewarding, productive, and pleasant when large numbers of people understand, appreciate, and seek out interclass contact and communication conducted in a mode of good will."[5] The sheer scale of foot traffic in the Zona suggests something of the importance of the site in the life of the wider city. In an essay entertaining the social benefits of tourism, with its class and status mixing in the Zona Rosa, Matthew Gutmann noted that the district's Insurgentes metro stop is among the busiest in the city, with thousands coming and going daily.[6] "The Zona," said one reveler, "belongs to everybody."

Yamil, who made frequent two-hour trips from Puebla to participate in Mexico City's nightlife, put matters succinctly, expressing something like a "right to the city"[7] for gays, lesbians, bisexuals, trans people, and LGBT youth: "The bugas [straights] have the family, church, and other public institutions. Why can't we have the Zona?" And then he added: "It's not like we were excluding anybody. You didn't have to show your gay ID when you got off the metro stop to enter the portals to the Zona. There were plenty of straight people who came with their gay friends. Everybody was welcome. Rich and poor, tourists and natives, young and old, *locas* [queens], *machos*, *travestis* [drag queens], *marimachas* [butch dykes], *mayates* [hustlers], trans women . . . Everyone was welcome."

Yamil describes a place that is understood to be "gay," but in the broadest sense of the word, a sense that overlaps with what Mexicans mean when they use the term "ambiente." Such places mix without homogenizing varied forms of sexual and gender diversity. If places like the Zona could speak, they would say: "You know who you are. You grew up alone, atomized. You were an outsider. You felt weird or rejected your whole life. Now welcome to a place that was made for you."

In Praise of Contact

Pilgrimages to cruisy sites like Greenwich Village or the Zona Rosa, then, are about sex, of course, but they are not only about sex: they are also about social intercourse. The vibrancy of life in the city, certainly the vibrancy of *gay* life in the city, depends on the existence of public spaces that throw together people from different walks of life in a field of open possibilities. Why not then plan and promote such places of "human contact," as Delany audaciously proposed: loci alternative to both the "networking" sites of economic life and the intensifying spaces of private, domestic, and family life?[8] Such spaces of contact and mixing, not the carefully curated racial-ethnic enclaves that have become the default arrangement on the Left today,[9] give an all-people's, utopian character to gay longings. We need social spaces that are for everybody.

I return to the theme of longings. I do not hastily fold these assertions into a "political" claim. Such claims have come all too easily to cultural studies scholarship, as to queer theory and its successors, which over time have essentially debased the currency of the term "political." Revelers are not engaging in politics when they make merry. They are neither lobbying nor protesting, nor are they accumulating and organizing social forces in anticipation of future collective actions that might affect the distribution of power and resources. Foremost, they are having fun. Frequently, they are trying to get laid (an important subvariant of having fun). Above all, what they aim for is *enjoyment*. But that is not nothing, and I want to suggest instead something about the *social* valences of such sites. These open contact zones attract, bond, combine, and recombine various categories and types of persons in conversation, dance, flirtation, and sex, facilitating a wide variety of evanescent experiences. They are beneficial, in that they conduce to empathic understandings among people who might not otherwise come into contact with one another. By dint of these characteristics and without much in the way of political intent, these experiences implicitly put into play tangible "principles of hope,"[10] if you will: concrete practices for transcending both the limitations of stodgy homophobic norms *and* the limits to gay identity, its association with status commodities, imported forms of life, and a strictly middle-class form of cosmopolitanism.

By that I mean that you don't have to spend money to chat, socialize, cruise, and participate in the daily spectacle that begins in the late afternoon and unfolds into the late evening. Some do not. You don't have to dress the part, either, by wearing designer labels or sporting a stylish coiffure. Many do not. The challenge is to work creatively with what resources you have, combining colors and textures with flare. It helps to be attractive, of course. Let me be clear: gay scenes are not egalitarian spaces; they are youth oriented, looks conscious, and they sort participants into very definite hierarchies of attractiveness and desirability. But you might also make your way on the scene by being entertaining, or charming, or interesting, or kind, or generous. It goes without saying that not every longing will be satisfied, but in the give-and-take of social exchange, you employ such gifts as you might possess. Precisely what makes these exchanges exciting is that they structure a portion of one's day as *play*, with opportunities for moves and countermoves. You might meet friends, or you might make acquaintances at the site. You might relax, strolling and taking in the views without overt sexual interest. Or you might have various kinds of amorous adventures. The same drag shows and stripper routines might become boring after repeated viewings, in which case other niches beckon. What is certain is that within the space of a few blocks, people from a wide variety of different social classes, status groups, and ethnic backgrounds will respond to your gambits.

Also, there is this: connections made and romances forged in places like the Zona might become lifelong friendships or long-term relationships. Nightlife is diversionary, but it is not only diversionary.

La Nueva Zona Rosa

Shifting, morphing sexual geographies in Mexico City illustrate something of the ebb and flow of neoliberal modalities over time. First, a deregulated, anything-goes sensibility (during the Fox sexenio) was conducive to the unprecedented florescence of public gay life. Rainbow flag–adorned bars flourished under the initial wave of political liberalization. Then came a repressive moment, corresponding not so much to an old-school rejection of homosexuality as to a privatized version of gay life. (Thus the curious fact that authorities left intact certain kinds of venues: small bars do not spill over into sidewalks and streets, and what happens in sex clubs is, on this definition, *private*, happening behind closed doors.)

This is a story that has unfolded in many locales over the years. It is the story of what happens when small businesses come into conflict with larger-scale corporations, when gay nightlife is in the crosshairs of urban redevelopment and gentrification plans—and, no doubt, when elites fret over the visibility of certain unauthorized kinds of gay life. A dash of sex panic is often put into play here by bien-pensant liberals no less often than by social conservatives, who perpetually expand and fortify the frontiers of "childhood" and inflate the need to "protect" it.[11] Of course, in the Zona there were new plot twists along the way: partial reopenings, which were periodically engulfed in various sorts of crises and scandals. Clubs that were part of the storied Cabaretito chain (owned by Tito Vasconcelos and his husband, David Rangel) were closed and reopened various times. Depopulation invited mayhem, and neither the Zona nor other parts of the city (including affluent neighborhoods) were immune to the economic stresses and social dislocations of the period as a rising tide of drug violence and personal insecurity enveloped the country. The horrific kidnapping and murder of twelve people in one of the Zona's clubs in 2013—part of a city-spanning war between drug distribution networks—resulted in a renewed wave of shutdowns (to say nothing of well-founded nervousness about violent crime in the city).

Eventually, after years of microstruggles, skirmishes, and changing municipal administrations, city authorities seemed to have decided that the Zona was not really susceptible to the sort of gentrification they had envisioned—that they had gone too far in shutting down too much of the gay scene there—and relented. Rebuilding and rebranding after the 2017 earthquake, the city launched a new campaign festooning the "New Zona Rosa." The new Zona looked a lot like the old Zona. Old megabars reopened; new ones were christened. The flow of people on sidewalks resumed—but never quite with the same intensity as during the first millennial decade's zenith. For, by this time, demographic shifts were under way, and new communications media were deepening their roots in society. Mexico's median age was now closing in on thirty. More and more, gay sex life (the nucleus of gay nightlife) had been channeled online into hookup apps, first Manhunt and then Grindr, or was happening in bathhouses and private parties scattered across the city.

OPERATIVOS

Meanwhile, eighty miles away in Puebla, similar dynamics were playing out under the auspices of the newly elected center-right PAN (Partido

Acción Nacional) government, which took office in 2011. Unlike the tolerant business conservatism of the Fox administration, Puebla's PAN was anchored in religiously tinged social conservatism. Municipal authorities under the new administration immediately began pressing bars and café-bars across the city's historic center (*centro histórico*) on their paperwork, licenses, and inspections. These proved vulnerable points for many of the establishments that catered to young, working-class, and LGBT audiences. This was especially true of the newer, livelier, youth-oriented gay establishments that dotted the centro and that were giving downtown streets the festive feel and sensibility of a smaller-scale Zona Rosa.

"Look," explained Yuli, the middle-aged owner of Luciérnaga, "I've owned different bars in the centro over many years. I could spend months or even years getting all my paperwork in order. But then I'd still have to pay bribes to move it along and get it approved. So I did what everyone else did: I just paid my bribes and under the PRI, they left me alone." Yuli intimates here how, under the PRI, corruption could be an ally as well as an enemy. "Now, under the PAN, I still pay my bribes—but they don't leave me alone! I don't understand what they want."

What the PAN wanted would become clearer as the city ramped up its "stings" and *operativos*, staging surprise site visits at the gay bars and cafés that were under scrutiny. These "operations" seldom came as complete surprises. Once operativos started in one part of the city, ambulatory vendors quickly spread word from bar to bar, well ahead of city inspectors. I was parked in my usual spot at the bar one evening when a team of three inspectors entered Luciérnaga, not altogether unexpectedly. The cheerful indigenous grandmother who sold flowers and acted as eyes and ears of the street had preceded the officials by an hour.

"We'd like to talk to you about your balconies," the head inspector began. "Are they unsafe?" asked Yuli, alarmed. "No," the inspector replied, "but your clients are kissing and hugging and making scandal there." (*Escándalo* is a capacious term in Spanish, connoting both loud noise and the sorts of offenses against morality marked by English speakers with the more restricted term "scandal.") "My clients don't have any other place to come and be with their friends or to go with their dates," Yuli countered, appealing to ideas of inclusivity and nondiscrimination. "Yes," the inspector replied, "but they can do that *inside* the bar, and you can lock the doors to the balconies so that what happens inside stays inside. Please show some respect for the families who are passing by on the street below." My eyes no doubt widened upon hearing this. I was tempted to join the conversation but did not: I could only cause more problems for Yuli by pointing out the inspector's rank bias. And so, impotently, I fumed.

After some cursory discussion of the electrical system and wiring, the inspector returned to his real preoccupations: "And don't you think that most of your clients are too young to be in a place like this?" He snuck a side glance at me, clearly not too young. "Every one of my clients has his IFE," Yuli said defensively, referring to Mexico's voter registration card, which attested that the holder was at least eighteen years old. "If you want, you can check." Now technically, Yuli operated with a café license, one of the few pieces of paperwork that was in order, and her approvals included a liquor license, meaning that minors could in fact enter and order food or coffee or soft drinks but not alcohol. But tonight, as over the preceding weeks, in response to the city's waxing campaign against gay gathering places, she had begun screening clients and refusing entry to the high school students who often came in small, mixed groups (gay, straight; male, female). She could thus state confidently that everyone present was eighteen or older.

"Yes," the head inspector said, surveying the crowd of mostly twenty-somethings, "but even so, don't you think they're still too young?" The other inspectors nodded gravely.

Upscaling the Centro

PAN officials continued tightening the screws on gay nightlife in downtown Puebla. Within a few more weeks, the city had shut down Luciérnaga. Yuli tried reopening under another name a few blocks away, but the new place lasted only a few months before the city shut it down, too. Word went around that she was blacklisted.

Most of the gay bars clustered in the centro were pushed out of business in similar fashion, as owners found themselves engulfed in challenges to their paperwork. Although it was several blocks away from the centro proper on a busy boulevard, Lalo's, a small bar that had catered to subproletarian hustlers and trans women for many years, was one of the first to go. Glitter, a café-bar catering to students with a large lesbian clientele, was soon gone, as well. The number of gay establishments in the historic center, then, was cut back to three, each separated from the others by several blocks, none near the zócalo, none on busy thoroughfares.

Accelerating the campaign against places where young and working-class people gathered, the state's PAN-ista governor ordered the closure of all the bars and nightclubs that had been clustered in the Los Sapos section of town, aiming to develop an upscale tourist zone on the scenic plaza. The governor's plans wildly overestimated the city's appeal as a destination for high-end tourism and ultimately failed, along with his scheme to develop a line of ski resort–type suspended cableways linking the centro to the Cinco de Mayo battleground site up the hill. (The gondola scheme was nixed by UNESCO, which threatened to revoke the city's designation as a World Heritage Site.) In the end, not even a Starbucks would locate in Los Sapos. Instead, rustic furniture retailers extended their domain from nearby blocks, occupying niches along the scenic site. I'd wager that the city was actually generating more employment, tourism, and revenues when the downtown site hosted cheap, lively forms of nightlife for diverse publics.

Meanwhile, gay NGOs were securing legal rights and recognitions. The state of Puebla appended LGBT protections to its human rights laws in response to protests over the brutal murder of a trans woman in 2012 and would later update its marriage practices—reluctantly under court order in 2017, then later, under progressive governance, by amendment to the state's marriage laws in 2020. Despite these recognitions of civil rights and protections, things remained largely unchanged with regard to the city's approach to public space, respectability, and socializing among people of different classes and ages in the centro.

In Puebla, then, florescence gave way to repression, as happened in Mexico City—but was never followed by a second boom. Newly fashioned alarms about youth and alcohol were put on public display, while behind-the-scene conversations suggested that policies were driven, at least in part, by other concerns. Gay nightlife was efficiently driven out of downtown public spaces, scattered into far-flung bars and clubs in distant suburbs, and channeled into hookup apps. Dive bars in general were also driven out, suggesting a two-prong attack both on gay gathering places and on the presence of young and working-class revelers in the centro.

"I hear it's only the bad places that the city is shutting down," commented a straight, upper-middle-class acquaintance, no doubt intending to goad me. But why not own it? These were indeed collectively "bad," disreputable places from the viewpoint of administrative elites. Their habitués were disproportionately "bad" people: queers without money, aspirants to gayness, members of suspect social classes. The decor, the sound systems, the cheap-drink offerings, were not in keeping with the image to which the developers aspired: a Disneyfied colonial-era theme park, middle-class family zone. A few people (including my husband and I) gained legal rights and protections under marriage equality, it is true; but thousands of LGBT and working-class people lost access to safe, centric social spaces near public transportation where they might meet friends and make acquaintances with people from different walks of life.

The Quality of Gay Life

Perhaps my zeal for certain kinds of social spaces, anchored by small businesses, will seem naive. I come back to quality of life, not as it is imagined in middle- and upper-middle-class hygienic fantasies, but as it might be experienced by (mostly) young LGBT people (mostly) without resources. I think about the deep friendships I forged in Luciérnaga and similar cafébars. I also think about how gay youth manage crises of various sorts—and the importance of certain kinds of settings for their development as fully rounded human beings.

Oscar, now in his thirties, waxes nostalgic and expresses a palpable sense of loss: "Kids today don't have the same experience that we had. Luciérnaga was a welcoming space, part café, part bar, part community center. Everyone greeted Yuli as 'Tía' [aunt] when they entered. No matter what you were going through at home, you could count on her sympathetic ear and sound advice—and on the support of networks of friends there. All that is gone now. And although there remain two bars downtown [in 2021], none of them have replaced Luciérnaga. The kids in high school or college come out alone now, they suffer and endure alone, there's no place for them to be together with others—and there's no one like Yuli to tell them, 'Be patient, be careful, give your parents time, don't do anything rash. . . .' And if they can get through that, all they know today is Suburbia [an expensive club located in a distant *colonia*] or Grindr."

Or they fall back on the less defined, ever-present, nonpublic ambiente, reconfigured and retrofitted to a postgay world: floating scenes, dicey places, unlit corners . . . Gaiety had represented a different sort of striving at the start of the new millennium, before aspirants were pushed to settle into and settle for the chopped-up and distributed version of modernity, with its perpetual deferrals of the dream of enlightened understanding, personal freedom, and material abundance.

Monsiváis's paradoxical apothegm about those who feel the need to come closer to the nuclei of modernity remains apposite: "and everything continues to be the same except that it is very different."[12]

Conclusion

THE HORIZONS OF GAY IDENTITY

We are troubled on every side, yet not distressed; we are
perplexed, but not in despair.

—St. Paul, second letter to the church at Corinth

We shall not say: Abandon your struggles, they are mere
folly; let us provide you with true campaign-slogans.
Instead, we shall simply show the world why it is struggling, and consciousness of this is a thing it must acquire
whether it wishes or not.

—Karl Marx to Arnold Ruge, September 1843

The challenge of what I have attempted here puts me in mind of Johann
Sebastian Bach's Two-Part Inventions, a set of brisk, instructional key-
board compositions in which each hand pursues its own independent
melodic narratives. The two storylines periodically come together, pose
questions of each other and venture answers, with one hand occasionally
borrowing the other's syntax to reveal the unifying harmonics that put
them in conversation and make for a unified piece.

On the one hand, then, I acknowledge the depth and specificity—the
authenticity—of gay life, of what people aspire to or refuse when they
approach the question of identity, of how gay men desire and love and
connect or are frustrated. How could I not? This, the struggle to be gay, is
a big part of my life, too, after all. On the other hand, I try to show how
the very real dilemmas and partial resolutions—the storylines—of gay
life could unfold only at this specific moment, under these social and

political-economic conditions, in conversation with the long arcs of other happenings and narratives. Among those immediate material conditions are the speeding-up of capitalism and the intensification of brute exploitation. This, the contemporary class condition of society, furnishes our collective imaginations and sets the horizons of the imaginable.

Bach, a master of contrapuntal music, was no stranger to the so-called deceptive cadence, a musical progression in which the dominant chord does not resolve to the tonic chord to give a sense of closure but instead seems to leave things up in the air, suggesting that this is not quite the end of the piece (and sometimes opening the way to lengthy digressions). Many of this book's chapters come to this sort of open-ended ending. This, the book's conclusion, will not close off a set of arguments about the unfinishedness of struggles with a pat ending, a tidy pronouncement on where the human condition is headed, or even a clear delineation of a line of march. The dialectic is not yet played out; we can only mark some of its valences and take stock of our understanding of it. Class struggles surge and retreat; social movements rise, stall, and fall. We can only hazard a few guesses about what forms any of this might take on the near horizon. We are headed for another world, one way or another, but whether the future world will be better or worse than the present one is unclear.

It is said that Bach contemplated the human condition, up close and empathically, with "benevolent understanding."[1] I hope that something similar might be said of the work of this sentimental gay socialist.

What, then, has been shown? In broad outlines:

First, I have demonstrated the salience of class in gay people's social and symbolic worlds. The class structure reverberates in immediate experiences of want and need; it resonates in people's institutional surroundings; it shapes and constrains their options, including their ability to exercise sexual freedom or to obtain cultural capital (education); and it channels their aspirations, especially if they are working-class or poor. These constraints and channelings happen in ways both simple and complex, but much of what working-class men aspire to when they aspire to gayness is middle-classness and the freedoms and enjoyments thought to be associated with it.

Second, I have shown the strong draw of political-economic developments on sexual subcultures and evolving gay scenes. It might seem obvious how, say, the availability of liquor licenses for certain types of small businesses affects what kinds of urban nightlife flourish or fail; it might seem less obvious how markets and their shaping, specific kinds of commodities, and forms of work and enterprise constitute important elements of nocturnal imaginaries. The changing scenes I describe variously exhibit these connections.

Third, I trace a development that might at first blush seem paradoxical: the conquest of important LGBT rights and protections, in the name of equality, occurred at a time when Mexico was becoming more and more unequal.[2] There is no incongruity here. Although the new spirit of capitalism cannot help but produce ever-wider economic inequalities, its enlightened managers cannot abide inequalities resulting from arbitrary discrimination, which is contrary to market principles. Antipathy to these latter kinds of inequality serves as a new source of legitimation for the neoliberal regime. Yet neoliberal anti-discrimination policies over time do not inevitably translate into greater freedoms for your average gay person on the street, any more than they mean improvements in the lives of dark-skinned people, a large majority of whom are working-class.

Fourth, I have examined some of the ways racial hierarchies, sexual mores, and class predicaments hang together and interact under changing conditions—how dynamics in one field serve as templates for identity work in the other fields. These interdynamics, I hold, can only be understood when connected with a global system whose dominant logic has to do with profit making and that today increasingly points to the priority of social class in structuring social relations.

Fifth, I have drawn out scenes and scenarios to suggest some of the ways modernity serves as both ideology and material condition in gay men's struggles. Modernity is ideology in the sense that it is an idea, a story that people tell and retell under changing conditions. Indeed, it is a metanarrative: the big story that makes sense of many other stories. Its force as ideology is not mysterious. In relegating some of us to the time of the now and others to the time of the past, even though we pass one another on the street or meet in smoky cafés, it affirms, rationalizes, and reinforces hierarchy. But modernity is also a material condition, in the sense that the term describes an ongoing political-economic process: how economic motives and institutional arrangements progressively dismantle obstacles to capital accumulation (as David Harvey would say of neoliberalism), disembedding social relations from local settings and submitting them to ongoing inspection (as Anthony Giddens would say of modernity's intrinsically globalizing force), and constantly "revolutionizing" production (as Marx would say of capitalism's ceaseless agitations).[3] Mexicans' frustrated pursuit of modernity, in the ideological sense, which seems like the pursuit of a receding mirage in the desert, is hardly unique among countries similarly situated in modernity in the political-economic sense; people in other countries of the global south make pilgrimages to the same altar.[4] (In telling themselves that they are trapped in "tradition" and must make their way to the promised land of "modernity," such aspirants are perhaps actually the ideal subjects of modernity: they undertake constant reflexive work on themselves and their surroundings.)

Sixth, none of the above conditions enclose us like insects in amber. I have stressed the unfinishedness of gay identity. Striving, frustration, and discontent are important parts of this unfinishedness. And if the paradoxes and predicaments of gay life seem to be unhappy or cruel, this is, paradoxically, because struggle is a precondition for our flourishing. (Has humankind ever known anything, so far, that was better, more productive, than struggle?)

In sum, all that has been shown has to do with the material foundations for identity formation, with how political-economic conditions structure identity and its discontents. In laying this out, I have frequently invoked the phrase "not only in Mexico" to indicate the transnational nature of the dynamics I sketch. And across the text I have used terms like "we" and "us" in shifting senses: we, scholars and students who inform our thinking with comparative studies, without which our perspectives would be parochial and truncated; we, globally connected denizens of changing subcultures who are linked together on unequal terms in the new era of globalization, of course, but also by the long history of colonialism and capitalism . . . Through close attention to the particular—showing how my subjects grapple with their crises, how they struggle to make a living, how they strive for dignity in the terms available to them—I hope I have made a compelling case for a renewed form of socialist universalism, a view that neither denies nor minimizes the specificity of people's experiences with racism, postcolonial condition, homophobia, and so on, but that sees them in light of the ongoing cleavage of society into classes. (This also involves hope, however attenuated, for a socialist future.)

Last, then, I have tried to show that the existing compendium of analytical frameworks in the field of LGBT studies are inadequate for the present historical conjuncture. We have forgotten how to think universally or—perhaps to say the same thing—dialectically. We have become expert at stoking divisions within the working class and avoiding confrontation with capital at a time when our models ought to be doing the opposite. We use words like "neoliberalism" when we might simply say "capitalism," or "globalization" when we might pause to take stock of just what we are actually describing.

Commenting on the way LGBT questions have entered into academic arguments about globalization, Bruno Perreau sketches an optimistic brief in *Queer Theory: The French Response*: "Queer theory analyzes the resonance in each individual of multiple forms of affiliation and disaffiliation, of subjectification and subjection. Ultimately, it holds that each individual is a territory whose borders oscillate with those of the world."[5]

It will be clear that Perreau's luminous turn of phrase expresses an unfulfilled wish. His reference to unstable territories and oscillating borders follows a long examination of how authors associated with queer of color critique—who at least attempted to put some meat on the bones of queer theory by attending to empire, global circuits, and forms of inequality derived from race, ethnicity, and immigrant status—ended up, after all, attempting to establish fixed identities, fortified borders, "stable territories" of us and them: white gay homonationalists (a post-9/11 term that combines "homosexual" with "nationalist" to describe normative, intolerant, and racist positions) on the one side, and (nonnormative) queers of color on the other.[6] The gist of Perreau's incisive critique of this literature is that we commit an intellectual error bordering on sophistry if we selectively fast-freeze *some* of the ideas and practices that are common at a given moment into a monolithic white Western or Northern sexual culture, as opposed to (and opposed by) a nonwhite Southern or non-Western culture or cultures.[7] In reality, sexualities everywhere are multiply traversed by fluctuating norms, sexual cultures by changing inequalities. By the same token, repression resonates in class hierarchies with varying intensities, disproportionately affecting queers without money, to be sure, but it does not leave middle-class gays unscathed. (This point was once poignantly made to me by an immigrant, a refugee from right-wing terror. Reflecting on his experiences in the Southern cone and on his network of gay friends in the United States, he stopped short my denunciation of white middle-class gays' relative privilege by saying, "I don't know anyone who hasn't had to give up something he loved because he loved men. Not a one."[8] And I might add: I don't know very many gay men, white, black, or Latino, working- or middle-class, who haven't been assaulted—"queer-bashed"—or threatened with physical violence.)

It will also be clear that I haven't found much use here for the concepts associated with queer of color critique, which, Perreau argues in his discussion of Jasbir Puar's *Terrorist Assemblages*, are long on associative reasoning and short on evidence.[9] But my own approach takes a step further back from the manifestos and broadsides of the post-9/11 period and instead sees the wider field of queer theory over the longer run as symptomatic of a problem it never could quite name. With the exception of a handful of works—among them, Lauren Berlant's *The Queen of America Goes to Washington City* and Rosemary Hennessy's *Profit and Pleasure*—[10] queer theory during its 1990s heyday chartered the airy heights of abstract models of discourse and performativity, never really grappling with the conditions of its own existence: that historical moment when neoliberal reforms and post-Fordist techniques linked to globalization were completing the task of tearing up the social contract that had prevailed since the end of World War II.

This process was stretched out over decades, and it seems pertinent to adumbrate it here. The rollback of working-class gains actually began as early as the 1960s, when deindustrialization and waning union power had the effect of dismantling the on-ramps to social mobility for inner-city black people at the height of the civil rights era[11]—and in the process also opened up disinvested urban spaces for the explosion of gay ghettos in the 1970s. Reagan-era changes of the 1980s then dramatically undermined the power of the working class everywhere, eviscerating the welfare state policies and social compacts that had underwritten stable employment at union wages for large sections of the populace. Free trade and mechanization accelerated during the Clinton years, relegating vast swaths of the

eastern midlands to contingent, low-wage employment and social abandonment, beginning the process of pushing down life expectancies for
white working-class people across wide geographies.[12] By kicking out
from under it all the props (starting with the "male wage") that had sustained the institutional hegemony of the heterosexual nuclear family,
these changes also (inadvertently) made way for the proliferation of "non-
heteronormative" subject positions and sexual identities, for the multipli-
cation of family forms, for the triumph of cultural politics and the scholarly staging of queer performativities, and so on.[13]

In the throes of events, a working-class community-based researcher
and independent scholar like Allan Bérubé could discern a connection
between "this massive redistribution of wealth and widening class
divide . . . [and] queer studies," challenging his audience at a 1995 queer
studies conference to make class central to their analytical frameworks.[14]
But most academics were loath to listen and remained oblivious to real-
world material conditions affecting the vast majority. To make matters
worse, queer theory was never up to the task of understanding either what
motivates many gay subjects (love)[15] or what constrains their freedom
(economic inequality—which was being exacerbated by the same neoliberal policies that were freeing us from yesterday's sexual conventions by
breaking down the Fordist social contract).

This book, then, has expressed my own wish for the field of LGBT studies: The task—understanding how people make and unmake identities in
a changing world—remains unfinished; the intellectual vocation remains
open for those who would hear the call. The related and still urgent "task
of distinguishing freedom from constraint in love, of learning to trace the
shifting and uncertain boundaries between the self and the world, is a diz-
zying and, indeed, an endless undertaking," as David Halperin wrote in a
distinguished essay at the dawn of a consistently constructionist approach
to identity in gay studies.[16] We can't hope to get traction on such a project
without taking into account the class condition of society, the tug and tow
of economic crosscurrents, the momentum of the intensification of inequalities. The task is perhaps especially challenging when the thoughts,
wishes, and theories of our real-world subjects do not hew to the paths
that we would prescribe for them or are immersed in bundles of promises
associated with "modernity." I have probed here some of my subjects'

messy, awful, beautiful, and contradictory struggles for modern identities. Some of those struggles seem ensnared in what critics usually gloss as "consumerism." No doubt. But who would tell the people that their longing for enlightened understanding, personal freedom, and material comfort are symptoms of their embourgeoisement? Who would tell them that they are mistaken about their wants when their needs are so great? Who would lay out all the forms of error and misidentification to which they might fall prey in order to instruct them on the proper path?

I have hewed to a seemingly quirky path, avoiding assertions about what sorts of longings are good for my subjects and what sorts are bad for them. In the first place, it has always seemed to me presumptuous for academics to stage themselves as the ones who know and their subjects as those who need enlightenment, especially when we are writing about matters involving local knowledge. Moralizing misses the point, because our subjects struggle with the conditions and concepts they encounter in the world, not with those that we might wish for them. But, more importantly, moralizing forecloses the analysis at precisely the point where matters might become interesting.

Over the course of decades, LGBT studies and queer theory have discerned the elements of identity as variously opposed dynamics held in tension: in biopolitical scripts and their reversal; in discourse and counterdiscourse; in stigma and its disavowal; in psychic life's identifications and disidentifications. I have tried to reorient and recast these oppositions. What if we now staked a new course and thought about identity instead as a different sort of predicament, above all one caught in the circuits of production and consumption? To transpose Eve Sedgwick's pithy claims about the indispensability of shame, a "negative" emotion that she argued was not merely repressive but also constitutive of gay identity formation,[17] what if we discerned instead a sort of tacit alliance between the lived experiences of consumerism and its everyday vernacular critique, between aspirations to class climbing and their inevitable frustrations, between conformism and nonconformism, between pretense and facticity, between internalized racisms or homophobias and their renunciation, such that one is not undone or subverted by the other but instead takes the other as ballast and support? I mean here to describe an approach to the struggles not only of gay men in Mexico but also of LGBT people across far-flung, globally linked cultures. If LGBT/queer studies historically has tended to posit abstract subjects who wrestle with "normativity" (ideal norms), we might begin again, more concretely, with real-world subjects who wrestle with their class position and its implications under changing circumstances.

The idea is challenging, at least for staid forms of criticism, seeing how it brings together something we (supposedly) like (gay identity) with something we (say we) don't like (certain modes of commodification and hierarchization). But if I am right, the paradoxes and contradictions I've traced here are not only *there*, in the world, outside our selves and our identities, but also *here*, part of the internal dynamics of self-making. This realization need not signal a new version of the ersatz populism that marked the history of cultural studies (consumption as resistance). Pathos and irony, Carlos Monsiváis's preferred registers when writing about such matters, seem closer to the mark. In any case, the predicaments I've laid out are by no means unique to gay subcultures. All manner of working-class life forms take root in the same dynamics, as even a cursory glance at youth subcultures shows.

We cannot say in advance where these internal skirmishes and idea-tional microstruggles will end up. What, then? We have clung for too long to the false notion that gay or queer identities are by nature oppositional, counterhegemonic, anti-normative. We have chased this idea across shift-ing populations and subpopulations, producing as our exhibits a succes-sion of multiply intersectional groups and subgroups, as first one and then another demographic eventually fails the standards of whatever we might plausibly mean by "transgressive." This transgressive conceit—crystalized in the word "queer," after all, which, unlike "gay," signals a refusal to imag-ine an end to stigma and rejection once and for all—bars the way to the perspectives we need; increasingly, it stands as an accusation against a growing majority of LGBT people who can never be deemed sufficiently queer to pass constantly changing litmus tests. In lieu of the academic fantasy of militantly oppositional subcultures contesting heteronormativ-ity or homonormativity or intersectional racialized cisgender norms or what have you, we might instead try to understand how ordinary people (I mean here the popular classes in their broadest and most inclusive sense) make do in the face of various forms of adversity: sexual repression, economic hardship, compounded social inequalities (including varied forms of discrimination), and unmet needs and wants. This seems to me a very different starting point for our inquiries. Reflexive moralizing serves to head off this train of ideas at the pass and to fortify the unreflexive class authority of academics. It is the enemy of unflinching analysis. Trying to find out whose positioning and repositioning in the muck and mire of inequalities best embodies resistant, transgressive principles (or, in recent academic trends, exemplary forms of victimization) is a losing proposition. This search is where radicalism regresses to liberalism and then ultimately, because it opposes class interests and majoritarian logics, transmutes into reactionary intrigue.

And here I extend a provocation I develop in the second part of this book, that is, the idea that we are at our most *authentic* when we strive to be something that we are not. Above all, my subjects struggle to be not poor, not prole, a precondition in their minds for being gay—but they do so without the material means to achieve this aim. Their struggles take in the desire to renounce preexisting stigmatized identities of various sorts ("puto," indigeneity, assorted associations with the popular classes). I have tried to put aside accumulated scholarly reflexes on these matters (instant decoloniality; extended lamentations over increasingly reified forms of victimhood deemed more worthy of denunciation than brute exploitation; hasty declarations that this or that constitutes an act of political resistance; waving the magic wand of hybridity over scenes of violence and disjuncture). Now I am not quite ready to say that we are at our *best* when we gape open-endedly at what we cannot have, or when we struggle within conceits that are racist or homophobic or class bound (in the latter cases, these are shackled with a high degree of self-loathing); only that these "undergoings," sufferings, strivings, are part of an ongoing work whose outcome is not predetermined. That is to say, it remains to be seen whether these wantings cleave to the scene "as a near-inexhaustible source of transformational energy"[18] or whether they set us running in circles like dogs chasing their own tails. But either way, what sometimes flashes in these struggles, and is of acute interest to socialist scholarship, are oblique principles of solidarity. I say "oblique," but these principles are very much out there in public view; they undergird everyday jokes, banter, and crude jests, if only we listen to them.

Gay social, political, and theoretical imaginaries have stalled and stagnated, and if we have any hope of revivifying them, we must give up the kinds of radicalism that are no longer radical and get in the way of the kind of radicalism we need. Like the dark humanism embodied in crude jokes, relinquishing the pose of anti-normativity potentially opens up our perspectives to wider solidarities and connects us with other struggles for dignity and a decent life. This work has been an experiment in that undertaking, and not the last, I hope. The "limits" to gay identity are spelled out in the preceding chapters; but what remains is gaiety's horizon of open-ended promise.

Every book contains within it loose ends and traces of books not written. This one is no exception. These traces haunt the author at the end of a project and give rise to wistful feelings. For instance, my informants' workplace experiences surface from time to time in the preceding pages, but I did not "shadow" them (as the sociologists would say) in their workaday routines. A book taking workplaces as its main site could no doubt reveal more about the imbrications of labor, sexuality, and identity. My subjects also talk a great deal about money and spending, and the meaning of expenditure surfaces as a recurring theme in their reflections here. They mock tightfistedness or reticence about money with standard insults: "Róger, eres muy pobre" (Roger, you are very poor; meaning, you are very stingy). They are also constantly engaged in lending and borrowing and saving schemes among networks of friends and neighbors. A book more directly focused on the experience of spending money, and the expectations around it, would yield fresh insights.

My friends engage a great deal in a form of banter and insult trading that they call *joteando*, queering or fagging. Such verbal performances are often rendered in an arch tone, gendering as feminine words that usually have no gender ("¿Qué está pasanda?") and drawing on a panoply of sexist, racist, homophobic, and class-based tropes. I have a hard time listening to these exchanges, but people tell me that they make cruel jokes about being robbed by a hookup or getting HIV so that these experiences won't hurt so much. Of course, these sorts of banter have much in common with camp, especially the practice of "reading," and also with the Dozens and similar verbal genres. A very different sort of book might work outward from the narratives of joteando and related forms of jest to disentangle how gender, race, and class come together in the lifeworlds of working-class gay men.

Although my book is about working-class gay life, I have repeatedly cast glances at the lives of middle-class gay men, sometimes to point up overlapping experiences, sometimes to show differences. A more expressly comparative work could inquire more deeply into the contentments and frustrations of each subset to answer ancillary questions about personal life under contemporary capitalism and the truncated, marketized forms of freedom it offers. Perhaps almost everyone, not just working-class people, or gays, are subject to the dynamics of longing and frustration that I describe.

Last, a recurring thread of this text takes up questions related to what Barbara and John Ehrenreich called the professional-managerial class: "salaried mental workers who do not own the means of production and whose major function ... [is] the reproduction of capitalist culture."[19] Educated people from working-class backgrounds often aspire to become licensed professionals; young social movement activists are usually aspirants to this class and sometimes strive for tenured academic appointments; and academic discourses invariably represent conversations among this class's members. A very different sort of book about the material foundations of identity would foreground class dynamics by expressly tracking this class's communication flows across national and cultural borders via NGOs, foundations, and transnational organizations.

Ongoing developments in Mexico suggest intensification of some of the trends I have tracked. I can only cast glances at them here.

The protracted COVID-19 pandemic, with its rolling lockdowns, closures, and comparatively high mortality rate in Mexico, shrank the GDP by 8.3 percent and disrupted study and employment for millions across the country.[20] These convulsions pushed up unemployment rates and exacerbated experiences of precarity; the resulting hardships have reverberated in gay scenes. It's no secret that many gay men consume recreational drugs, perhaps at levels that are higher than the general population. But now, in place of the usual party drugs (cocaine, ecstasy), one increasingly sees young men smoking crack or crystal methamphetamine, especially in bathhouses and other *lugares de encuentro* (meeting places) where working-class men gather. Accompanying this shift to drugs associated with working-class despair and resignation, I hear reports of increases in petty theft—wallets snatched, cell phones pilfered—in gay settings. At the same time, a growing number of acquaintances are testing positive for HIV, a condition that no longer carries a death sentence but does spell out a future of medication, treatment, and, for some, complications. Some of my informants tell me that they don't expect to turn fifty, in any event. To my horror, such talk of premature death, circulating along networks of friends, seems to be reinforcing fatalistic outlooks, strategies of resignation, and feelings of guilt, shame, and self-loathing. No doubt drug abuse, theft, unprotected sex, and defeatism are always there, in the background of gay life, but their frequency or intensity is an index of hard times. I cannot help but think that if gay men at least had less precarious economic lives—stable employment, livable wages, affordable rent—they could gather around them more reliable support networks and make their ways through the trials and tribulations of being gay with less harm and self-injury.

At the same time, many mid-twentieth-century strivings associated with modernity and its pursuit seem exhausted and worn-out today. This is true in Mexico no less than in the United States—and not for the first time, if we recall how quickly postmodernism followed on the heels of the new social movements in intellectual cultures of the North Atlantic.

Today, many of my friends and subjects in Mexico complain about the banalities of the gay scene, its association with appearances and vanity, its monotonous musical offerings, and specifically about meaningless, mechanistic, or boring sex. They unplug from Grindr or disengage from bars and lugares de encuentro—but usually only for a while. For such discontents are built into the proposition, and they carry forward the core idea of the sexual revolution, which has taken up one of the durable subplots of late modernity: the idea that sex should be instructive, special, consciousness expanding, ego shattering, that it should involve an intense emotional connection with an other or others. Sophisticates among us might try to console ourselves with Foucauldian bromides—whoever seeks the truth in sex misunderstands what she or he is looking for—yet even Foucault sought implausible things in sex: "limit experiences" that would "test" the body and allow one to transcend the limits of self-identity.[21] And here, again, I cannot help but think that if more people had stabler and more secure lives, the gay scene might involve more realistic pursuits of adventure and experience, with fewer desperate and inevitably frustrated searches for excitement and stimulation. Of course, this is by no means guaranteed.

Meanwhile, social movement activists, largely based in NGOs and universities, have intensified their rhetoric and protests, much of it aimed at the center-left government. This development bears closer inspection. Leftist groups and social activists generally supported Andrés Manuel López Obrador in his third and successful bid for president in 2018—but not all of them. The Zapatistas, for example, pointedly declined to endorse or even meet with the candidate. The organization's barbed broadsides had little effect: AMLO still piled up huge majorities in indigenous precincts in Chiapas. And nationwide, his landslide victory swept every state except Guanajuato, finally breaking the old political order and giving AMLO's new party, Morena (acronym for National Regeneration Movement, which also means "brown-skinned woman"), and its electoral allies constitutional supermajorities in both chambers of Congress.

Relations with social movement activists soured when AMLO canceled contracts with NGOs to deliver a wide array of the state's social, health, and welfare services, a practice encouraged under Fox and his neoliberal successors. NGOs—some as small as two activists connected to the world by the internet, some as large as Walmart's charitable apparatus serving families with disabled children—were everywhere and had their fingers in everything related to health and social welfare. There are arguments to be made for this distributed and parceled-out arrangement, to be sure. Gay men who might avoid HIV testing in large public hospitals might seek out testing and counseling in small LGBT community centers, for example. If large public health centers often have an officious and sterile feel about them, small feminist-run community centers provide warmer and arguably more effective peer counseling. And, if scope and outreach pose problems for the delivery of some services, who has wider reach than Walmart? Yet, for all their advantages, these arrangements wittingly or unwittingly advanced a privatized logic: they passed public money through private hands. Viewing such practices as neoliberal forms of clientelism and invitations to corruption, AMLO briskly eliminated them, recentralizing diffuse structures and shoring up the administrative state while also expanding and improving the state's provision of social, health, education, and welfare services. Whatever services nongovernmental organizations would henceforth provide would be strictly a nongovernmental affair.

By 2020, then, many of the same activists who had supported AMLO in 2018 were intensifying their rhetoric and aiming at least some of their protests against the center-left government. Feminist groups, the largest and best-organized sector of social movement activists, figured prominently in these efforts. A wave of protests against femicide was widely reported in the local and international press, and these protests were invariably spun as a black eye for the government. Human Rights Watch headlined its news release "Mexican Government Paralyzed in the Face of a Wave of Femicides."[22] Such taglines echoed across the mediascape.

Now, it is manifestly true that Mexican women experience coercion, oppression, and violence in their everyday lives. But they are less likely to be victims of lethal violence than are men. Roughly 88 percent of homicide victims are male, 12 percent are female—and these ratios have remained basically unchanged for decades, though homicide numbers overall have climbed considerably. This, the wider backdrop for surging rates of violence against women, went largely unreported in news stories and human rights briefings. Worse, wide-eyed journalists filed stories about "sharp increases" in femicide, that small subset of women's murders in which a woman is killed because of her gender, never noting that these sharp increases are likely a statistical kink produced by the recent, gradual, and ongoing adoption of the term *feminicidio* in reporting by local and national authorities. Shrill rhetoric and distorted statistics flickered along international NGO, activist, and journalist networks, intensifying the sense of crisis as Mexican feminists adopted a US victims' rights approach to women's oppression, wherein horrifying predations against helpless victims stand as synecdoche for wider systems of crime and oppression.[23] News footage of riots from three consecutive International Women's Days further fired up the movement.

In short order, globally savvy graffiti scrawled on Mexico City's public monuments and Puebla's limestone buildings were taking cues from

Chile's 2019 rebellion and borrowing catchphrases from America's 2020 protests. I was surprised to find "acab" (all cops are bastards) scribbled at various sites. Some of the postings in Mexico City in 2022 were so incendiary that I was uncertain as to whether they represented false-flag operations or Dadaist works of art. "Plant a bomb." "Abolish everything." Much of the rhetoric in broadsides and at protests seemed performatively tailored to university audiences, and I was struck by the form of loathing expressed by some activists in private conversations, who snickered that it had taken López Obrador fourteen years to receive his *licenciatura* (bachelor's degree)—his terminal degree, at that.

Collectively, I suggest, these developments mark a delamination of activist groups, staffed by aspiring professionals, from the constituencies they purport to represent.[24] These developments are in sync with wider trends evident in the municipal, gubernatorial, and legislative off-year elections in 2021, which revealed a growing political divide between educated middle-class and less educated working-class social sectors. (Morena mostly kept its support in the pueblos and working-class barrios, but the PRI and especially the PAN clawed back some municipal posts and seats in the Chamber of Deputies, especially in middle-class or affluent districts.) Perhaps, too, they mark the ironic end of what Nancy Fraser calls "progressive neoliberalism,"[25] not with a whimper of co-optation but in the bang of ultraradical histrionics disconnected from popular constituencies.

This seems to me to culminate in a series of lost opportunities, at a time when the material needs of the popular classes are increasingly clear. I cannot help but think that the bulk of the forms of violence and abuse that afflict women and children would be greatly attenuated if women had sufficient income and resources to leave violent or abusive relationships. I cannot help but think that teenage girls—or boys—and gay youth in volatile family situations first and foremost need shelter, alternative housing, counseling, and remediation. I cannot help but think that organizers and activist groups could better connect to their supposed constituents if they disconnected from international foundation circuits and instead foregrounded in their thinking the sorts of grubby material conditions that limit people's freedom. Not to put too fine a point on it, but we need fewer particularist claims about how rights might attach to people based on their identities and more universalist demands for social provisions to which everyone is entitled.

Last, I earlier surveyed struggles over governance in Mexico's presidential federal republic, a gradual and uneven transition from center-left dictatorship to neoliberal kleptocracy to meaningful democracy: shifting horizons for the construction of gay and other identities. This business, too, remains unfinished and undecided.

In the run-up to the 2018 elections, López Obrador ran a flawless campaign, railing at rampant corruption, inveighing against the neoliberal policies of the past thirty-five years, and promising a sweeping transformation of government and society. His election in 2018 represented the coming to power of a no-longer-"new" Left that had been incubated in the student movements of 1968 and had struggled for an electoral breakthrough since the stolen election of 1988. On election night, as voting results came in and it became clear that there would be no computer crashes, crowds of working-class people laughed, shouted, and wept for joy in the streets while upper-middle-class people nervously waited to find out whether AMLO would prove to be the populist thug they feared. The president-elect, who had avoided social issues like same-sex marriage and abortion rights during the campaign, reinforced his core message and struck an inclusive note: "The state will cease to be a committee at the service of a minority," he declared in his victory speech, "and will represent all Mexicans, rich and poor, those who live in the country and in the city, migrants, believers and nonbelievers, to people of all philosophies and sexual preferences."[26] (The invocation of sexual "preferences" instead of "orientations" reflected the speaker's age and no doubt his distance from social movement activism. Even so, it represented a remarkable breakthrough.)

The new administration immediately set about advancing working-class interests in a variety of ways. In his first month in office, AMLO boosted the minimum wage. By its second year, the Morena government had passed a string of new health, education, and welfare programs *and* a potentially transformative labor law reform, giving workers the right to elect their union officials by secret ballot and to approve collective bargaining agreements.[27] Mexican workers saw their incomes increase by

6 percent—the poorest quintile by 24 percent.[28] Alas, these gains were eroded and reversed by the subsequent COVID pandemic, which roiled the country in 2020 and 2021. But even under the best of circumstances, Mexico's economy remains defined by the country's post-NAFTA positioning as "America's factory," a position that suppresses wages, and this is unlikely to change dramatically in the short term. AMLO's campaign promise not to raise taxes also considerably restricts the state's ability to redress social inequalities, though the government has funded new initiatives in part by clamping down on tax evasion by large corporations. Attempts at winding down the narco war with a combination of amnesties, opportunities, and military pressures have produced mixed results so far.

The standard-issue left critique, often lobbed by non-Mexican observers, is that AMLO made too many compromises with elites, intending to curb their opposition and neutralize them during the campaign, and that these accommodations prevent him from instituting a broadly transformative program. This assessment, it seems to me, misdiagnoses the situation. The Mexican working class was not clamoring for nationalization of the factories, expropriation of foreign owners, an assertively anti-imperialist posture, or even an aggressively Keynesian or social democratic approach to spending and governance. Their sights were set instead on the durable workings of a crony-capitalist regime defined by graft, corruption, and takings; they were focused on their struggles against a parasitical elite who controlled the media, fixed elections, and cut juicy deals among themselves.[29] In my view, then, AMLO's "transformation" will be judged primarily by his success or failure in shutting down nodal points for the transfer of public funds into private wealth, and secondarily by the effects of mildly redistributive policies, some clawing back of the public interest as against unpopular privatizations, and attempts to improve the baseline for poor and working-class people in health, education, and welfare services. Cumulatively, these would represent real gains for the toiling majority, with most LGBT people included among them.

Mexico today, then, like much of the world, seems to be on hold, on pause, waiting for something—no one is quite sure for what. Heroic collective struggles worthy of commemoration in murals or folk songs or counter-cultural poetry have been whittled down to the daily grind of atomized men and women who do not seem to have the winds of history at their backs. (Anyway, the soothsayers pronounced the end of history decades ago.) Gone, too, is the sense of vertiginous change, experienced as exhilarating or dehumanizing or both, associated with marketization, cultural opening, and political liberalization; these changes have been routinized and automatized now. Yet, somehow, in spite of barriers and carefully placed obstacles, all of the elements of another social transformation seem to be in place, but the will to undertake a thoroughgoing reconstruction is not; the reformers are timid and cautious, their ambitions tempered by memories of authoritarianism and turbulence, fear of upsetting the apple cart. All of the elements of the gay scene are there, too, but in lieu of yesteryear's expansive vistas of freedom, when a dappled humanity spilled outside bars and cafés and filled the sidewalks to make a joyful noise, prospects today are comparatively privatized and scaled back to comport with subdued neoliberal sensibilities.

Dreams of a better life once animated the great causes of the modern age. Today those longings seem contained, not by the monastic cells of asceticism or rigid norms but, on the contrary, in the hedonistic pursuit of pleasure, parceled out according to purchasing power—reprieves from workaday drudgery at paltry wages. No one knows how long we will live in this velvet cage, whether the spirit of old rebellions will arise again or when new social movements might use the term "worldmaking" in a credible sense.[30] Troubled but not distressed, most people assimilate the contradictions and get on with it. Perplexed but not despairing, the socialist takes in the news of the world and whispers his morning prayer: "We develop new principles for the world out of the world's own principles."[31]

This book is a series of meditations on the struggle to be gay, in Mexico, for example, and about some of the ways gay life has taken shape there along the wavering border between the local ambiente and the globally connected cosmopolis. But gay life isn't intrinsically interesting, except to those of us who have a specific—that is to say, carnal—interest in it. And we sometimes bore even ourselves with repetitious music at the same predictable clubs haunted by the same tired queens pursuing unfeeling sex. Gay life becomes profoundly more interesting—even to nongays—by dint of its connection with shared elements of the modern human condition (the struggle for autonomy, self-possession, acceptance, dignity, and connection) on the one hand and its placement in world-spanning political-economic and cultural currents (modernization, urbanization, privatization, liberalization, and so on) on the other. Released from striving, liberated from surplus longing, deprived of the struggle narrative through which we make sense of our goals and predicaments, what would our lives be like? We would be just another variety of desiring in a pluralistic and accepting world.

This, then, is the far horizon, the outer limit, of gayness: that we might hope in some happy future to become utterly, fabulously, deliriously boring someday.

Notes

BOOK EPIGRAPHS

Ernst Bloch, Introduction, in *The Principle of Hope,* vol. 1, trans. Neville Plaice, Stephen Plaice, and Paul Knight (Cambridge, MA: MIT Press, 1995), 4.

Sigmund Freud, *Letters of Sigmund Freud,* copyright © 1960. Reprinted by permission of Basic Books, an imprint of Hachette Book Group, Inc.

INTRODUCTION: WHEN THE MUSIC STOPS

1. Bobby Benedicto recounts the circulation of similar perceptions and discussions in Manila. "The Haunting of Gay Manila: Global Space-Time and the Specter of *Kabaklaan*," *GLQ* 14, nos. 2–3 (2008): 317–38 (323–26).

2. Aaron O'Neill, "Mexico—Median Age of the Population 1950-2050," Statista, September 7, 2021, https://www.statista.com/statistics/275555/median-age-of-the-population-in-mexico/; Erin Duffin, "Median Age of the U.S. Population 2020," Statista, April 1, 2022, https://www.statista.com/statistics/241494/median-age-of-the-us-population/; Aaron O'Neill, "Germany—Average Age of the Population 1950-2050," Statista, September 8, 2021, https://www.statista.com/statistics/624303/average-age-of-the-population-in-germany/.

3. Lauren Berlant and Michael Warner used the term "worldmaking" to describe all the ways that nonstraight people might create virtual worlds, "queer

counter-publics," counterposed to the official straight world of kinship and private intimacy. See Berlant and Warner, "Sex in Public," in "Intimacy," special issue *Critical Inquiry* 24, no. 2 (Winter 1998): 558). Although they do not directly cite him, the authors no doubt tip their hats to Harvard philosopher Nelson Goodman's *Ways of Worldmaking* (Indianapolis: Hackett, 1978).

4. For work that does indeed take such factors into account, see Héctor Carrillo, *Pathways of Desire: The Sexual Migration of Mexican Men* (Chicago: University of Chicago Press, 2017); and Carrillo, *The Night Is Young: Sexuality in Mexico in the Time of AIDS* (Chicago: University of Chicago Press, 2002).

5. See Lancaster, *Life Is Hard: Machismo, Danger, and the Intimacy of Power in Nicaragua* (Berkeley: University of California Press, 1992), 235–78.

6. In his comments on Douglas Crimp's paper treating Andy Warhol's depiction of Mario Montez in "Screen Test #2," Jack (previously known as Judith) Halberstam criticizes what he sees as the cultural appropriation of other, nonwhite people's suffering, chiding the white gay male participants at the Gay Shame conference in these terms: "Curious indeed that this shame, the other's shame, so seamlessly becomes 'ours' . . . . . . How perfect!" Halberstam expresses no curiosity about whether Warhol's and Montez's shared working-class Catholic backgrounds might produce shared experiences of suffering, constituting a commonality between filmmaker and subject, nor does he inquire into how, exactly, white gay men might respond to Montez's performances. Instead, he assumes that since Montez was Puerto Rican, all of his performances must be expressions of Puerto Ricanness, then goes on to ventriloquize nonwhite perspectives to say something essentially banal: "Who is this 'we,' white boy?" Judith Halberstam, "Shame and White Gay Masculinity," *Social Text* 23, Nos. 3–4 (84–85) (Fall–Winter 2005): 225.

7. Bruno Perreau, *Queer Theory: The French Response* (Stanford, CA: Stanford University Press, 2016), 143.

8. See Mikhail M. Bakhtin, *The Dialogic Imagination: Four Essays by M. M. Bakhtin*, ed. Michael Holquist, trans. Caryl Emerson and Michael Holquist (Austin: University of Texas Press, 1982).

9. Samuel R. Delany, *Times Square Red, Times Square Blue* (New York: New York University Press, 1999), 111, 123.

10. The third of these terms is probably less well understood than the first two, though they, too, are complex. In the heyday of liberation theology, radical Christians conceived their mission in terms of "accompaniment." The Vatican II Reforms' "preferential option for the poor" meant that the Church was to be *there*, in solidarity with the poor; to walk beside them, to bring them support, and to keep them company in their struggles. Paul Rabinow has developed a rather more abstruse version of anthropology as accompaniment and some of the forms of collaboration it might entail. An atheist, I have nonetheless taken my cue from the liberation theologians since my first fieldwork in Sandinista Nicaragua. It will

perhaps stretch the term to apply it to mostly working-class gay men, but I should like to think that in my present work I have *accompanied* my subjects, learned from them, in friendship and solidarity. See Paul Farmer, *In the Company of the Poor: Conversations with Dr. Paul Farmer and Fr. Gustavo Gutierrez* (Maryknoll, NY: Orbis Books, 2013). See also Paul Rabinow, *The Accompaniment: Assembling the Contemporary* (Chicago: University of Chicago Press, 2011).

11. I am indebted to Alexandro José Gradilla (in conversation) for this apposite phrase, "gentrification of everyday sexual practices."

12. V. N. Vološinov, *Marxism and the Philosophy of Language* (1930), trans. Ladislav Matejka and I. R. Titunik (New York: Seminar Press, 1973), 74–77. For a more optimistic view of the alien word, see Bakhtin, *Dialogic Imagination*, 276–79.

13. One thinks, for example, of "On the Jewish Question," which, despite its early provenance (1844), has remained a touchstone for thinking about identity and inequality. Karl Marx, in *Karl Marx: Selected Writings*, revised ed., ed. David McLellan (Oxford: Oxford University Press, 2000), 46–70.

14. Raymond Williams, "Base and Superstructure in Marxist Cultural Theory," *New Left Review* 1, no. 82 (November–December 1973): 8.

15. As David Harvey puts it: "The social relation that lies at the root of the Marxian value theory is the class relation between capital and labor. . . . The conception of class evolves in the course of investigating the process of commodity production and exchange." *The Limits to Capital* (1999; reprinted, London: Verso, 2018), 24.

16. Gayatri Spivak, "Can the Subaltern Speak?" in *Marxism and the Interpretation of Culture*, ed. Lawrence Grossberg and Cary Nelson (Urbana: University of Illinois Press, 1988), 288. For clear presentation of queer of color critique, see Roderick A. Ferguson, *Aberrations in Black: Toward a Queer of Color Critique* (Minneapolis: University of Minnesota Press, 2004).

17. Martin F. Manalansan IV, *Global Divas: Filipino Gay Men in the Diaspora* (Durham, NC: Duke University Press, 2003), 32.

18. Siegfried Kracauer, *The Salaried Masses: Duty and Distraction in Weimar Germany* (1929), trans. Quintin Hoare, Introduction by Inka Mülder-Bach (London: Verso, 1998), 30.

19. Michael Warner, ed., *Fear of a Queer Planet: Queer Politics and Social Theory* (Minneapolis: University of Minnesota Press, 1993), vii, xxiv.

20. See Rosemary Hennessy's important critique of this tradition, in *Profit and Pleasure: Sexual Identities in Late Capitalism* (New York: Routledge, 2000), esp. 53–54.

21. Matt Brim, *Poor Queer Studies: Confronting Elitism in the University* (Durham, NC: Duke University Press, 2020), 11.

22. Allan Bérubé, *Coming Out Under Fire: The History of Gay Men and Women in World War II* (1990), 20th anniversary ed., with a new foreword by

John D'Emilio and Estelle Freedman (Chapel Hill: University of North Carolina Press, 2010); Bérubé, *My Desire for History: Essays in Gay, Community, and Labor History*, ed. with an introduction by John D'Emilio and Estelle B. Freedman (Chapel Hill: University of North Carolina Press, 2011).

23. Kath Weston, *Render Me, Gender Me: Lesbians Talk Sex, Class, Color, Nation, Studmuffins* (New York: Columbia University Press, 1997); George Chauncey, *Gay New York: Gender, Urban Culture, and the Making of the Gay Male World, 1890–1940* (New York: Basic Books, 2019).

24. Christopher Chitty, *Sexual Hegemony: Statecraft, Capital, and Sodomy in the Rise of the World System*, ed. Max Fox, with an introduction by Christopher Nealon (Durham, NC: Duke University Press, 2020).

25. Didier Eribon, *Returning to Reims* (2009), introduction by George Chauncey, trans. Michael Lucy (Los Angeles: Semiotext(e), 2013).

26. Alberto Prunetti, "Workers Telling Their Own Stories Can Rebuild Working-Class Pride," *Jacobin*, January 7, 2022, https://jacobinmag.com/2022/01/didier-eribon-retour-a-reims-movie-class.

27. Víctor Macías-González, "Homosexuales," in *Hampones, pelados y pecatrices: Sujetos peligrosos de la Ciudad de México (1940–1960)*, ed. Susana Sosenski and Gabriela Pulido (Cuidad de México: Fondo de Cultura Económica, 2019), 109–58.

28. Carrillo, *Pathways of Desire*, 40.

29. Guillermo Núñez Noriega, *Just Between Us: An Ethnography of Male Identity and Intimacy in Rural Communities of Northern Mexico* (Tucson: University of Arizona Press, 2014), 12.

30. Mauricio List Reyes, *Jóvenes corazones gay en la ciudad de México: Género, identidad y socialidad en hombres gay* (Puebla, México: Benemérita Universidad Autónoma de Puebla, 2005), 122.

31. Audre Lorde uses the term in her influential broadsides, in *Sister Outsider: Essays and Speeches* (1984; reprinted, Berkeley: Crossing Press, 2007), 115, 187.

32. On my reading, Brim sometimes does this, in *Poor Queer Studies*.

33. Max Weber, *From Max Weber: Essays in Sociology*, trans., ed., and with an introduction by Hans Gerth and C. Wright Mills (Oxford: Oxford University Press, 1946), 180–95.

34. Friedrich Engels, *The Origin of the Family, Private Property, and the State, in the Light of the Researches of Lewis H. Morgan*, prepared by Professor Eleanor Burke Leacock (New York: International, 1972).

35. David Harvey, "Accumulation by Dispossession," in *The New Imperialism* (Oxford: Oxford University Press, 2003), 137–82.

36. Marx, *Karl Marx*, 521–23; "Letter to Sigfrid Meyer and August Vogt," in *Karl Marx and Friedrich Engels, Selected Correspondence*, 2nd ed., ed. S. W. Ryazanskaya, trans. I. Lasker (New York: Progress, 1975), 220–24.

37. See the essays in Robert McKee Irwin, Michelle Rocío Nasser, and Ed McCaughan, eds., *The Famous 41: Sexuality and Social Control in Mexico, 1901* (New York: Palgrave Macmillan, 2003).

38. See Víctor Macías-González, "The Transnational Homophile Movement and the Development of Domesticity in Mexico City's Homosexual Community, 1930–1970," *Gender History* 23, no. 3 (October 2014): 519–44. See also Héctor Carrillo's discussion in *Pathways of Desire*, 40. Mexican scholars have been closely studying this period. See, for example, Nathaly Rodríguez, *De sedientos seres: Una historia social del homoerotismo masculino, Ciudad de México, 1917–1952* (Puebla, México: Universidad Iberoamericana Puebla, 2020).

39. Carlos Monsiváis, *Mexican Postcards*, ed., trans., and with an introduction by John Kraniauskas (London: Verso, 1997).

40. Jose Esteban Muñoz, *Cruising Utopia: The Then and There of Queer Futurity* (New York: New York University Press, 2009).

41. Queer is many things, but it isn't just any old thing you like: a longing for the future or utopia or what have you. "Queer," if it is to have any meaning at all (and suspending for the moment the difference among its vernacular, political, and academic inscriptions) *includes* the residue of stigma and exclusion: it is a sensibility shared by all nonauthorized sexualities, disapproved genders, or shunned ways of sexual being. If anything, it is *dystopic*, at least from the point of view of the repurposed signs that give it meaning, a resignation to the idea that things are not going to change much for most of us. What has been radical about the project called queer was its attempt to wrestle joy and meaning out of difficult situations very much in the here and now. These labors have not been without effect, but the fact that this territory has been reconstituting itself, progressively peeling large variants of L, G, B, and T away from "queer," suggests that we have already reached its limits. We now face a very different future.

42. This phrase, so apposite for my purposes, appears in Jedediah Britton-Purdy's op-ed, "The Republican Party Is Succeeding Because We Are Not a True Democracy," *New York Times*, January 3, 2022, https://www.nytimes.com/2022/01/03/opinion/us-democracy-constitution.html.

PART I. PREDICAMENT AND CRISIS

Epigraphs

Alasdair MacIntyre, *After Virtue*, © 1981, by the University of Notre Dame. Reprinted by permission of the publisher.

Raymond Williams, *Marxism and Literature*, © 1977, by Oxford University Press. Reprinted by permission of the publisher.

CHAPTER 1. MOMENT OF TRUTH

1. J. L. Austin, *How to Do Things with Words: The William James Lectures Delivered at Harvard University in 1955* (Oxford: Oxford University Press, 1975), 12–24, esp. 16.

2. Jon Binnie, *The Globalization of Sexuality* (London: Sage, 2004), 34. See also Binnie, "Class, Sexuality, and Space: A Comment," *Sexualities* 14, no. 1 (2011): 21–26.

3. Martin F. Manalansan IV, "In the Shadows of Stonewall: Examining Gay Transnational Politics and the Diasporic Dilemma," *GLQ* 2 (1995): 434.

4. Queer theorists have debated the merits of "guilt" versus "shame" as affective registers. I cast my lot with shame here: the term presupposes a relationship with other's perceptions, whereas "guilt" suggests an internalized judgment. See, for instance, David M. Halperin and Valerie Traube's postconference collection, *Gay Shame* (Chicago: University of Chicago Press, 2009).

5. James Clifford, *The Predicament of Culture: Twentieth-Century Ethnography, Literature, and Art* (Cambridge, MA: Harvard University Press, 1988).

6. Jason de León delves this landscape of risk and abandonment in *The Land of Open Graves: Living and Dying on the Migrant Trail*, with photographs by Michael Wells (Berkeley: University of California Press, 2015).

7. Fredric Jameson, *The Political Unconscious: Narrative as a Socially Symbolic Act* (New York: Cornell University Press, 1981), 88.

8. See Nancy Scheper-Hughes, *Saints, Scholars, and Schizophrenics: Mental Illness in Rural Ireland* (Berkeley: University of California Press, 1979).

9. Ellen Lewin, *Filled with the Spirit: Sexuality, Gender, and Radical Inclusivity in a Black Pentecostal Church Coalition* (Chicago: University of Chicago Press, 2018).

10. Judith Stacey, "Cruising to Familyland: Gay Hypergamy and Rainbow Kinship," *Current Sociology* 52, no. 2 (2004): 181–97.

CHAPTER 2. A PRELIMINARY ANSWER TO THE QUESTION

1. Anthony Giddens, *Modernity and Self-Identity: Self and Society in the Late Modern Age* (Stanford, CA: Stanford University Press, 1991).

CHAPTER 3. LIFE'S RICH PAGEANT

1. Max Weber, *From Max Weber: Essays in Sociology*, trans., ed., and with an introduction by Hans Gerth and C. Wright Mills (Oxford: Oxford University Press, 1946), 180–95.

2. "Historic Centre of Puebla" UNESCO World Heritage Convention, retrieved September 7, 2022, https://whc.unesco.org/en/list/416.

3. Global Data Lab, "Mexico: Subnational HDI," Institute for Management Research, Radboud University, retrieved April 16, 2023, https://globaldatalab .org/shdi/table/shdi/MEX/.

4. The International Labour Organization estimates that nearly 60 percent of the workforce labors in the informal sector in Mexico; the figure is around 75 percent for the state of Puebla. Programme for the Promotion of Formalization in Latin America and the Caribbean, "Informal Employment in Mexico: Current Situation, Policies, and Challenges," International Labour Organization, 2014, https://www.ilo.org/wcmsp5/groups/public/---americas/---ro-lima/documents/publication/wcms_245889.pdf, 1, 5. The government of Mexico gives a current estimate (fourth quarter, 2022) of Puebla's informal employment at 71.3 percent. Gobierno de México, "Puebla: State," Data México, retrieved April 16, 2023, https://datamexico.org/en/profile/geo /puebla-pu.

5. Angela McRobbie, *Be Creative: Making a Living in the New Culture Industries* (Cambridge: Polity, 2016).

6. See the essays in *The Women, Gender, and Development Reader*, 2nd ed., ed. Nalini Visvanathan, Lynn Duggan, Nan Wiegersma, and Laurie Nisonoff (New York: Zed Books, 2011). See also Silvia Lopez Estrada, "Work, Family, and Gender Relations on the Northern Border of Mexico," in *Gender Transitions along Borders: The Northern Borderlands of Mexico and Morocco*, ed. Marlene Solis (London: Routledge, 2016), 31–40, esp. 36.

7. Carlos Decena, *Tacit Subjects: Belonging and Same-Sex Desire among Immigrant Dominican Men* (Durham, NC: Duke University Press, 2011).

8. Eve Kosofsky Sedgwick, *Tendencies* (Durham, NC: Duke University Press, 1993), 62–63.

CHAPTER 4. COMMONPLACES

1. See Pierre Bourdieu, "The Forms of Capital," in *Handbook of Theory and Research for the Sociology of Education*, ed. John G. Richardson (Westport, CT: Greenwood, 1986), 243–48.

2. To fuse lines from Denise Riley's *Am I That Name? Feminism and the Category of "Women" in History* (New York: Macmillan, 1988) and Didier Eribon's *Insult and the Making of the Gay Self* (Durham, NC: Duke University Press, 2004).

3. Raymond Williams, "Base and Superstructure in Marxist Cultural Theory," *New Left Review* 1, no. 82 (November–December 1973): 4.

CHAPTER 5. PRECARIOUS LIVES

1. Max Weber, *The Protestant Ethic and the Spirit of Capitalism* (1930), trans. Talcott Parsons, introduction by Anthony Giddens (New York: Routledge, 2001), 23–24.

2. Karl Polanyi, *The Great Transformation: The Political and Economic Origins of Our Time* (1944) (Boston: Beacon Press, 2001), 35–44.

3. E. P. Thompson, *Customs in Common: Studies in Traditional Popular Culture* (New York: New Press, 1993), 188–98. After reproducing his famous 1980 paper on moral economy (185–258), Thompson addresses criticisms and extensions of his concept (259–351).

4. My doctoral dissertation and first book, *Thanks to God and the Revolution: Popular Religion and Class Consciousness in the New Nicaragua* (New York: Columbia University Press, 1988), was much indebted to this scholarship, which shows how "conservatism" can become the springboard for revolutionary action. See, especially, Eric Wolf, *Peasant Wars of the Twentieth Century* (Norman: University of Oklahoma Press, 1969).

5. Pierre Bourdieu, *Outline of a Theory of Practice* (1972), trans. Richard Nice (Cambridge: Cambridge University Press, 1977), esp. 72–95.

6. Antony S. R. Manstead, "The Psychology of Social Class: How Socioeconomic Status Impacts Thought, Feelings, and Behaviour," *British Journal of Social Psychology* 57, no. 2 (2018): 267–91.

7. See, for instance, Annick Prieur, *Mema's House, Mexico City: On Transvestites, Queens, and Machos* (Chicago: University of Chicago Press, 1998). See also Pierre Bourdieu's short book on gender, *Masculine Domination*, trans. Richard Nice (Stanford, CA: Stanford University Press, 2003).

8. Didier Eribon, *Returning to Reims*, trans. Michael Lucey (Los Angeles: Semiotext(e), 2013).

9. Jennifer Scheper-Hughes, "The Niño Jesús Doctor: Novelty and Innovation in Mexican Religion," *Nova Religio: The Journal of Alternative and Emergent Religions* 16, no. 2 (November 2012): 4–28.

10. Ana Raquel Minian, *Undocumented Lives: The Untold Story of Mexican Migration* (Cambridge, Massachusetts: Harvard University Press, 2018), 7–8, 92, 95; Héctor Carrillo, *Pathways of Desire: The Sexual Migration of Mexican Gay Men* (Chicago: University of Chicago Press, 2017), 52, 151–52.

11. Oscar Lewis, "Culture of Poverty," in *On Understanding Poverty: Perspectives from the Social Sciences*, ed. Daniel Patrick Moynihan (New York: Basic Books, 1969), 187–220; Daniel Patrick Moynihan, "The Negro Family: The Case for National Action" (Washington, DC: Office of Policy Planning and Research, US Department of Labor, 1965).

12. J. D. Vance, *Hillbilly Elegy: A Memoir of a Family and Culture in Crisis* (New York: Harper, 2016).

13. Theodor Adorno, *Negative Dialectics* (1966), trans. E. B. Ashton (New York: Routledge, 1973), 149–50. Such views of the working class as a fixed subculture have been useful for corporatist and fascist political projects, which flatter and domesticate the working class, casting its "grievances" in chauvinistic terms. This, as Slavoj Žižek reminds us, is diametrically opposed to the way Marx understood class dynamics. To cast the distinction in contemporary terms: the goal of liberal identity politics is to bring about "peaceful coexistence," "mutual respect and recognition" among various subject positions and interest groups. Class struggle is a different sort of antagonism. It aims not to conserve the classes intact in a balanced and harmonized relation with one another but to destroy the system that produces class differences. Slavoj Žižek, "Class Struggle against Classism," *Philosophical Salon* (*Los Angeles Review of Books*), May 10, 2021, https://thephilosophicalsalon.com/class-struggle-against-classism/. One thus searches Marx's and Engels's writings in vain for passages that either chauvinistically flatter or condescendingly disparage the working class in cultural terms.

14. Vivek Chibber, *The Class Matrix: Social Theory after the Cultural Turn* (Cambridge, MA: Harvard University Press, 2022).

15. Karl Marx, "The German Ideology," in *Karl Marx: Selected Writings*, revised ed., ed. David McLellan (Oxford: Oxford University Press, 2000), 176.

16. Eduardo L. Menéndez y Renée B. Di Pardo, "Violencias y Alcohol: Las Cotidianidades de las Pequeñas Muertes," *Relaciones* 19, no. 74 (Primavera 1998): 2–71; *Informe General de la Consulta sobre Alcoholismo y Pueblos Indígenas* (Ciudad de México: Comisión Nacional para el Desarrollo de los Pueblos Indígenas, 2008); José Manuel Herrera Paredes and Carla Aparecida Arena Ventura, "Consumo de alcohol y violencia doméstica contra las mujeres: un estudio con estudiantes universitarias de México," *Revista Latino-Americana de Enfermagem* 18 (Spec) (May–June 2010): 557–64.

17. UN Office on Drugs and Crime's International Homicide Statistics database, "Intentional Homicides (per 100,000 People)—Mexico," accessed October 2, 2022, https://data.worldbank.org/indicator/VC.IHR.PSRC.P5?end=2020&locations=MX&start=2006.

18. Instituto Nacional de Estadística, Geografía e Informática (INEGI), *Censo de Población y Vivienda 2020—Cuestionario Básico* (Aguascalientes, México: INEGI, 2020).

19. "Mexico's University Graduate Numbers Are Well below OECD Average," *Mexico City News*, August 23, 2018, https://mexiconewsdaily.com/news/graduate-numbers-well-below-oecd-average/.

20. See Michael Denning, "Wageless Life," *New Left Review* 66 (November–December 2010): 97.

21. Michael Denning uses this phrase throughout "Wageless Life."

22. I again channel Raymond Williams here, in "Base and Superstructure in Marxist Cultural Theory," *New Left Review* 1, no. 82 (November–December 1973): 4.

23. The conversation, which probably never occurred, supposedly went as follows. Fitzgerald: The rich are different from you and me. Hemingway: Yes, they have more money.

24. Judith Butler, "Performativity, Precarity, and Sexual Politics," *AIBR: Revista de Antropología Iberoamericana* 4, no. 3 (Septiembre–Diciembre 2009): i–xiii.

25. Ernst Bloch, "Nonsynchronism and the Obligation to Its Dialectics" (1935), *New German Critique* (Spring 1977): 22–38.

26. Not only in Mexico. See James Ferguson, "Of Mimicry and Membership: Africans and the 'New World Society,'" *Cultural Anthropology* 17, no. 4 (2002): 551–69.

27. Errico Malatesta, "An Anarchist Programme (1920)," Marxists Internet Archive, accessed May 21, 2023, https://www.marxists.org/archive/malatesta /1920/program/program.htm.

CHAPTER 6. FABLE OF RAPPORT

1. See the discussion in James Clifford, "On Ethnographic Authority," *Representations*, no. 2 (Spring 1983): 132.

2. The idea that I found a home in Puebla cuts against prevailing conceits in the liberal academy and, in some circles, might even be construed as a settler-colonialist gesture. I trust that I have not made myself at home unreflexively, like a boorish and presumptuous houseguest who takes up too much space and inconveniences the owners of the house. I only note in passing the obvious facts: people of different social classes and origins variously vacation, travel, move around, and relocate, sometimes taking up their dwellings in places where they weren't born. Their motives are varied and their experiences involve multiplex inequalities, occasions for the crisscrossing of understandings and misunderstandings. Prima facie denunciations of these experiences on the Left reify identities of various kinds, mirroring nativist anti-immigrant, border-fortifying rhetoric on the Right; their moral tone sometimes borders on old-fashioned prohibitions against race mixing.

CHAPTER 7. IDENTITY AND ITS DISCONTENTS

1. John Mason Hart, *Revolutionary Mexico: The Coming and Process of the Mexican Revolution* (Berkeley: University of California Press, 1989), 129–62.

2. Eric Wolf, *Peasant Wars of the Twentieth Century* (Norman: University of Oklahoma Press, 1969), 33; George McCutchen McBride, *The Land Systems of Mexico* (New York: American Geographical Society, 1923), 154.

3. See Robert McKee Irwin, "The Famous 41: The Scandalous Birth of Modern Mexican Homosexuality," *GLQ: A Journal of Lesbian and Gay Studies* 6, no. 3 (2000), 353; Carlos Monsiváis, "El mundo soslayado," in Salvador Novo, *La estatua de sal* (Mexico City: Consejo Nacional para la Cultura y las Artes, 1998), 19–21.

4. Robert McKee Irwin, Edward J. McCaughan, and Michelle Rocío Nasser, eds., *The Famous 41: Sexuality and Social Control in Mexico, 1910* (New York: Palgrave Macmillan, 2003).

5. Irwin, "The Famous 41," 354.

6. Robert Buffington, "Homophobia and the Mexican Working Class, 1900–1910," in Irwin, McCaughan, and Nasser, *The Famous 41*, 194.

7. Irwin, "The Famous 41," 363.

8. Roger N. Lancaster, *Life Is Hard: Machismo, Danger, and the Intimacy of Power in Nicaragua* (Berkeley: University of California Press, 1992), 235–78.

9. Irwin, "The Famous 41," 365.

10. Víctor Macías-González, "The *Lagartijo* at The High Life: Masculine Consumption, Race, Nation, and Homosexuality in Porfirian Mexico," in Irwin, McCaughan, and Nasser, *The Famous 41*, 227–28); Buffington, "Homophobia and the Mexican Working Class," 361–62; Irwin, "The Famous 41," 361–62.

11. Wolf, *Peasant Wars of the Twentieth Century.*

12. Marjorie Becker, *Setting the Virgin on Fire: Lázaro Cárdenas, Michoacán Peasants, and the Redemption of the Mexican Revolution* (Berkeley: University of California Press, 1995). See also Enrique Krauze's chapter on Cárdenas in *Mexico: Biography of Power—A History of Modern Mexico, 1810-1996* (New York: Harper Perennial, 1998), 438–89.

13. José Vasconcelos, *The Cosmic Race* (1925), bilingual ed., translated and annotated by Didier Tisdel Jaén (Baltimore: Johns Hopkins University Press, 1997).

14. Carlos Monsiváis, "Notas sobre la cultura mexicana en el siglo XX," in *Historia General de México*, obra preparada por el Centro de Estudios Históricos (Cuidad de México: El Colegio de México, 2000), 986.

15. Benedict Anderson, *Imagined Communities: Reflections on the Origins and Spread of Nationalism* (1983), revised ed. (London: Verso, 2006).

16. In "La Trampa de las Castas," Pilar Gonzalbo finds inconsistencies, irregularities, ambiguities, and exceptions to the supposed rules, as well as mobility between caste categories. She suggests that the caste system was never rigorously followed in viceregal New Spain; much less did it result in a system of rigorous segregation. In Solange Alberro and Pilar Gonzalbo Aizpuru, *La Sociedad Novohispana: Estereotipos y Realidades* (Ciudad de México: Colegio de México, 2013), 17–154.

17. Guillermo Bonfil Batalla, *México Profundo: Reclaiming a Civilization* (1987), trans. Philip A. Dennis (Austin: University of Texas Press, 1996), 3.

18. Bonfil Batalla, 17–18.

19. Bonfil Batalla, *México Profundo*, 128.

20. It is worth noting that Claudio Lomnitz sees a more dynamic historical process here, with ideas about death being imbricated in the postcolonial making of the nation. Lomnitz, *Death and the Idea of Mexico* (New York: Zone Books, 2005), for example, 24, 28, 46, 483.

21. Or, as Jean Baudrillard curmudgeonly quipped in a different context: "Liberation has left everyone in an undefined state (it is always the same: once you are liberated, you are forced to ask who you are)." Baudrillard, *America* (New York: Verso, 2010), 46.

22. Karl Marx, *Pre-capitalist Economic Formations*, ed. E. J. Hobsbawm (New York: International, 1965), esp., Hobsbawm's introduction, 34, 63, 69–70.

23. Cedric Johnson, "An Open Letter to Ta-Nehisi Coates and the Liberals Who Love Him," *Jacobin*, February 3, 2016, https://jacobin.com/2016/02/ta-nehisi-coates-case-for-reparations-bernie-sanders-racism/.

24. René Flores and Edward Telles, "Social Stratification in Mexico: Disentangling Color, Ethnicity, and Class," *American Sociological Review* 77, no. 3 (June 2012): 490.

25. Johnson "An Open Letter."

26. Bonfil Batalla, *México Profundo*, 18.

27. See, for instance, Víctor Macías-González, "The Transnational Homophile Movement and the Development of Domesticity in Mexico City's Homosexual Community, 1930-1970," *Gender and History* 26, no. 3 (November 2014): 519–44. See also his chapter, "Homosexuales," in *Hampones, pelados y pecatrices. Sujetos peligrosos de la Ciudad de México (1940–1960)*, ed. Susana Sosenski and Gabriela Pulido (Cuidad de México: Fondo de Cultura Económica), 109–58.

28. Joanna Wuest, "After Liberation: Sex, Social Movements, and Capital since the New Left," *Polity* 54, no. 3 (2022): 478–502.

29. See Eric Zolov, *Refried Elvis: The Rise of the Mexican Counterculture* (Berkeley: University of California Press, 1999), 217–24.

30. Walter Benn Michaels, *The Trouble with Diversity: How We Learned to Love Identity and Ignore Inequality*, 10th anniversary ed. (New York: Picador, 2016).

31. Nancy Fraser, "Feminism, Capitalism, and the Cunning of History," *New Left Review* 56 (March–April 2009): 97–117.

32. Marshall Berman, *All That Is Solid Melts into Air: The Experience of Modernity* (New York: Penguin, 1982), 92, 94.

33. John D'Emilio, "Capitalism and Gay Identity," in *The Gender Sexuality Reader: Culture, History, Political Economy*, ed. Roger N. Lancaster and Micaela di Leonardo, 468, 474–75 (New York: Routledge, 1997).

CHAPTER 8. *THEY* LIVED IN A
DIFFERENT TIME FROM *US*

1. Ramon Lobato, *Shadow Economies of Cinema: Mapping Informal Film Distribution* (New York: Palgrave Macmillan, 2019), 81.

2. See George M. Cowan's classic ethnographic piece, "Mazateco Whistle Speech," *Language* 24, no. 3 (July–September 1948): 280–86.

3. The benchmark essay is, of course, Eric R. Wolf, "Closed Corporate Peasant Communities in Mesoamerica and Central Java," *Southwestern Journal of Anthropology* 13, no. 1 (Spring 1957): 1–18.

4. The 1910 rural and urban numbers are drawn from the national census: INEGI, 1910 census, accessed May 6, 2023, https://en.www.inegi.org.mx /programas/ccpv/1910/. INEGI gives a 21 percent rural figure for 2020. "Población rural y urbana, 2020," Cuéntame de México, accessed April 29, 2023, https://cuentame.inegi.org.mx/poblacion/rur_urb.aspx?tema=P. Using other criteria, the OECD calculates the current rural population at 36 percent. OECD, "Income Inequality," 2021, OECD Data, accessed April 29, 2023, https://www .oecd.org/gov/oecdruralpolicyreviewsmexico.htm. The most recent figures on indigenous self-description and language are taken from the 2015 Intercensal Survey. INEGI, "Etnicidad: Lengua indígena," in *Principales resultados de la Enquesta Intercensal 2015*, accessed April 29, 2023, https://www.senado.gob .mx/comisiones/asuntos_indigenas/eventos/docs/etnicidad_240216.pdf.

5. Guillermo Bonfil Batalla, *México Profundo: Reclaiming a Civilization* (1987), trans. Philip A. Dennis (Austin: University of Texas Press, 1996), 20.

6. Bonfil Batalla, 17, 20, 46.

7. Robert Brain writes about love and intimacy in Chinautleco friendships (Guatemala) in his quirky, readable *Friends and Lovers* (New York: Basic, 1976), 39–42. Walter Williams surveys tolerant attitudes among the lowland Maya and the region's mestizos in *The Spirit and the Flesh: Sexual Diversity in American Indian Culture* (Boston: Beacon Press, 1986), 140–151. Lynn Stephen surveys gender and sexual diversity in "Sexualities and Genders in Zapotec Oaxaca," in James N. Green and Florence E. Babb, coordinators, "Gender, Sexuality, and Same-Sex Desire in Latin America," special issue, *Latin American Perspectives* 29, no. 2 (March 2002): 41–59.

8. Carlos Monsiváis, *Los ídolos a nado: Una antología global* (Barcelona: Debate Feminista, Random House Mondadori, 2011), 129–30.

9. Lauren Berlant, *Cruel Optimism* (Durham, NC: Duke University Press, 2011), 1, 23–24.

10. Raymond Williams, *Marxism and Literature* (Oxford: Oxford University Press, 1977), 128–35.

11. Eve Kosofsky Sedgwick, "Queer Performativity: Henry James's *The Art of the Novel*," *GLQ* 1, no. 1 (1993): 15.

CHAPTER 9. PUTOS

1. C. J. Pascoe, *Dude, You're a Fag: Masculinity and Sexuality in High School* (2007), with a new preface (Berkeley: University of California Press, 2012).

2. Henry Romero, "Mexico's wages are so paltry that human-rights and legal groups are sounding the alarm," *Business Insider*, March 1, 2017, https://www.businessinsider.com/mexico-wages-incomes-poverty-2017-2

3. "Informal Employment in Mexico: Current Situation, Policies, and Challenges," FORLAC: Programme for the Promotion of Formalization in Latin America and the Caribbean, International Labour Organization, 2014.

4. OECD, "Average Wages," OECD Data, accessed April 30, 2023, https://data.oecd.org/earnwage/average-wages.htm; OECD, "Hours Worked," OECD Data, accessed April 30, 2023, https://data.oecd.org/emp/hours-worked.htm.

5. OECD, "Income Inequality," 2021 or latest available, OECD Data, accessed April 29, 2023, https://data.oecd.org/inequality/income-inequality.htm.

6. World Bank Group, "Poverty and Equity Brief: Latin America and the Caribbean—Mexico, World Bank, October 2021, https://databankfiles.worldbank.org/public/ddpext_download/poverty/987B9C90-CB9F-4D93-AE8C-750588BF00QA/AM2021/Global_POVEQ_MEX.pdf.

7. This is a recurring theme for Carlos Monsiváis. See his essay "Would So Many Millions of People Not End Up Speaking English? The North American Culture of Mexico," in *The Latin American Cultural Studies Reader*, ed. Ana del Sarto, Alicia Ríos, and Abril Trigo (Durham, NC: Duke University Press, 2004), esp. 206, 213, 219–220.

8. Octavio Paz, *The Labyrinth of Solitude* [1950] *and Other Writings*, trans. Lysander Kemp, Yara Milos, and Rachel Phillips Belash (New York: Grove Press, 1985), 194; Carlos Fuentes, *Myself with Others: Selected Essays* (New York: Farrar, Straus and Giroux, 1988), 23.

9. Lauren Berlant, *Cruel Optimism* (Durham, NC: Duke University Press, 2011).

10. Maggie Nelson, *On Freedom: Four Songs of Care and Restraint* (Minneapolis: Graywolf Press, 2021); Tim Dean, *Unlimited Intimacy: Reflections on the Subculture of Barebacking* (Chicago: University of Chicago Press, 2009).

11. Karl Marx, "The Fetishism of Commodities," from *Capital*, in *Karl Marx: Selected Writings*, revised ed., ed. David McLellan (Oxford: Oxford University Press, 2000), 472–81.

12. Georg Lukács, *History and Class Consciousness: Studies in Marxist Dialectics*, trans. Rodney Livingstone (Cambridge, MA: MIT Press, 1972); Theodor Adorno and Max Horkheimer, *Dialectic of Enlightenment: Philosophical Fragments* (1944; reprinted, Stanford, CA: Stanford University Press, 2002), 94–136.

13. Stuart Hall, "Encoding, Decoding," in *Culture, Media, Language,* ed. Stuart Hall, Dorothy Hobson, Andrew Lowe and Paul Willis (London: Hutchinson, 1980), 128–38.

14. Thorstein Veblen, *Theory of the Leisure Class* (1899; reprint, Oxford: Oxford University Press, 2007); Jean Baudrillard, "The System of Objects" (1968) and "For a Critique of the Political Economy of the Sign" (1972), in *Jean Baudrillard: Selected Writings,* 2nd ed., ed. Mark Poster (Stanford, CA: Stanford University Press, 2001), 13–31, 60–100.

15. Adolph Reed Jr., "Antiracism: A Neoliberal Alternative to a Left," *Dialectical Anthropology* 42 (2018): 105–15.

16. Grant Farred, *Martin Heidegger Saved My Life* (Minneapolis: University of Minnesota Press, 2015).

17. Mauricio Cabrera, "Todos Somos Putos," *Juanfutbol,* 20 June 2014, accessed July 26, 2021, https://juanfutbol.com/articulo/maca/todos-somos-putos. Cabrera's original post has been removed, though one can still find extensive quotations from the article online.

18. "Revealed: 6,500 Migrant Workers Have Died in Qatar since World Cup Awarded," *The Guardian,* February 23, 2021, https://www.theguardian.com /global-development/2021/feb/23/revealed-migrant-worker-deaths-qatar-fifa-world-cup-2022.

CHAPTER 10. POSTCARDS FROM THE AMBIENTE

1. Ernst Bloch, "Nonsynchronism and the Obligation to Its Dialectics" (1935), *New German Critique,* no. 11 (Spring 1977): 22.

2. Stephen O. Murray and Wayne R. Dynes, "Hispanic Homosexuals: A Spanish Lexicon," in *Latin American Male Homosexualities,* ed. Stephen O. Murray (Albuquerque: University of New Mexico Press, 1995), 181, 189.

3. Stephen O. Murray and Manuel Arboleda G., "Stigma Transformation and Relexification: 'Gay' in Latin America," in *Male Homosexuality in Central and South America,* ed. Stephen O. Murray (New York: Gay Academic Union, 1987), 131.

4. Carlos Monsiváis, "De las variedades de la experiencia homoerótica," *Debate Feminista* 35 (Abril 2007): 166–67.

5. Patty Kelly, *Lydia's Open Door: Inside Mexico's Most Modern Brothel* (Berkeley: University of California Press, 2008), 121–150.

6. Howard Richler, *How Happy Became Homosexual: And Other Mysterious Semantic Shifts* (Vancouver: Ronsdale Press, 2013), 41–42.

7. Franklin Kameny, "Gay Is Good," in *We Are Everywhere: A Historical Sourcebook of Gay and Lesbian Politics,* ed. Mark Blasius and Shane Phelan

(New York: Routledge, 1997), 366–77; Carl Wittman, *A Gay Manifesto* (New York: Red Butterfly, 1970).

8. V. N. Vološinov, *Marxism and the Philosophy of Language* (1930), trans. Ladislav Matejka and I. R. Titunik (New York: Seminar Press, 1973).

9. Barry Adam, "Homosexuality without a Gay World: Pasivos y Activos en Nicaragua," *Out/Look* 1 no. 4 (1989): 74–82.

10. Gordon Brent Ingram, "Ten Arguments for a Theory of Queers in Public Space," introductory talk for the panel "Queer Space: Sites of Existence, Sites of Resistance," Queer Frontiers Conference, International Lesbian and Gay Archives, University of Southern California, Los Angeles, 1995.

11. Carlos Monsiváis, "Juan Gabriel y aquel apoteósico y polémico concierto en Bellas Artes," *Proceso*, August 29, 2016 (first published May 12, 1990), https://www.proceso.com.mx/cronica/2016/8/29/juan-gabriel-aquel-apoteosico-polemico-concierto-en-bellas-artes-169702.html.

12. Anthony Giddens, *The Consequences of Modernity* (Cambridge: Polity Press, 1990), 28–33.

13. Anthony Giddens, *Modernity and Self-Identity: Self and Society in the Late Modern Age* (Stanford, CA: Stanford University Press, 1991), 70–87.

14. Johannes Fabian, *Time and the Other: How Anthropology Makes Its Object* (New York: Columbia University Press, 1983).

15. Roger N. Lancaster, "Subject Honor and Object Shame: The Construction of Male Homosexuality and Stigma in Nicaragua," *Ethnology* 27, no. 2 (April 1988): 111–25; Lancaster, *Life Is Hard: Machismo, Danger, and the Intimacy of Power in Nicaragua* (Berkeley: University of California Press, 1992), 235–78. I would be remiss not to say how conversations with Richard Parker, who was also a graduate student at Berkeley at the time, helped shape these ideas. See Richard Parker, *Bodies, Pleasures, and Passions: Sexual Culture in Contemporary Brazil* (Boston: Beacon Press, 1991).

16. See, for instance, Ana Maria Alonso and Maria Teresa Korek, "Silences: 'Hispanics,' AIDS, and Sexual Practices," and Tomás Almaguer, "Chicano Men: A Cartography of Homosexual Identity and Behavior," in *The Lesbian and Gay Studies Reader*, ed. Henry Abelove, Michèle Aina Barale, and David M. Halperin (New York: Routledge, 1993), 110–26, 255–73.

17. In subsequent analyses, I used pluralizing phrases like "sexualities in Latin America" instead of "Latin American sexuality" and gave more textured views of how popular sexual understandings vary. See, for example, Lancaster, "Tolerance and Intolerance in Sexual Cultures in Latin America," in *Passing Lines: Immigration and (Homo)Sexuality*, ed. Brad Epps, Kaja Valens, and Bill Johnson González (Cambridge, MA: David Rockefeller Center on Latin American Studies and Harvard University Press, 2005), 255–74.

18. Dennis Altman, *Global Sex* (Chicago: University of Chicago Press, 2001); Altman, "Rupture or Continuity: The Internationalization of Gay Identities," *Social Text* 48 (Autumn 1996): 82.

19. Lisa Rofel, *Desiring China: Experiments in Neoliberalism, Sexuality, and Public Culture* (Durham, NC: Duke University Press, 2007), 90; Rofel, "Qualities of Desire: Imagining Gay Identities in China," *GLQ* 5, no. 4 (1999): 454.

20. Martin F. Manalansan IV, *Global Divas: Filipino Gay Men in the Diaspora* (Durham, NC: Duke University Press, 2003), 6.

21. Altman, "Rupture or Continuity."

22. Héctor Carrillo notes this repeatedly in *The Night Is Young: Sexuality in Mexico in the Time of AIDS* (Chicago: University of Chicago Press, 2017), 15–16, 96.

23. Octavio Paz, *The Labyrinth of Solitude and Other Writings* (1950), trans. Lysander Kemp, Yara Milos, and Rachel Phillips Belash (New York: Grove Press, 1985), 194; Carlos Fuentes, *Myself with Others: Selected Essays* (New York: Farrar, Straus and Giroux, 1988).

24. This will stand as a concise and passable summary of scores of interviews I conducted in 2006–7. When I asked respondents to compare and contrast the two countries in a Fulbright-funded project titled "How Mexicans See the United States," they invariably devised these and similar sorts of associations.

25. Carlos Monsiváis, "Would So Many Millions of People Not End Up Speaking English? The North American Culture and Mexico," in *The Latin American Cultural Studies Reader*, ed. Ana Del Sarto, Alicia Ríos, and Abril Trigo (Durham, NC: Duke University Press), 231–32.

26. Monsiváis, "Would So Many Millions of People Not End Up Speaking English?" 219, 223.

27. Carrillo, *The Night Is Young*.

28. Louisa Schein, "Of Cargo and Satellites: Imagined Cosmopolitanism," *Postcolonial Studies* 2, no. 3 (1999): 345–75.

29. Nestor García Canclini, *Hybrid Cultures: Strategies for Entering and Leaving Modernity*, trans. Christopher L. Chiappari and Silvia L. Lopez (Minneapolis: University of Minnesota Press, 1995).

30. David Valentine, *Imagining Transgender: An Ethnography of a Category* (Durham, NC: Duke University Press, 2007), e.g., 3–6, 62, 119–21.

31. Stuart Hall and Tony Jefferson, eds., *Resistance through Rituals: Youth Subcultures in Post-war Britain*, 2nd ed. (NY: Routledge, 1993); Dick Hebdige, *Subculture: The Meaning of Style* (1979; reprinted, New York: Routledge, 1988).

32. Michael Warner, "Queer and Then? The End of Queer Theory," *Chronicle of Higher Education*, January 1, 2012, https://www.chronicle.com/article/queer-and-then/.

CHAPTER 11. URBAN TRIBES

1. See John Ross, "Mexico City's Urban Tribes Go on the Warpath against Emos," *Counterpunch*, April 8, 2008, https://www.counterpunch.org/2008/04/08/mexico-city-s-urban-tribes-go-on-the-warpath-against-emos/.

2. Alexis Madrigal, "Anti-emo Riots Break Out across Mexico," *Wired*, March 27, 2008, https://www.wired.com/2008/03/anti-emo-riots/; Daniel Hernandez, "Emo Bashing: Mexico's Latest Urban-Youth Craze," *LA Weekly*, April 9, 2008, http://www.laweekly.com/music/emo-bashing-mexicos-latest-urban-youth-craze-2152920.

3. Ross, "Mexico City's Urban Tribes Go on the Warpath."

4. Carlos Monsiváis, "Would So Many Millions of People Not End Up Speaking English? The North American Culture and Mexico," in *The Latin American Cultural Studies Reader*, ed. Ana Del Sarto, Alicia Ríos, and Abril Trigo (Durham, NC: Duke University Press, 2004), 219.

5. Monsiváis, 221.

CHAPTER 12. A TALE OF TWO CITIES

1. INEGI (Instituto Nacional de Estadística, Geografía e Informática), "Estadísticas a Propósito del 14 de Febrero: Datos Nacionales," Comunicado de Prensa Núm 92/20, 13 de Febrero 2020.

2. Josh Rogin, "Giuliani Made Millions Consulting for Mexico's Most Anti-Trump Politician," *Washington Post*, November 29, 2016, https://www.washingtonpost.com/news/josh-rogin/wp/2016/11/29/giuliani-made-millions-consulting-for-mexicos-most-anti-trump-politician/.

3. Paul Berman, "Labyrinth of Solitude," *New York Times Magazine*, August 2, 1998, sec. 6, p. 50.

4. Lauren Berlant and Michael Warner, "Sex in Public," *Critical Inquiry* 24 (Winter 1998): 563.

5. Samuel R. Delany, *Times Square Red, Times Square Blue* (New York: New York University Press, 1999), 111.

6. Matthew Gutmann, "Seed of the Nation: Men's Sex and Potency in Mexico," in *The Gender/Sexuality Reader: Culture, History, Political Economy*, ed. Roger N. Lancaster and Micaela di Leonardo (New York: Routledge, 1997), 194–206.

7. David Harvey, "The Right to the City," *New Left Review* 53 (September–October 2008): 23–40.

8. Delany, *Times Square Red, Times Square Blue*, 179.

9. Over the years, denunciations of tourism, cultural appropriation, settler colonialism, and microaggressions have stacked up. Segments of Left academic culture have waxed increasingly suspicious of interracial relationships and

pessimistic about desegregationist goals and ideals, culminating in calls for racially and ethnically segregated safe spaces or healing spaces. See Emily DeRuy, "The Fine Line between Safe Space and Segregation," *The Atlantic*, August 17, 2016, https://www.theatlantic.com/education/archive/2016/08/finding-the-line-between-safe-space-and-segregation/496289/; and Sarah Viren, "The Safe Space That Became a Viral Nightmare," *New York Times Magazine*, Education Issue, September 7, 2022, https://www.nytimes.com/2022/09/07/magazine/arizona-state-university-multicultural-center.html.

10. Ernst Bloch, *The Principle of Hope*, 3 vols. (1954, 1955, 1959), trans. Neville Plaice, Stephen Plaice, and Paul Knight (Cambridge, MA: MIT Press, 1995).

11. Roger N. Lancaster, *Sex Panic and the Punitive State* (Berkeley: University of California Press, 2011).

12. Carlos Monsiváis, "Would So Many Millions of People Not End Up Speaking English? The North American Culture and Mexico," in *The Latin American Cultural Studies Reader*, ed. Ana Del Sarto, Alicia Ríos, and Abril Trigo (Durham, NC: Duke University Press), 232.

CONCLUSION: THE HORIZONS OF GAY IDENTITY

Epigraph 2: "Marx to Ruge, Kreuznach, September 1843," letters from the Deutsch-Französische Jahrbücher, https://www.marxists.org/archive/marx/works/1843/letters/43_09.htm.

1. Jeremy Denk, "Why I Hate the 'Goldberg Variations,'" *Deceptive Cadence*, NPR, March 19, 2012, https://www.npr.org/sections/deceptivecadence/2012/03/16/148769794/why-i-hate-the-goldberg-variations.

2. Miguel del Castillo Negrete Rovira, "Income Inequality in Mexico, 2004–2014," *Latin American Policy* 8, no. 1 (2017): 93–113. Del Castillo finds that after corrections are made, and contrary to the official data that are usually cited, social inequality is high and increasing in Mexico, owing to public policies implemented from the mid-1980s on.

3. David Harvey, *A Brief History of Neoliberalism* (Oxford: Oxford University Press, 2007), esp. 9–38; Anthony Giddens, *The Consequences of Modernity* (Cambridge: Polity Press, 1990), esp. 20–23, 36–45. Karl Marx and Friedrich Engels summarize the modernizing dynamism of capitalism in *The Communist Manifesto*: "The bourgeoisie cannot exist without constantly revolutionizing the instruments of production, and thereby the relations of production, and with them the whole relations of society." In *Karl Marx: Selected Writings*, revised ed., ed. David McLellan (Oxford: Oxford University Press, 2000), 248.

4. See Achille Mbembe's arguments in *On the Postcolony* (Berkeley: University of California Press, 2001). See also Olúfẹ́mi Táíwò, *How Colonialism Preempted Modernity in Africa* (Bloomington: Indiana University Press, 2010);

and Táíwò, *Africa Must Be Modern: A Manifesto* (Bloomington: Indiana University Press, 2014).

5. Bruno Perreau, *Queer Theory: The French Response* (Stanford, CA: Stanford University Press), 143.

6. Perreau, 143.

7. Perreau, 127, 131.

8. In an instructive reprise of intersectional identitarian arguments, Jack Halberstam asserts that white gay men should be ashamed of themselves whenever they draw analogies between their sense of loss (as *white* gay men) and that of others (black and brown gay men). As a demographic, generic white men supposedly start with many advantages, such that their *gay* sense of loss can only be tied up with a loss of privilege. (Judith Halberstam, "Shame and White Gay Masculinity," *Social Text* 23, nos. 3–4 [84–85] [Fall–Winter 2005]: 219–33.) Briskly distinguishing the good gays from the bad gays (223) and employing racial-ethnic identity as both analysis and analysand (224), Halberstam ultimately bars the path to fellow feeling and empathy (225), which can only figure as projections or deflections in the game of privilege maintenance. The author does carve out the usual convenient exception: masculinity, or "butchness," is politically productive and commendable when women do it, but deplorable when men do it (226); thus, despite their superficial semblance to men, they, even white butches, might be entitled to speak with authority about loss. Whatever the merits of analytically pitting tomboys against sissies (see David M. Halperin and Valerie Traub, "Introduction: Beyond Gay Pride," in *Gay Shame*, ed. David M. Halperin and Valerie Traub [Chicago: University of Chicago Press, 2009], 35), in the competition for acknowledgment of oppression, conspicuously absent in this broadside is any recognition of social class. Privilege maintenance here might be better understood as the work of members of the professional class, who posit identities, assert grievances, and administer chastisements so as to preside over their adjudication and ranking. This sort of parsing and tallying is good for shoring up interest groups under the banner of "diversity, equity, and inclusion," which is to say that it has favored placement in the neoliberal university, but is the opposite of the work of cultivating solidarities.

9. Jasbir Puar, *Terrorist Assemblages: Homonationalism in Queer Times* (Durham, NC: Duke University Press, 2017).

10. Lauren Berlant, *The Queen of America Goes to Washington City: Essays on Sex and Citizenship* (Durham, NC: Duke University Press, 1997); Rosemary Hennessey, *Profit and Pleasure: Sexual Identities in Late Capitalism* (New York: Routledge, 2000).

11. Touré Reed, *Toward Freedom: The Case against Race Reductionism* (London: Verso, 2020), 73–75, 77–100.

12. See Anne Case and Angus Deaton, *Deaths of Despair and the Future of Capitalism* (Princeton, NJ: Princeton University Press, 2020).

13. I am condensing here my concluding arguments in *The Trouble with Nature: Sex in Science and Popular Culture* (Berkeley: University of California Press, 2003), 306–48.

14. Allan Bérubé, *My Desire for History: Essays in Gay, Community, and Labor History*, ed. John D'Emilio and Estelle B. Freedman (Chapel Hill: University of North Carolina Press, 2011), 241.

15. At least until recently, the field rarely broached the subject of love, not deeming it sufficiently disruptive. See David M. Halperin, "Queer Love," *Critical Inquiry* 45 (Winter 2019): 396–419.

16. David M. Halperin, *One Hundred Years of Homosexuality and Other Essays on Greek Love* (New York: Routledge, 1990), 40.

17. Eve Kosofsky Sedgwick, "Queer Performativity: Henry James's *The Art of the Novel*," *GLQ* 1, no. 1 (1993), esp. 4–5.

18. I continue to channel Sedgwick here, rewiring her arguments about the productiveness of shame in "Queer Performativity," 4.

19. Barbara Ehrenreich and John Ehrenreich, "The Professional-Managerial Class," *Radical America* 11, no. 2 (March–April 1977): 13.

20. Economic Commission for Latin America, "Economic Survey of Latin America and the Caribbean, 2021: Mexico," 1, accessed May 6, 2023, https://repositorio .cepal.org/bitstream/handle/11362/47193/83/EI2021_Mexico_en.pdf.

21. Mitchell Dean and Daniel Zamora, *The Last Man Takes LSD: Foucault and the End of Revolution* (London: Verso, 2021), 10–11. See also James Miller's earlier book, *The Passion of Michel Foucault* (New York: Anchor, 1994), 30–35.

22. José Miguel Vivanco, "Mexican Government Paralyzed in the Face of a Wave of Femicides," Human Rights Watch, March 3, 2020, https://www.hrw .org/news/2020/03/03/mexican-government-paralyzed-face-wave-femicides.

23. See my previous work on the victims' rights approach: *Sex Panic and the Punitive State* (Berkeley: University of California Press, 2011), esp. 195, 200, 206–7.

24. René Rojas marks a similar delamination in Chile, where social movement activists larded a proposed constitutional reform with identitarian planks and blew a historic opportunity. "Chile's Vote Was a Rebuke of the 21st-Century Left; Will We Listen?" *Jacobin*, December 5, 2022, https://jacobin.com/2022/12 /chiles-vote-was-a-rebuke-of-the-21st-century-left-will-we-listen?.

25. See Nancy Fraser, "The End of Progressive Neoliberalism," *Dissent*, January 2, 2017, https://www.dissentmagazine.org/online_articles/progressive-neoliberalism-reactionary-populism-nancy-fraser.

26. Roger Lancaster, "Dreams of a Better Mexico," *Jacobin*, July 6, 2018, https://jacobin.com/2018/07/lopez-obrador-election-victory-morena.

27. Jason Vazquez, "Backgrounder: AMLO and Mexican Labor Law Reform," *OnLabor: Workers, Unions, Politics*, March 19, 2021, https://onlabor.org /backgrounder-amlo-and-mexican-labor-law-reform/.

28. Viri Ríos, "¿López Obrador ha reducido la desigualdad en México?" *New York Times*, February 17, 2020, https://www.nytimes.com/es/2020/02/17/espanol/opinion/desigualdad-mexico-amlo.html.

29. López Obrador was especially candid about these matters in post-2006 discussions of the "power mafia." See his *La mafia que se adueno de Mexico . . . y el 2012* (Barcelona: Grijalbo Mondadori, 2006).

30. "Velvet cage" plays off Max Weber's discussion of the "iron cage" in *The Protestant Ethic and the Spirit of Capitalism* (London: Routledge, 1992), 123–24.

31. "Marx to Ruge, Kreuznach, September 1843."

Bibliography

Adam, Barry. "Homosexuality without a Gay World: Pasivos y Activos en Nicaragua." *Out/Look* 1, no. 4 (1989): 74–82.

Adorno, Theodor. *Negative Dialectics* (1966). Translated by E. B. Ashton. New York: Routledge, 1973.

Adorno, Theodor, and Max Horkheimer. *Dialectic of Enlightenment: Philosophical Fragments.* 1944. Reprinted, Stanford, CA: Stanford University Press, 2002.

Almaguer, Tomás. "Chicano Men: A Cartography of Homosexual Identity and Behavior." In *The Lesbian and Gay Studies Reader,* edited by Henry Abelove, Michèle Aina Barale, and David M. Halperin, 255–73. New York: Routledge, 1993.

Alonso, Ana Maria, and Maria Teresa Korek. "Silences: 'Hispanics,' AIDS, and Sexual Practices." In *The Lesbian and Gay Studies Reader,* edited by Henry Abelove, Michèle Aina Barale, and David M. Halperin, 110–26. New York: Routledge, 1993.

Altman, Dennis. *Global Sex.* Chicago: University of Chicago Press, 2001.

———. "Rupture or Continuity: The Internationalization of Gay Identities," *Social Text* 48 (Autumn 1996): 77–94.

Anderson, Benedict. *Imagined Communities: Reflections on the Origins and Spread of Nationalism* (1983). Revised edition. London: Verso, 2006.

Austin, J. L. *How to Do Things with Words: The William James Lectures Delivered at Harvard University in 1955.* Oxford: Oxford University Press, 1975.

Bakhtin, Mikhail. *The Dialogic Imagination: Four Essays by M. M. Bakhtin.* Edited by Michael Holquist. Translated by Caryl Emerson and Michael Holquist. Austin: University of Texas Press, 1981.

Baudrillard, Jean. *America.* New York: Verso, 2010.

———. "The System of Objects" (1968), and "For a Critique of the Political Economy of the Sign" (1972). In *Jean Baudrillard: Selected Writings,* 2nd edition, edited and with an introduction by Mark Poster, 13–31, 60–100. Stanford, CA: Stanford University Press, 2001.

Becker, Marjorie. *Setting the Virgin on Fire: Lázaro Cárdenas, Michoacán Peasants, and the Redemption of the Mexican Revolution.* Berkeley: University of California Press, 1995.

Benedicto, Bobby. "The Haunting of Gay Manila: Global Space-Time and the Specter of *Kabaklaan.*" *GLQ* 14, nos. 2–3 (2008): 317–38.

Berlant, Lauren. *The Queen of America Goes to Washington City: Essays on Sex and Citizenship.* Durham, NC: Duke University Press, 1997.

———. *Cruel Optimism.* Durham, NC: Duke University Press, 2011.

Berlant, Lauren, and Michael Warner. "Sex in Public." In "Intimacy," special issue. *Critical Inquiry* 24, no. 2 (Winter 1998): 547–66.

Berman, Marshall. *All That Is Solid Melts into Air: The Experience of Modernity.* New York: Penguin, 1982.

Berman, Paul. "Labyrinth of Solitude." *New York Times Magazine,* August 2, 1998, sec. 6, p. 50.

Bérubé, Allan. *Coming Out Under Fire: The History of Gay Men and Women in World War II* (1990). 20th Anniversary Edition. With a new foreword by John D'Emilio and Estelle Freedman. Chapel Hill: University of North Carolina Press, 2010.

———. *My Desire for History: Essays in Gay, Community, and Labor History.* Edited, with an introduction, by John D'Emilio and Estelle B. Freedman. Chapel Hill: University of North Carolina Press, 2011.

Binnie, Jon. "Class, Sexuality, and Space: A Comment." *Sexualities* 14, no. 1 (2011): 21–26.

———. *The Globalization of Sexuality.* London: Sage, 2004.

Bloch, Ernst. "Nonsynchronism and the Obligation to Its Dialectics" (1935), *New German Critique,* no. 11 (Spring 1977): 22–38.

———. *The Principle of Hope.* 3 volumes (1954, 1955, 1959). Translated by Neville Plaice, Stephen Plaice, and Paul Knight. Cambridge, MA: MIT Press, 1995.

Bonfil Batalla, Guillermo. *México Profundo: Reclaiming a Civilization* (1987). Translated by Philip A. Dennis. Austin: University of Texas Press, 1996.

Bourdieu, Pierre. "The Forms of Capital." In *Handbook of Theory and Research for the Sociology of Education,* edited by John G. Richardson, 241–58. Westport, CT: Greenwood, 1986.

———. *Masculine Domination*. Translated by Richard Nice. Stanford, CA: Stanford University Press, 2003.

———. *Outline of a Theory of Practice* (1972). Translated by Richard Nice. Cambridge: Cambridge University Press, 1977).

Brain, Robert. *Friends and Lovers*. New York: Basic Books, 1976.

Brim, Matt. *Poor Queer Studies: Confronting Elitism in the University*. Durham, NC: Duke University Press, 2020.

Britton-Purdy, Jedediah. "The Republican Party Is Succeeding Because We Are Not a True Democracy." *New York Times*, January 3, 2022. https://www .nytimes.com/2022/01/03/opinion/us-democracy-constitution.html

Buffington, Robert. "Homophobia and the Mexican Working Class, 1900–1910." In *The Famous 41: Sexuality and Social Control in Mexico, 1910*, edited by Robert McKee Irwin, Edward J. McCaughan, and Michelle Rocío Nasser, 193–225. New York: Palgrave MacMillan, 2003.

Butler, Judith. "Performativity, Precarity, and Sexual Politics." *AIBR: Revista de Antropología Iberoamericana* 4, no. 3 (September–December 2009): i–xiii.

Cabrera, Mauricio. "Todos Somos Putos." *Juanfutbol*, June 20, 2014. Accessed July 26, 2021. https://juanfutbol.com/articulo/maca/todos-somos-putos (Cabrera's original post has been removed from the website, though one can still find extensive quotations from the article online).

Carrillo, Héctor. *The Night Is Young: Sexuality in Mexico in the Time of AIDS*. Chicago: University of Chicago Press, 2002.

———. *Pathways of Desire: The Sexual Migration of Mexican Men*. Chicago: University of Chicago Press, 2017.

Case, Anne, and Angus Deaton. *Deaths of Despair and the Future of Capitalism*. Princeton, NJ: Princeton University Press, 2020.

Chauncey, George. *Gay New York: Gender, Urban Culture, and the Making of the Gay Male World, 1890–1940*. New York: Basic Books, 2019.

Chibber, Vivek. *The Class Matrix: Social Theory after the Cultural Turn*. Cambridge, MA: Harvard University Press, 2022.

Chitty, Christopher. *Sexual Hegemony: Statecraft, Capital, and Sodomy in the Rise of the World System*. Edited by Max Fox, with an introduction by Christopher Nealon. Durham, NC: Duke University Press, 2020.

Clifford, James. "On Ethnographic Authority." *Representations*, no. 2 (Spring 1983): 118–46.

———. *The Predicament of Culture: Twentieth-Century Ethnography, Literature, and Art*. Cambridge, MA: Harvard University Press, 1988.

Cowan, George M. "Mazateco Whistle Speech." *Language* 24, no. 3 (July– September 1948): 280–86.

Dean, Mitchell, and Daniel Zamora. *The Last Man Takes LSD: Foucault and the End of Revolution*. London: Verso, 2021.

Dean, Tim. *Unlimited Intimacy: Reflections on the Subculture of Barebacking.* Chicago: University of Chicago Press, 2009.

Decena, Carlos. *Tacit Subjects: Belonging and Same-Sex Desire among Immigrant Dominican Men.* Durham, NC: Duke University Press, 2011.

Delany, Samuel R. *Times Square Red, Times Square Blue.* New York: New York University Press, 1999.

Del Castillo Negrete Rovira, Miguel. "Income Inequality in Mexico, 2004–2014." *Latin American Policy* 8, no. 1 (2017): 93–113.

De León, Jason. *The Land of Open Graves: Living and Dying on the Migrant Trail.* With photographs by Michael Wells. Berkeley: University of California Press, 2015.

D'Emilio, John. "Capitalism and Gay Identity." In *The Gender/Sexuality Reader: Culture, History, Political Economy,* edited by Roger N. Lancaster and Micaela di Leonardo, 467–76. New York: Routledge, 1997.

Denk, Jeremy. "Why I Hate the 'Goldberg Variations.'" *Deceptive Cadence.* NPR, March 19, 2012. https://www.npr.org/sections/deceptivecadence/2012/03/16/148769794/why-i-hate-the-goldberg-variations.

Denning, Michael. "Wageless Life." *New Left Review* 66 (November–December 2010): 79–97.

DeRuy, Emily. "The Fine Line between Safe Space and Segregation." *The Atlantic,* August 17, 2016. https://www.theatlantic.com/education/archive/2016/08/finding-the-line-between-safe-space-and-segregation/496289/.

Duffin, Erin. "Median Age of the U.S. Population 2020." Statista, April 1, 2022. https://www.statista.com/statistics/241494/median-age-of-the-us-population/.

Economic Commission for Latin America. "Economic Survey of Latin America and the Caribbean, 2021: Mexico." Accessed May 6, 2023. https://repositorio.cepal.org/bitstream/handle/11362/47193/83/EI2021_Mexico_en.pdf.

Ehrenreich, Barbara, and John Ehrenreich. "The Professional-Managerial Class." *Radical America* 11, no. 2 (March–April 1977): 7–32.

Engels, Friedrich. *The Origin of the Family, Private Property, and the State, in the Light of the Researches of Lewis H. Morgan.* Prepared by Professor Eleanor Burke Leacock. New York: International, 1972.

Eribon, Didier. *Insult and the Making of the Gay Self.* Durham, NC: Duke University Press, 2004.

———. *Returning to Reims* (2009). Introduction by George Chauncey. Translated by Michael Lucy. Los Angeles: Semiotext(e), 2013.

Fabian, Johannes. *Time and the Other: How Anthropology Makes Its Object.* New York: Columbia University Press, 1983.

Farmer, Paul. *In the Company of the Poor: Conversations with Dr. Paul Farmer and Fr. Gustavo Gutierrez.* Maryknoll, NY: Orbis Books, 2013.

Farred, Grant. *Martin Heidegger Saved My Life*. Minneapolis: University of Minnesota Press, 2015.

Ferguson, James. "Of Mimicry and Membership: Africans and the 'New World Society.'" *Cultural Anthropology* 17, no. 4 (2002): 551–69.

Ferguson, Roderick A. *Aberrations in Black: Toward a Queer of Color Critique*. Minneapolis: University of Minnesota Press, 2004.

Flores, René, and Edward Telles. "Social Stratification in Mexico: Disentangling Color, Ethnicity, and Class." *American Sociological Review* 77, no. 3 (June 2012): 486–94.

Fraser, Nancy. "The End of Progressive Neoliberalism." *Dissent*, January 2, 2017. https://www.dissentmagazine.org/online_articles/progressive-neoliberalism-reactionary-populism-nancy-fraser.

———. "Feminism, Capitalism, and the Cunning of History." *New Left Review* 56 (March–April 2009): 97–117.

Fuentes, Carlos. *Myself with Others: Selected Essays*. New York: Farrar, Straus and Giroux, 1988.

García Canclini, Nestor. *Hybrid Cultures: Strategies for Entering and Leaving Modernity*. Translated by Christopher L. Chiappari and Silvia L. Lopez. Foreword by Renato Rosaldo. Minneapolis: University of Minnesota Press, 1995.

Giddens, Anthony. *The Consequences of Modernity*. Cambridge: Polity Press, 1990.

———. *Modernity and Self-Identity: Self and Society in the Late Modern Age*. Stanford, CA: Stanford University Press, 1991.

Global Data Lab. "Mexico: Subnational HDI." Institute for Management Research, Radboud University. Retrieved April 16, 2023. https://globaldatalab.org/shdi/table/shdi/MEX/.

Gobierno de México. "Puebla." Data México. Accessed May 7, 2023. https://datamexico.org/en/profile/geo/puebla-pu.

Gonzalbo, Pilar. "La Trampa de las Castas." In *La Sociedad Novohispana: Estereotipos y Realidades*, by Solange Alberro and Pilar Gonzalbo Aizpuru, 17–154. Ciudad de México: Colegio de México, 2013.

Goodman, Nelson. *Ways of Worldmaking*. Indianapolis: Hackett, 1978.

Gutmann, Matthew. "Seed of the Nation: Men's Sex and Potency in Mexico." In *The Gender/Sexuality Reader: Culture, History, Political Economy*, edited by Roger N. Lancaster and Micaela di Leonardo, 194–206. New York: Routledge, 1997.

Halberstam, Jack/Judith. "Shame and White Gay Masculinity." *Social Text* 23, nos. 3–4 (84–85) (Fall–Winter 2005): 219–33.

Hall, Stuart. "Encoding, Decoding." In *Culture, Media, Language*, edited by Stuart Hall, Dorothy Hobson, Andrew Lowe and Paul Willis, *Culture, Media, Language*, 128–38. London: Hutchinson, 1980.

Hall, Stuart, and Tony Jefferson, eds. *Resistance through Rituals: Youth Subcultures in Post-war Britain.* 2nd edition. New York: Routledge, 1993.

Halperin, David M. *How to Be Gay.* Cambridge, MA: Belknap Press of Harvard University Press, 2012.

———. *One Hundred Years of Homosexuality and Other Essays on Greek Love* New York: Routledge, 1990.

———. "Queer Love." *Critical Inquiry* 45 (Winter 2019): 396–419.

Halperin, David M., and Valerie Traub. "Introduction: Beyond Gay Pride." In *Gay Shame,* edited by David M. Halperin and Valerie Traub, 3–40. Chicago: University of Chicago Press, 2009.

Halperin, David M., and Valerie Traube, eds. *Gay Shame.* Chicago: University of Chicago Press, 2009.

Hart, John Mason. *Revolutionary Mexico: The Coming and Process of the Mexican Revolution.* Berkeley: University of California Press, 1989.

Harvey, David. *A Brief History of Neoliberalism.* Oxford: Oxford University Press, 2007.

———. *The Limits to Capital.* 1999. Reprinted, London: Verso, 2018.

———. *The New Imperialism.* Oxford: Oxford University Press, 2003.

———. "The Right to the City." *New Left Review* 53 (September–October 2008): 23–40.

Hebdige, Dick. *Subculture: The Meaning of Style.* 1979. Reprint, New York: Routledge, 1988.

Hennessy, Rosemary. *Profit and Pleasure: Sexual Identities in Late Capitalism.* New York: Routledge, 2000.

Hernandez, Daniel. "Emo Bashing: Mexico's Latest Urban-Youth Craze." *LA Weekly,* April 9, 2008. http://www.laweekly.com/music/emo-bashing-mexicos-latest-urban-youth-craze-2152920.

Herrera Paredes, José Manuel, and Carla Aparecida Arena Ventura. "Consumo de alcohol y violencia doméstica contra las mujeres: un estudio con estudiantes universitarias de México." *Revista Latino-Americana de Enfermagem* 18 (Spec) (May–June 2010): 557–64.

"Historic Centre of Puebla." UNESCO World Heritage Convention. Retrieved September 7, 2022. https://whc.unesco.org/en/list/416.

Instituto Nacional de Estadística, Geografía e Informática (INEGI). *Censo de Población y Vivienda 2020—Cuestionario Básico.* INEGI, 2020.

———. "Estadísticas a Propósito del 14 de Febrero: Datos Nacionales," Comunicado de Prensa Núm 92/20, 13 de Febrero 2020.

———. 1910 census. May 6, 2023, http://en.www.inegi.org.mx/app/buscador/default.html?q=1910+census.

———. "Población rural y urbana, 2020." Cuénatme de México. Accessed April 29, 2023, https://cuentame.inegi.org.mx/poblacion/rur_urb.aspx?tema=P.

———. "Etnicidad: Lengua indígena," in *Principales resultados de la Enquesta intercensal 2015* (main results from the 2015 Intercensal Survey). Accessed April 29, 2023. https://www.senado.gob.mx/comisiones/asuntos_indigenas /eventos/docs/etnicidad_240216.pdf.

Informe General de la Consulta sobre Alcoholismo y Pueblos Indígenas. Ciudad de México: Comisión Nacional para el Desarrollo de los Pueblos Indígenas, 2008.

Ingram, Gordon Brent. "Ten Arguments for a Theory of Queers in Public Space." Introductory talk for the panel "Queer space: Sites Of Existence, Sites Of Resistance." Queer Frontiers Conference, International Lesbian and Gay Archives, University of Southern California, Los Angeles, 1995.

Irwin, Robert McKee. "The Famous 41: The Scandalous Birth of Modern Mexican Homosexuality." *GLQ: A Journal of Lesbian and Gay Studies* 6, no. 3 (2000): 353–76.

Irwin, Robert McKee, Edward J. McCaughan, and Michelle Rocío Nasser, eds. *The Famous 41: Sexuality and Social Control in Mexico, 1910.* New York: Palgrave Macmillan, 2003.

Jameson, Fredric. *The Political Unconscious: Narrative as a Socially Symbolic Act.* New York: Cornell University Press, 1981.

Johnson, Cedric. "An Open Letter to Ta-Nehisi Coates and the Liberals Who Love Him," *Jacobin*, February 3, 2016. https://jacobin.com/2016/02/ta-nehisi-coates-case-for-reparations-bernie-sanders-racism/.

Kameny, Franklin. "Gay Is Good." In *We Are Everywhere: A Historical Source-book of Gay and Lesbian Politics*, edited by Mark Blasius and Shane Phelan, 366–77. New York: Routledge, 1997.

Kelly, Patty. *Lydia's Open Door: Inside Mexico's Most Modern Brothel.* Berkeley: University of California Press, 2008.

Kracauer, Siegfried. *The Salaried Masses: Duty and Distraction in Weimar Germany* (1929). Translated by Quintin Hoare. Introduction by Inka Mülder-Bach. London: Verso, 1998.

Krauze, Enrique. *Mexico: Biography of Power—A History of Modern Mexico, 1810–1996.* New York: HarperPerennial, 1998.

Lancaster, Roger N. "Dreams of a Better Mexico." *Jacobin*, July 6, 2018. https:// jacobin.com/2018/07/lopez-obrador-election-victory-morena.

———. *Life Is Hard: Machismo, Danger, and the Intimacy of Power in Nicaragua.* Berkeley: University of California Press, 1992.

———. *Sex Panic and the Punitive State.* Berkeley: University of California Press, 2011.

———. "Subject Honor and Object Shame: The Construction of Male Homosexuality and Stigma in Nicaragua." *Ethnology* 27, no. 2 (April 1988): 111–25.

———. *Thanks to God and the Revolution: Popular Religion and Class Consciousness in the New Nicaragua.* New York: Columbia University Press, 1988.

———. "Tolerance and Intolerance in Sexual Cultures in Latin America." In *Passing Lines: Immigration and (Homo)Sexuality*, edited by Brad Epps, Kaja Valens, and Bill Johnson González, 255–74. Cambridge, MA: David Rockefeller Center on Latin American Studies and Harvard University Press, 2005.

———. *The Trouble with Nature: Sex in Science and Popular Culture*. Berkeley: University of California Press, 2003.

Lewin, Ellen. *Filled with the Spirit: Sexuality, Gender, and Radical Inclusivity in a Black Pentecostal Church Coalition*. Chicago: University of Chicago Press, 2018.

Lewis, Oscar. "Culture of Poverty." In *On Understanding Poverty: Perspectives from the Social Sciences*, edited by Daniel Patrick Moynihan, 187–220. New York: Basic Books, 1969.

List Reyes, Mauricio. *Jóvenes corazones gay en la ciudad de México: Género, identidad y socialidad en hombres gay*. Puebla, México: Benemérita Universidad Autónoma de Puebla, 2005.

Lobato, Ramon. *Shadow Economies of Cinema: Mapping Informal Film Distribution*. New York: Palgrave Macmillan, 2019.

Lomnitz, Claudio. *Death and the Idea of Mexico*. New York: Zone Books, 2005.

Lopez Estrada, Silvia. "Work, Family, and Gender Relations on the Northern Border of Mexico." In *Gender Transitions along Borders: The Northern Borderlands of Mexico and Morocco*. Edited by Marlene Solis, 31–40. London: Routledge, 2016.

López Obrador, Andrés Manuel. *La mafia que se adueno de Mexico . . . y el 2012*. Barcelona: Grijalbo Mondadori, 2006.

Lorde, Audre. *Sister Outsider: Essays and Speeches*. 1984. Reprint, Berkeley: Crossing Press, 2007.

Lukács, Georg. *History and Class Consciousness: Studies in Marxist Dialectics*. Translated by Rodney Livingstone. Cambridge, MA: MIT Press, 1972.

Macías-González, Víctor. "Homosexuales." In *Hampones, pelados y pecatrices. Sujetos peligrosos de la Ciudad de México (1940-1960)*, edited by Susana Sosenski and Gabriela Pulido, 109–58. Cuidad de México: Fondo de Cultura Económica, 2019.

———. "The *Lagatijo* at The High Life: Masculine Consumption, Race, Nation, and Homosexuality in Porfirian Mexico." In *The Famous 41: Sexuality and Social Control in Mexico, 1910*, edited by Robert McKee Irwin, Edward J. McCaughan, and Michelle Rocío Nasser, 227–49. New York: Palgrave Macmillan, 2003.

———. "The Transnational Homophile Movement and the Development of Domesticity in Mexico City's Homosexual Community, 1930-70." *Gender and History* 26, no. 3 (November 2014): 519–44.

Malatesta, Errico. "An Anarchist Programme (1920)." Marxists Internet Archive. Accessed May 21, 2023, https://www.marxists.org/archive/malatesta/1920 /program/program.htm.

Madrigal, Alexis. "Anti-emo Riots Break Out across Mexico." *Wired*, March 27, 2008. https://www.wired.com/2008/03/anti-emo-riots/.

Manalansan, Martin F., IV. *Global Divas: Filipino Gay Men in the Diaspora*. A John Hope Franklin Center Book. Durham, NC: Duke University Press, 2003.

———. "In the Shadows of Stonewall: Examining Gay Transnational Politics and the Diasporic Dilemma," *GLQ* 2 (1995): 425–38.

Manstead, Antony S. R. "The Psychology of Social Class: How Socioeconomic Status Impacts Thought, Feelings, and Behaviour." *British Journal of Social Psychology* (2018): 267–291.

Marx, Karl. "The German Ideology." In *Karl Marx: Selected Writings*, revised Edition, edited by David McLellan, 175–208. Oxford: Oxford University Press, 2000.

———. *Karl Marx: Selected Writings*. Revised edition. Edited by David McLellan. Oxford: Oxford University Press, 2000.

———. "Marx to Ruge, Kreuznach, September 1843." Letters from the Deutsch-Französische Jahrbücher. Accessed May 6, 2023. https://www.marxists.org /archive/marx/works/1843/letters/43_09.htm.

———. "On the Jewish Question." In *Karl Marx: Selected Writings*, revised ed., edited by David McLellan, 46–70. Oxford: Oxford University Press, 2000.

———. *Pre-capitalist Economic Formations*. Edited, with an introduction, by E. J. Hobsbawm. New York: International, 1965.

Marx, Karl, and Friedrich Engels. "The Communist Manifesto." In *Karl Marx: Selected Writings*, Revised Edition. Edited by David McLellan. Oxford: Oxford University Press, 2000), 245–72.

———. *Karl Marx and Friedrich Engels: Selected Correspondence*. 2nd edition. Edited by S. W. Ryazanskaya. Translated by I. Lasker. New York: Progress, 1975.

Mbembe, Achille. *On the Postcolony*. Berkeley: University of California Press, 2001.

McBride, George McCutchen. *The Land Systems of Mexico*. New York: American Geographical Society, 1923.

McRobbie, Angela. *Be Creative: Making a Living in the New Culture Industries*. Cambridge: Polity, 2016.

Menéndez y Renée B. Di Pardo, Eduardo L. "Violencias y Alcohol: Las Cotidianidades de las Pequeñas Muertes." *Relaciones* 19, no. 74 (Primavera 1998): 2–71.

Michaels, Walter Benn. *The Trouble with Diversity: How We Learned to Love Identity and Ignore Inequality*. 10th anniversary edition. With a new afterword. New York: Picador, 2016.

Miller, James. *The Passion of Michel Foucault*. New York: Anchor, 1994.

Minian, Ana Raquel. *Undocumented Lives: The Untold Story of Mexican Migration*. Cambridge, MA: Harvard University Press, 2018.

Monsiváis, Carlos. "De las variedades de la experiencia homoerótica." *Debate Feminista* 35 (Abril 2007): 163–92.

———. *Los ídolos a nado: Una antología global*. Barcelona: Debate Feminista, Random House Mondadori, 2011.

———. "Juan Gabriel y aquel apoteósico y polémico concierto en Bellas Artes." *Proceso*, August 29, 2016 (first published May 12, 1990). https://www
.proceso.com.mx/cronica/2016/8/29/juan-gabriel-aquel-apoteosico-
polemico-concierto-en-bellas-artes-169702.html.

———. *Mexican Postcards*. Edited, translated, and with an introduction by John Kraniauskas. London: Verso, 1997.

———. "El mundo soslayado." In Salvador Novo, *La estatua de sal*, 13–72. Cuidad de México: Consejo Nacional para la Cultura y las Artes, 1998.

———. "Notas sobre la cultura mexicana en el sigloXX." In *Historia General de México*, obra preparada por el Centro de Estudios Históricos, 957–1076. Cuidad de México: El Colegio de México, 2000.

———. "Would So Many Millions of People Not End Up Speaking English? The North American Culture of Mexico." In *The Latin American Cultural Studies Reader*, edited by Ana del Sarto, Alicia Ríos, and Abril Trigo, 203–32. Durham, NC: Duke University Press, 2004.

Moynihan, Daniel Patrick. "The Negro Family: The Case for National Action." Washington, DC: Office of Policy Planning and Research, US Department of Labor, 1965.

Muñoz, Jose Esteban. *Cruising Utopia: The Then and There of Queer Futurity*. New York: New York University Press, 2009.

Murray, Stephen O., and Manuel Arboleda G. "Stigma Transformation and Relexification: 'Gay' in Latin America." In *Male Homosexuality in Central and South America*, edited by Stephen O. Murray, 130–38. New York: Gay Academic Union, 1987.

Murray, Stephen O., and Wayne R. Dynes. "Hispanic Homosexuals: A Spanish Lexicon." In *Latin American Male Homosexualities*, edited by Stephen O. Murray, 180–92. Albuquerque: University of New Mexico Press, 1995.

Nelson, Maggie. *On Freedom: Four Songs of Care and Restraint*. Minneapolis: Graywolf Press, 2021.

Núñez Noriega, Guillermo. *Just Between Us: An Ethnography of Male Identity and Intimacy in Rural Communities of Northern Mexico*. Tucson: University of Arizona Press, 2014.

O'Neill, Aaron. "Mexico—Median Age of the Population 1950–2050." Statista, September 7, 2021.https://www.statista.com/statistics/275555/median-age-of-
the-population-in-mexico/.

———. "Germany—Average Age of the Population 1950–2050." Statista, September 8, 2021. https://www.statista.com/statistics/624303/average-age-of-the-population-in-germany/.

OECD (Organisation for Economic Co-Operation and Development). "Average Wages." From *OECD Employment Outlook, 2022*. OECD Data. Accessed April 30, 2023, https://data.oecd.org/earnwage/average-wages.htm

———. "Hours Worked." From *OECD Employment Outlook, 2022*. OECD Data. Accessed April 30, 2023, https://data.oecd.org/emp/hours-worked.htm.

———. "Income Inequality," 2021 or latest available. OECD Data. Accessed April 29, 2023, https://data.oecd.org/inequality/income-inequality.htm.

———. *OECD Rural Policy Reviews: Mexico*. May 2007. https://www.oecd.org/gov/oecdruralpolicyreviewsmexico.htm.

Parker, Richard. *Bodies, Pleasures, and Passions: Sexual Culture in Contemporary Brazil*. Boston: Beacon Press, 1991.

Pascoe, C. J. *Dude, You're a Fag: Masculinity and Sexuality in High School* (2007). With a new preface. Berkeley: University of California Press, 2012.

Paz, Octavio. *Labyrinth of Solitude and Other Writings* (1950). Translated by Lysander Kemp, Yara Milos, and Rachel Phillips Belash. New York: Grove Press, 1985).

Perreau, Bruno. *Queer Theory: The French Response*. Stanford, CA: Stanford University Press, 2016.

Polanyi, Karl. *The Great Transformation: The Political and Economic Origins of Our Time* (1944). Foreword by Joseph E. Stiglitz. Introduction by Fred Block. Boston: Beacon Press, 2001.

Prieur, Annick. *Mema's House, Mexico City: On Transvestites, Queens, and Machos*. Chicago: University of Chicago Press, 1998.

Programme for the Promotion of Formalization in Latin America and the Caribbean. "Informal Employment in Mexico: Current Situation, Policies, and Challenges." International Labour Organization. 2014. https://www.ilo.org/wcmsp5/groups/public/---americas/---ro-lima/documents/publication/wcms_245889.pdf.

Prunetti, Alberto. "Workers Telling Their Own Stories Can Rebuild Working-Class Pride," *Jacobin*, January 7, 2022. https://jacobinmag.com/2022/01/didier-eribon-retour-a-reims-movie-class.

Puar, Jasbir. *Terrorist Assemblages: Homonationalism in Queer Times*. Durham, NC: Duke University Press, 2017.

Rabinow, Paul. *The Accompaniment: Assembling the Contemporary*. Chicago: University of Chicago Press, 2011.

Reed, Adolph, Jr. "Antiracism: A Neoliberal Alternative to a Left." *Dialectical Anthropology* 42 (2018): 105–15.

Reed, Touré. *Toward Freedom: The Case against Race Reductionism.* London: Verso, 2020.

Richler, Howard. *How Happy Became Homosexual: And Other Mysterious Semantic Shifts.* Vancouver: Ronsdale Press, 2013.

Riley, Denise. *Am I That Name? Feminism and the Category of "Women" in History.* New York: Macmillan, 1988.

Ríos, Viri. "¿López Obrador ha reducido la desigualdad en México?" *New York Times,* February 17, 2020. https://www.nytimes.com/es/2020/02/17/espanol /opinion/desigualdad-mexico-amlo.html.

Rodríguez, Nathaly. *De sedientos seres: Una historia social del homoerotismo masculino, Ciudad de México, 1917–1952.* Puebla, México: Universidad Iberoamericana Puebla, 2020.

Rofel, Lisa. *Desiring China: Experiments in Neoliberalism, Sexuality, and Public Culture.* Durham, NC: Duke University Press, 2007.

———. "Qualities of Desire: Imagining Gay Identities in China." *GLQ* 5, no. 4 (1999): 451–74.

Rojas, René. "Chile's Vote Was a Rebuke of the 21st-Century Left; Will We Listen?" *Jacobin,* December 5, 2022. https://jacobin.com/2022/12/chiles-vote-was-a-rebuke-of-the-21st-century-left-will-we-listen?.

Romero, Henry. "Mexico's Wages Are So Paltry That Human-Rights and Legal Groups Are Sounding the Alarm." *Business Insider,* March 1, 2017. https://www.businessinsider.com/mexico-wages-incomes-poverty-2017-2.

Ross, John. "Mexico City's Urban Tribes Go on the Warpath against Emos." *Counterpunch,* April 8, 2008. https://www.counterpunch.org/2008/04/08 /mexico-city-s-urban-tribes-go-on-the-warpath-against-emos/.

Schein, Louisa. "Of Cargo and Satellites: Imagined Cosmopolitanism." *Postcolonial Studies* 2, no. 3 (1999): 345–75.

Scheper-Hughes, Jennifer. "The Niño Jesús Doctor: Novelty and Innovation in Mexican Religion." *Nova Religio: The Journal of Alternative and Emergent Religions* 16, no. 2 (November 2012): 4–28.

Scheper-Hughes, Nancy. *Saints, Scholars, and Schizophrenics: Mental Illness in Rural Ireland.* Berkeley: University of California Press, 1979.

Sedgwick, Eve Kosofsky. "Queer Performativity: Henry James's *The Art of the Novel.*" *GLQ* 1, no. 1 (1993): 1–16.

———. *Tendencies.* Durham, NC: Duke University Press, 1993.

Spivak, Gayatri. "Can the Subaltern Speak?" In *Marxism and the Interpretation of Culture,* edited by Lawrence Grossberg and Cary Nelson, 271–313. Urbana: University of Illinois Press, 1988.

Stacey, Judith. "Cruising to Familyland: Gay Hypergamy and Rainbow Kinship." *Current Sociology* 52, no. 2 (2004): 181–97.

Stephen, Lynn. "Sexualities and Genders in Zapotec Oaxaca." In "Gender, Sexuality, and Same-Sex Desire in Latin America." Special issue, *Latin American Perspectives* 29, no. 2 (March 2002): 41–59.

Táíwò, Olúfẹ́mi. *How Colonialism Preempted Modernity in Africa*. Bloomington: Indiana University Press, 2010.

———. *Africa Must Be Modern: A Manifesto*. Bloomington: Indiana University Press, 2014.

Thompson, E. P. *Customs in Common: Studies in Traditional Popular Culture*. New York: New Press, 1993.

United Nations Office on Drugs and Crime's International Homicide Statistics database. "Intentional Homicides (per 100,000 People)—Mexico." Accessed October 2, 2022. https://data.worldbank.org/indicator/VC.IHR.PSRC.P5?en d=2020&locations=MX&start=2006.

Valentine, David. *Imagining Transgender: An Ethnography of a Category*. Durham, NC: Duke University Press, 2007.

Vance, J. D. *Hillbilly Elegy: A Memoir of a Family and Culture in Crisis*. New York: Harper, 2016.

Vasconcelos, José. *The Cosmic Race* (1925). Bilingual edition. Translated and annotated by Didier Tisdel Jaén. Afterword by Joseba Gabilondo. Baltimore: Johns Hopkins University Press, 1997.

Vazquez, Jason. "Backgrounder: AMLO and Mexican Labor Law Reform." *OnLabor: Workers, Unions, Politics*, March 19, 2021. https://onlabor.org /backgrounder-amlo-and-mexican-labor-law-reform/.

Veblen, Thorstein. *Theory of the Leisure Class*. Oxford World's Classics. 1899. Reprint, Oxford: Oxford University Press, 2007.

Viren, Sarah "The Safe Space That Became a Viral Nightmare." *New York Times Magazine*, Education Issue, September 7, 2022. https://www.nytimes.com /2022/09/07/magazine/arizona-state-university-multicultural-center.html.

Visvanathan, Nalini, Lynn Duggan, Nan Wiegersma, and Laurie Nisonoff, eds. *The Women, Gender, and Development Reader*. 2nd edition. New York: Zed Books, 2011.

Vivanco, José Miguel. "Mexican Government Paralyzed in the Face of a Wave of Femicides." Human Right Watch, March 3, 2020. https://www.hrw.org /news/2020/03/03/mexican-government-paralyzed-face-wave-femicides.

Vološinov, V. N. *Marxism and the Philosophy of Language* (1930). Translated by Ladislav Matejka and I. R. Titunik. New York: Seminar Press, 1973.

Warner, Michael. "Queer and Then? The End of Queer Theory." *Chronicle of Higher Education*, January 1, 2012. https://www.chronicle.com/article/queer-and-then/.

Warner, Michael, ed. *Fear of a Queer Planet: Queer Politics and Social Theory*. Minneapolis: University of Minnesota Press, 1993.

Weber, Max. *From Max Weber: Essays in Sociology*. Translated, edited, and with an Introduction by Hans Gerth and C. Wright Mills. Oxford: Oxford University Press, 1946.

———. *The Protestant Ethic and the Spirit of Capitalism* (1930). Translated by Talcott Parsons. With an Introduction by Anthony Giddens. New York: Routledge, 2001.

Weston, Kath. *Render Me, Gender Me: Lesbians Talk Sex, Class, Color, Nation, Studmuffins*. New York: Columbia University Press, 1997.

Williams, Raymond. "Base and Superstructure in Marxist Cultural Theory." *New Left Review* 1, no. 82 (November–December, 1973): 3–16.

———. *Marxism and Literature*. Oxford: Oxford University Press, 1977.

Williams, Walter. *The Spirit and the Flesh: Sexual Diversity in American Indian Culture*. Boston: Beacon, 1986.

Wittman, Carl. *The Gay Manifesto*. New York: Red Butterfly, 1970.

Wolf, Eric R. "Closed Corporate Peasant Communities in Mesoamerica and Central Java." *Southwestern Journal of Anthropology* 13, no. 1 (Spring 1957): 1–18.

———. *Peasant Wars of the Twentieth Century*. Norman: University of Oklahoma Press, 1969.

World Bank Group. "Poverty and Equity Brief: Latin America and the Caribbean—Mexico." World Bank, October 2021. https://databankfiles.worldbank.org/public/ddpext_download/poverty/987B9C90-CB9F-4D93-AE8C-750588BF00QA/AM2021/Global_POVEQ_MEX.pdf.

Wuest, Joanna. "After Liberation: Sex, Social Movements, and Capital since the New Left." *Polity* 54, no. 3 (2022): 478–502.

Žižek, Slavoj. "Class Struggle against Classism." The Philosophical Salon. *Los Angeles Review of Books*, May 10, 2021, https://thephilosophicalsalon.com/class-struggle-against-classism/.

Zolov, Eric. *Refried Elvis: The Rise of the Mexican Counterculture*. Berkeley: University of California Press, 1999.

Index

www.ingramcontent.com/pod-product-compliance
Lightning Source LLC
Chambersburg PA
CBHW031056280326
41928CB00049B/532